MIGRATION MIRACLE

Jacqueline Maria Hagan

Migration Miracle

Faith, Hope, and Meaning on
the Undocumented Journey

HARVARD UNIVERSITY PRESS
Cambridge, Massachusetts, and London, England   2008

Library of Congress Cataloging-in-Publication Data

Hagan, Jacqueline Maria, 1954–
    Migration miracle : faith, hope, and meaning on the undocumented journey / Jacqueline Maria
Hagan.
        p. cm.
    Includes bibliographical references and index.
    ISBN 978-0-674-03085-5 (alk. paper)
    1. Immigrants—Religious life—United States. 2. Immigrants—United States—Interviews.
    3. United States—Emigration and immigration—Religious aspects. I. Title.

BV639.I4H23 2008
261.8'36—dc22   2008007135

For Joe

Contents

MIGRATION MIRACLE

Introduction

The mountaintop *ayuno* (fast) is only accessible by *foot*. To attend the morning-long fasting prayer service, we left at daybreak with our guide Pastor José Sapon, an energetic evangelical minister who, despite his youthful appearance, has guided his own independent ministry for some decades. We taxied to an unmarked spot along the northbound road leading out of Cuatro Caminos (four roads), a major transportation depot and historic trading center located on the outskirts of the Guatemalan highland town of San Cristóbal, Totonicapán. I was well familiar with the Maya community, having done my dissertation fieldwork there almost twenty years earlier. From Cuatro Caminos we proceeded by foot for several kilometers, winding our way through cornfields and up one of the five paths that lead to the Maya sacred grounds of Xe Cacal Xiguin. Our hour-long trek took us to a small clearing near the mountaintop, a secluded place where perhaps two dozen Maya men, women, and children sat on rocks or squatted on the cold ground. All were deep in prayer. Leading the service was Pastor Daniel Cua, a zealous young evangelical minister who believed God spoke to the group through him. The service began with an *oración* (a prayer and conversation with God), followed by *alabanzas con Dios* (a time of praise and worship during which the spirit of God is experienced by the attendees). With Bible in hand, Pastor Cua spoke in tongues and then translated into Quiché, a fading Maya language, while Pastor Sapon translated into Spanish for us. The attendees believed that God would listen harder to those who fasted before prayer and had come seeking counseling on a variety of basic problems. Many had traveled miles along mountain trails to find hope and solace. Some beseeched God to cure physical ailments while others requested guidance in family matters; still others prayed for divine intervention to help them locate jobs.

I had come to the ayuno in response to Pastor Sapon's claims that migration counseling was on the increase among ministries in the Guatemalan highlands, a phenomenon I had not observed during my fieldwork in the area in the late 1980s. Did any of the attendees in fact have migration petitions? They had. Dressed in the traditional Maya *huipil* and *corte*, a Maya woman stepped forward and asked the group to pray with her for the safety of her husband, from whom she had not heard since his departure for the United States some months earlier. Another Mayan, the father of a young migrant who had arrived in the United States several months earlier, offered prayers for his son's success in the United States. In another case, a father had not heard from his son in several weeks. Not knowing whether he had arrived safely, he requested that the pastor ask God if his son and companions were lost. To the obvious relief of the weeping father, the pastor informed him and the others that the journeying migrants were safe.

Eager to explore the phenomenon of migration counseling in the western highlands of Guatemala, I asked Pastor Sapon to escort us to other ayunos. At each sacred and cultural fasting ritual far from traditional church walls and institutional practices, participants raised pressing migration issues, especially concerns over the journey and a safe arrival. At an ayuno held Wednesday and Friday mornings in a humble adobe home in a Maya hamlet some twenty kilometers away from the sacred mountain-top celebration, the presiding pastor told us that only days before as many as several dozen migrants had come to participate in group prayer before setting off by foot toward the Mexican border. Another evangelical pastor told us that since the mid- to late-1990s, migration counseling had become a regular part of her prayer services. At times, she told us, her followers have even requested that she meet with their *coyote* (a guide who takes migrants across international borders in exchange for money), to determine whether the guide is honest or a scoundrel. When I asked local area clergy about their observed increase in migration counseling, they agreed that the rising demand for counseling paralleled the growth in migration streams leading north to the United States, which involved increased personal and financial hazards for prospective migrants. It was Pastor Sapon's explanation that resonated: "Because the investment is so high, the risk so much, and crossing the borders implies uncertainty, the majority of those in our community who make this voyage are focused on seeking divine intervention in their undertaking. Moreover, the poverty in this area is so great that people have no other alternative but to seek out God's miracles, regardless of the outcome."[1]

At this point, I realized that most migration scholars, with their emphasis on economic market structures and rational decision makers that assess cost-benefit analyses, had missed a crucial factor in models accounting for international migration from Mexico and Latin America—the central and intertwining role of culture, religion, and spirituality in the lives of the poor and working class who wrestle with the migration undertaking. When I returned to Houston in the fall of 2000, I drafted the Guatemalan case study and began to think about designing a larger study to gauge the role of culture; folk and everyday religious practices; and the church and clergy in the lives of undocumented migrants as they make their decisions to migrate and as they prepare for and undertake their journey.[2]

Since the arrival of the Puritans in the 1620s, various peoples, including Quakers, Jews, Catholics, and multiple Protestant sects, have migrated for religious reasons to what became the United States. Their stories have been well documented in the history of immigrants in America. What has not been recorded, however, is the story of how economically motivated migrants, such as the Latin American labor migrants featured in this book, rely on religion—their clergy, belief systems, faith, cultural expressions, and everyday religious practices—as resources to endure the migration undertaking. This was the story I was eager to explore.

While the beginning stage of the study was under way in Houston, I was invited to the Arizona-Mexico border by Reverend Robin Hoover, president of Humane Borders, a humanitarian interfaith coalition that strategically places water stations in the desert to quench the thirst of migrants along or near well-traveled paths across southern Arizona. My friend and colleague Helen Rose Ebaugh and I traveled to Arizona in the summer of 2002. While there, Rev. Hoover guided us through some of the most frequently traversed but dangerous crossing points along the U.S.-Mexico border, including the desert areas southwest of Tucson, that had begun to claim a disproportionate number of migrant lives during the hot summer months. Deaths had increased along the border as migrants sought to circumvent intensified enforcement and security efforts along well-established and historic crossing points. The tragic human consequences of these efforts to curtail unauthorized migration from Central America and Mexico were evident. While we were there, the first of many subsequent groups of migrants—seven men, women, and children—were found dead in the Altar desert corridor. Since then, many migrants have died in the desert in their desperate attempts to reach the United States to find jobs. These desert deaths contribute to the thousands of migrant crossing deaths that have been recorded since the onset of tighter border controls in the mid-1990s.[3]

We traveled the desert terrain on both sides of the border where the ground was so hot it melted the soles of Helen Rose's shoes. In Mexico, we visited several recently erected, faith-based shelters in Nogales and Agua Prieta that provide shelter and humanitarian assistance to crossing and deported migrants. At these places of hospitality we interviewed destitute, weary, and injured migrants and asked them about the ways in which they put their faith into practice during their travels. On the U.S. side of the border, we visited houses of refuge and interviewed priests, pastors, and leaders of coalitions of religious and advocacy groups, most of whom represent denominations that share a long tradition in social justice work and civic action. Some, like Reverend John Fife, have long been involved in immigration issues and can trace their roots to the U.S. Sanctuary Movement of the 1980s. Their humanitarian efforts today focus on life-saving aid for journeying migrants, such as the Samaritans, a coalition of Quakers, Jews, Methodists, Catholics, and Presbyterians who make regular trips to the desert in four-wheel drive vehicles equipped with food, water, and first-aid supplies. Away from the shelters and churches—in the desolate desert stretches of the crossing corridor—we visited abandoned migrant camps where we documented the many religious artifacts—crosses, prayer books, pictures, and other items—left by migrants as they scrambled to safety along I-10 in Arizona. I was reminded of the Atlantic crossing and coping strategies of the millions of Europeans who made their way to the United States at the turn of the twentieth century.[4]

My fieldwork in Guatemala testified to the centrality of faith and popular religious practices, as well as trusted clergy, in the lives of migrants as they separate from home and community and prepare for the journey north. The desert border experience reinforced my belief that migration scholarship has failed to capture adequately the role of religion and spirituality in the migration journey. Furthermore, the Arizona experience impressed upon me the importance of faith and religion as a coping mechanism among traveling migrants, and revealed the growing public face and supportive role of church and clergy, which provide for the humanitarian and counseling needs of journeying migrants and advocate on their behalf.

By and large, scholarship on religion and migration has focused on the role of religion in immigrant incorporation, with an eye toward explaining how religious affiliation and participation help immigrants face the challenges of adaptation in a new land. Both historical and contemporary accounts of immigrants in the United States describe the ways in which religious institutions in receiving areas act as vehicles through which immigrants weather the traumas and hardships of immigration and, at the same time, maintain their cultural heritage and reaffirm their ethnic identities. It is precisely because of the psychological traumas of immigration that immigrants turn to religion—the familiar—for comfort. Indeed, religion is so central to the immigration experience that the historian Timothy Smith conceptualizes it as a "theologizing experience."[5] In classic accounts of European immigration to the United States, for example, Oscar Handlin and William Herberg singled out the psychosocial benefits of religious membership for newcomers.[6] Ethnic churches provided solace and refuge from the trauma of the migration experience, so that within their walls immigrants, in the comfortable company of family and friends, could pray in their native languages and practice familiar cultural rituals. According to Handlin, immigrants became Americans by first becoming ethnic Americans, a process nurtured through ethnic churches.[7]

The massive influx of immigrants to the United States in recent decades has renewed scholarly interest in the intersection between immigration and religion, in particular, the institutional role of religion in immigrant incorporation. Accounts of contemporary immigration continue to point to the centrality of religious organizations as sources of social and economic support in the settlement experience of a variety of newcomer immigrant groups. Churches, synagogues, and temples scattered throughout the U.S. landscape provide an array of material services to ease immigrant settlement and shape integration. Upon arrival, newcomers rely on religious organizations for services that include housing referrals, job opportunities, and language training, as well as for knowledge that facilitates civic and political participation.[8] These places of worship, which are often erected or transformed by immigrants, also provide for fellowship with co-ethnics and a venue for expressing ethnic identity, thereby creating more religious and cultural diversity across America's religious geography.[9] Yet in the contemporary world religion is more than a vehicle for incorporation and identity reaffirmation. As sociologist Peggy Levitt reminds us, religion also enables us to stay closely connected to homeland and to members of shared culture, tradition, and faith throughout the world.[10]

While the classic and contemporary literature offers abundant accounts of the buffering and integrative roles of religion in immigrant incorporation, very few studies have systematically examined how religion interacts with earlier stages of the migration experience, both in sending communities and along the journey. This gap in migration and religion literature is surprising when it comes to poor and working class labor migrants from Latin America. We know that the poor and powerless, relative to other classes, have long turned to their faith and religion, especially their saints and revered icons, for solace, presence, guidance, and reflection in times of personal crisis. Lacking the power and economic resources to change their precarious situations to realize their aspirations, the religious poor naturally seek divine intervention in the form of tens of thousands of daily petitions and mementos deposited at churches throughout Latin America. These contemporary pilgrims thus demonstrate the people's reliance, when faced with personal problems or formidable challenges, on their faith and the presence of popular saints and holy images. The hundreds of local, regional, and national shrines that house revered popular images and dot the landscapes of urban and rural communities throughout Latin America attest to the Catholic practices of the religious in Mexico, Central America, and more generally in Latin America.

Many Latin Americans express their religion in ways that are not always sanctioned by or authorized by the institutional church. The religious practice of ayunos in Maya sacred grounds in the highlands of Guatemala illustrates the lasting strength and influence of folk religion among Latin Americans. In remote areas where the church was historically less successful in converting locals, such as border areas of Mexico and the United States, people have especially defied the church and created their own folk saints and popular holy images for psychological sustenance, some of whom, like Juan Soldado (Juan the Soldier), whose well-visited shrine is situated in a local public cemetery in Tijuana, are known as protectors of migrants.[11]

Evidence from other studies supports the contention that clergy and congregations both in communities of origin and of destination are not only aware of the material and spiritual needs of migrants but also attempt to specifically meet those needs. In a study of present-day Ghanaian Pentecostalism, Rijk Van Dijk showed that prospective migrants turn to healing and deliverance rituals held for them at prayer camps in Ghana for spiritual counsel and protection during their travel.[12] An increasing number of dioceses and parishes in migrant-sending communities in Mexico and Central America promote migration devotion by celebrating the Day of the Migrant and organizing masses, processions and patron saint rites in honor of migrant parishioners.[13] In the heyday of the U.S. Sanctuary Movement during the

1980s, refugees who fled political turmoil in Central America found refuge in Catholic and Protestant churches along the southwest border and in the interior United States.[14] Churches in the United States have long provided for the material and spiritual needs of newcomer immigrants.[15] Migrants, too, make sense of their journey without recourse to the church itself, turning instead to familiar cultural and personal religious practices. For example, in their historical analysis of a sample of Mexican *retablos* (small votive paintings) Jorge Durand and Douglas Massey show that migrants often returned to their home communities to give thanks to the saints and holy images of the Catholic Church for escaping harm during their journey north to the United States.[16]

My own research also attests to the importance of religion, faith, and everyday religious practices to migrants, but this book goes further, telling the story of how religion permeates the entirety of the migration experience, from decision making and departure through the dangerous undocumented journey from their home communities north to the United States, and beyond. The fieldwork I pursued in Guatemala and Arizona documented numerous accounts of migrants for whom religion was a critical resource, and I found ample evidence that evangelical clergy in the Guatemalan highlands incorporate migration counseling into their regular services. Although the Guatemalan case study documents the centrality of religion in the migration process, it has limitations in that its findings are based on the experiences of members of one community who rely on Maya folk religious practices and evangelical clergy for the spiritual support to endure hardship and peril in the trip north.[17] Thus this small case study led me to a larger question: is religion an identifiable resource in the contemporary migration process of other migrant groups of different religious, ethnic, and cultural backgrounds? When I returned from Guatemala, I expanded my research focus and set out to develop a project that would allow me to understand the multiple ways in which migrants have access to and draw on religious resources during various stages of the migration process, including 1) decision making and leave-taking, 2) the journey, and 3) the arrival. I designed a project to explore how migrants themselves interpret, create, and sometimes transform everyday religious practices to derive meaning for the decision to migrate and to seek spiritual guidance and protection from clergy and religious institutions during the process of international travel. I was also interested in exploring how migrants make sense of safe arrival through familiar religious practices. In this way, I illustrate the concept of religion in its broadest sense, to include all those beliefs and practices sanctioned by the church, as well as the rich diversity of everyday practices informed by culture and shared experience, and employed and transformed by the migrants themselves to derive meaning in the migration process.[18]

Interviews with clergy in Guatemala, Arizona, and Mexico impressed upon me that to truly understand the role of religion in the migration process, especially the journey, I needed to explore the responses of faith workers, agencies, and institutions to the realities of contemporary undocumented migration from Latin America. Religious institutions offer a unique vantage point on international migration because they transcend the boundaries of nation-states and often recognize migration as a fundamental human right. I was interested in exploring how different faith groups organized and rallied to support the rights of the migrants, especially in the context of militarized borders, and I sought information on the extent to which religious workers and groups had moved beyond the private confines of worship and counsel to broader public roles as advocates and protectors who challenge state policy. To capture the ways in which religious institutions, coalitions, organizations, and groups are mobilizing around migration issues and contesting state policies, I conducted close to one hundred interviews with religious leaders and faith workers in the Untied States, Mexico, and Central America.

Many of these interviews were conducted with clergy, missionaries, and faith workers of the Catholic Church, an institution that has a long history of social teachings that defend the right to migrate. In more recent years the public face of the Catholic Church has been front and center in the immigration debate and directly at odds with the state. The human rights activism of the Catholic hierarchy on migration may come as a surprise to the many who have watched with consternation the unyielding stance of the Roman Catholic Church on such issues as birth control, abortion, gay rights, celibacy, and women in the priesthood. Yet one of the major narrative threads that runs through this book is the way Catholic social theology is practiced at multiple levels of hierarchy and especially by faith workers who provide shelter and counseling for transit migrants.

To capture the perspectives and life experiences of those who are targeted by enforcement efforts but rarely are heard in the halls of policy making, I needed to expand my methodology. Shortly after my return from Arizona, beginning in the fall of 2002 and lasting through the summer of 2003, a research team of bilingual male and female students and professors at the University of Houston interviewed 202 undocumented Mexican, Guatemalan, Salvadoran, and Honduran migrants who undertook the deadly migrant trail across thousands of miles of jungle and desert and several international borders to reach the United States.[19] We focused on the migration journey of Central Americans and Mexicans for several reasons in addition to the easy geographic accessibility of these groups. Poor migrants with high levels of religiosity and low levels of education largely compose the flows from this region. Most are Catholic, but increasing numbers, especially indigenous Guatemalans, have converted to evangelical denominations in recent decades.[20] These groups represent a diverse range of Latino immigrants who vary by national origin, religious identity, and ethnicity—differences that are fundamental in the study's analysis. Because most migrants from Central America and Mexico lack the financial or educational resources to enter the United States through legal channels, they typically rely on some combination of resources from their own personal networks of family and friends, the guidance of coyotes, and knowledge they acquire on the road to enter as unauthorized migrants.

Central Americans and Mexicans also comprise a sizeable proportion of the growing number of unauthorized entrants to the United States each year. In the 1970s and 1980s, the undocumented population in the United States continued to grow by roughly 200,000 persons a year. Since then it has steadily climbed. During the 1990s, it increased by almost 500,000 a year, but since 2000, it has grown by roughly 850,000 persons a year. Well over half of yearly unauthorized entrants come from Mexico and an additional quarter from other parts of Latin America, including El Salvador, Guatemala, and Honduras.[21] As recent undocumented migrants from Latin America, they usually have no choice but to travel the dangerous journey of thousands of miles over several militarized borders to reach the United States, the journey I explore in depth in this book. Once in the United States, these labor migrants typically find low-wage jobs in service, manufacturing, and construction industries where at $21,000 their median household earnings amount to just enough to keep them out of poverty but far below the median U.S. household income of $45,000. In the United States, these newcomers continue to join well-established migrant communities in urban labor markets, such as Los Angeles and Houston, but increasingly also arrive in new settlement areas in labor markets in states such as North Carolina and Georgia.[22]

I selected the migrant sample to provide baseline data on the various ways in which different groups express faith by engaging in religious rituals and practices before, during, and after the migration journey. The large majority of the migrants interviewed (89 percent) arrived in the United States between 1990 and 2002, and within this group more than half arrived after 1995, when enforcement activities increased dramatically along the U.S.-Mexico border. Twenty percent arrived between 2000 and 2002, an accelerated period of tightened security along the Mexico-Guatemala border.[23] During this period, the border region also experienced a surge in programs to assist transit migrants, most of which have been developed by churches, interfaith organizations, and nongovernmental organizations (NGOs).[24] In an attempt to capture a range of religiosity among the sample, we conducted nearly half (49 percent) the interviews in religious settings, including places of worship and at Christian bookstores; the remainder (51 percent) took place in nonreligious environments such as workplaces, parks, labor pools, and other public settings.

A central question underlying this research is whether migrants make more use of and rely more strongly on religion when they feel little control over the situations they confront, that is, when risks are extremely high. Theological differences and local cultural practices may also influence the nature and extent to which migrants make use of religious practices in the migration process. Perhaps evangelical clergy are more responsive than their Catholic counterparts to the needs of their followers, or perhaps there is something unique about Maya folk practices that other ethnic groups may not share.

Table 1, which profiles the sample, captures these variations. Close to two-thirds of the sample are Mexicans, a percentage we targeted when designing the sample to reflect their larger undocumented flows. We interviewed both women and men to explore any gender differences in the journey and the role of religion in it. The sample is also a fairly young one: roughly one-third of the sample undertook the journey while they were still in their teens. Because undocumented migration is driven by a search for higher wages, we tend to think that most labor migrants from Central America and Mexico are young adult men of working age. This is no longer the case. Increasingly, women and children comprise these flows. By some estimates, as many as 50,000 undocumented children enter the United States each year from Central America and Mexico.[25]

Finally, to capture different religious origins and experiences of migrant groups, we interviewed both Protestants and Catholics. Although Latin

Table 1. Profile of study sample prior to migration

Characteristic	Percentage (n)
Region of Origin	
México	61 (123)
Central America[a]	39 (79)
Gender	
Female	39 (79)
Male	61 (123)
Age	
Under 20	34 (68)
20 to 29	38 (78)
30 to 39	21 (42)
40 and older	7 (14)
Religion when traveling	
Protestant[b]	25 (51)
Catholic[c]	73 (147)
Other (1 Christian, 2 Mormons, and 1 nonbeliever)	2 (4)
Church attendance	
Several times a week	27 (54)
About once a week	40 (80)
Several times a month	12 (24)
Several times a year	13 (27)
Did not attend	8 (17)
Participated in community religious activities	35 (70)
Practiced home religious activities	
None	23 (47)
One	24 (48)
Two	25 (50)
Three	10 (21)
Four or more	18 (36)

a. The Central American respondents consisted primarily of Salvadorans (32), Guatemalans (26), and Hondurans (19). One Costa Rican, one Nicaraguan, and one Panamanian are also in the total sample.

b. The Protestant respondents included Pentecostal, Evangelical, Apostolic, Jehovah's Witness, and Baptist; none claimed to be affiliated with more mainstream Protestant churches such the Episcopal or Presbyterian churches.

c. These include three charismatic Catholics.

America is still home to roughly half the world's 1 billion Catholics, the region has witnessed a dramatic surge in evangelical Protestantism since the mid-1980s. By some estimates 15 percent of Latin Americans belong to evangelical churches.[26] In Mexico, the country with the second largest number of Catholics in Latin America, almost 90 percent of the Mexican population identify themselves as Catholic. The number of Protestants in the country steadily increased for decades and leveled out at about 6 percent by 1990. The increase in Protestantism is more dramatic in Central America. Today, close to 25 percent of the population is Protestant. Mainline Protestant churches have had a minor presence in the region: most Protestants are evangelical and members of the many Pentecostal Protestant churches that have flourished in Central America in recent decades, the most popular of which is the Church of God (Iglesia de Dios). By the mid-1990s, roughly 15–20 percent of all Salvadorans, Nicaraguans, and Hondurans belonged to evangelical churches. Guatemala is home to the highest percentage of Protestants in Latin America, peaking at 26 percent by 1995.[27] Many who converted from Catholicism to Protestantism in Guatemala come from poor, indigenous communities in the western highlands, where elements of capital penetration and state militarization disrupted Maya identity and community and sent scores of Catholics fleeing to Pentecostal meetings and ayunos.[28]

Given the strong religious presence and identity in the region, it should not come as any surprise to find that the study sample is a fairly religious one. Roughly two-thirds of the respondents reported that they attend church at least once a week. In addition, more than a third of the sample participated in other community and church-based religious activities, including organizing Bible groups, youth programs, and church outreach programs for the those in need in the community. Much of the religious experiences and many of the rituals practiced among the sample are expressed outside the walls of churches and in the privacy of their own homes, practices that largely go undetected in congregational studies of religiosity. As the table shows, three of every four migrants responded that they observed religious practices in their homes or in the homes of others. Activities included individual and group prayers, ayunos, and home altar devotional practices.

We organized the interviews around a semistructured interview script that included more than one hundred questions designed to tap migrants' everyday experiences and assess the role of religion at each stage of the migration process. For example, respondents described the preparations they and their families made before migration; how they consulted their church and its leaders; and if they prayed to saints and holy icons and images. They described the religious practices in which they engaged before migrating, including any that involved pilgrimages, the making of migration petitions, or the creation of promises to be fulfilled if granted a safe arrival. The script addressed the conditions of the journey, including information about traveling companions, modes of transportation and routes, the length of their journeys, and a host of social and physical problems they may have faced along the way. The migrants recounted the popular and more traditional religious practices or activities in which they engaged en route and the religious organizations and churches from which they sought shelter and assistance during the journey. Respondents also provided information about their religious activities upon arrival, that is, how they expressed thanks for a safe arrival and if and how they fulfilled any promises they made to holy images and icons before migrating. Each of the interviews lasted from one to several hours, and the respondents were not remunerated for their time. Nonetheless, many welcomed the opportunity to speak about their faith and the adoption and construction of religious practices as coping mechanisms on the journey.

In time, the research design for the project altered and expanded, as preliminary findings from one data source led me in new and unexpected directions. The migrants repeatedly spoke of religious places, shrines, and sacred locations that they had either visited prior to departure or on the journey to pray to a holy image for protection, or had promised to visit in the future to give thanks for what they spoke of as the "miracle" of their safe arrival. Part of the subsequent fieldwork involved travel to a number of these shrines and holy places, to interview migrant pilgrims, clergy, and workers who manage the sites. In addition to the Maya Sacred grounds of Xe Cacal Xiguin, during summers and holidays in 2002, 2003, 2004, and 2005, I visited seventeen Catholic shrines and religious places in Mexico, Guatemala, Honduras, El Salvador, Costa Rica, and along the U.S.-Mexico border. In Mexico, Guatemala, Honduras, El Salvador, and Costa Rica, holy icons housed in Catholic shrines reflect popular images of Christ and the Virgin, such as La Virgen de Guadalupe in Mexico City; La Virgen de San Juan de los Lagos in Jalisco, Mexico; El Cristo Negro in Esquipulas, Guatemala; and La Virgen de Suyapa in Tegucigalpa, Honduras. Along the U.S.-Mexico border, we visited several popular shrines that are not recognized by the Catholic Church but have been erected by followers of *almas*, or souls who are believed to have miraculous powers to help common people in trouble, including migrants, coyotes, and border crossers more generally.[29]

At each of these shrines we conducted interviews with migrant pilgrims, with pastors who oversee the shrines, and with the curators and staff who maintain them. At these sanctuaries we collected records of petitions requesting assistance that were left by pilgrims, including migrants petitioning for a safe journey. Sometimes the petitions were handwritten, which allowed me to analyze them for migration content, but most of the time I relied on my own observations, the voices of migrants who told me of their requests, and those petitions recounted to clergy who counseled migrants before their departure. At these shrines we also collected "migration miracles," various expressions of thanks to a revered saint or icon in return for a safe journey to the United States, often including what migrants called a *milagro* (miracle) a divine intervention that allowed them to escape apprehension, assault, or even death. Sometimes the milagros were recounted by migrants we interviewed at the shrines; other times they were told to us by the priests and curators who are charged with caring for the multiple offerings of thanks. Sometimes the milagros were incorporated into services on the Day or Week of the Migrant or Emigrant, a special day or week set aside by the diocese to commemorate their resident emigrants. Believers leave many types of gifts in exchange for the miracle received. We saw flowers, ribbons, carvings, crutches, baby booties, clothing, small silver or wax objects of body parts (also called milagros in Mexico), and virtually any other object that could symbolize a favor granted. In some shrines, migrants record these miracles in ex-voto drawings or in books of miracles; in others, the legends are passed on by word of mouth from the migrants to those who watch over the shrines, like Señora Josefina, the protector of the room of miracles at the shrine of St. Toribio in Jalisco, Mexico.

Many of the interviews conducted with local and trusted priests and clergy took place at shrines or places of worship that migrants visited before departing from their home communities. A substantial number of the interviews with religious leaders, however, occurred at migrant shelters and hospitality houses that are situated along the crossing corridor that stretches from Guatemala to the southwest United States. At these shelters, we observed migrant religious practices, interviewed journeying migrants, and interviewed church ministers and directors or staff of migrant shelters that offer religious counsel and humanitarian and legal assistance. The field observations and interviews at shelters provided context and allowed me to explore institutional responses by various religious bodies to the religious practices of journeying migrants. I wanted to trace the ways in which local, national, and international faith-based groups and NGOs serving migrants had expanded in response to the growth in migration numbers and crossing dangers. I was interested as well in documenting the types of humanitarian and social services and social network opportunities they provide to transit migrants as well as their role in the larger migration process.

Among these religious interviews, I focused especially on the Scalabrinian congregation, the only transnational Catholic congregation devoted solely to the care of migrants. The Scalabrini have constructed a network of safe houses (Red Casas del Migrante) for journeying and deported migrants along the undocumented migrant trail that stretches from Central America to the United States. Early in the fieldwork, in the summer of 2002, I met a dynamic and fervent young Scalabrini priest, Father Francisco Pellizzari, who, despite his Italian and Argentinean roots, had found himself firmly established in the largest of the Scalabrinian migrant shelters in Latin America, the Casa del Migrante in Juárez, Mexico.[30] After a stimulating three-hour discussion, he gave me the names of other Scalabrinian missionaries to contact and introduced me to the provincial office that provided archival data on the Scalabrinians in the region, including back issues of their publication, *Migrante*, which supplies a wealth of information on regional migration trends and issues. Through Father Pellizzari and his initial contacts I interviewed several dozen Scalabrinians, about half of whom work the migrant trail. I was able, for example, in 2003 to interview Father Pedro Corbellini, the eighty-eight-year-old, Italian-born founder of the seminary for Scalabrinians in Mexico. Established in 1980, through the joint efforts of U.S and Mexican bishops, the seminary trains and prepares priests for ministering to the growing Latino diaspora and works closely with the Mexican church in providing for transit migrants.

In Mexico and Guatemala I visited the Scalabrinian *casas*, where we observed their humanitarian, spiritual, and social justice work, interviewed migrants, and spoke to staff that tend to their needs. I met Father Flor Maria Rigoni, a Scalabrini missionary who is renowned in Latin America for his tireless work with migrants. He educated me about the Scalabrini tradition—Samaritans of the migrant trail—and their social theology of liberating the migrants. He reminded me that Jesus was the first migrant. He poignantly showed me the sacred and human dimension of migrants from the Scalabrini perspective when he told me, "We see the face of us and of Jesus in the migrant." Descriptions and discussions of the Scalabrinian congregation and their migration work, which is largely based on a theology of migration that stresses liberalizing and transforming the lives of migrants, runs through many pages of this book.

The Catholic Church hierarchy in Guatemala, El Salvador, Mexico, the United States, and Rome supports many of the shrines and shelters in sending communities and along the migratory route. Indeed, the Scalabrini work closely with the local, regional, national, and transnational church hierarchies to develop their transit programs for journeying migrants. To understand these nested relationships I attended several regional, binational, and transnational conferences on regional migration that were sponsored by a broad coalition of civil society organizations, including churches, NGOs, and civil associations. I attended the fourth annual Binational Workshop on Pastoral Services for Migrants, held in Mexico City during the celebration of the Day of the Migrant in September 2003. Approximately seventy religious leaders attended this conference, sponsored by the Mexican Episcopal Commission for the Pastoral Care of Human Mobility, the U.S. Conference of Bishops, and the Vatican's Pontifical Council for the Pastoral Care of Migrants and Itinerant People, all of which support, promote, or direct migrant-related programs. The conference yielded a wealth of new data concerning the development of programs for migrants journeying in Mexico. At the conference, I interviewed priests from both sides of the border, directors of U.S. NGOs and Mexican civil associations, and U.S. and Mexican bishops who are active in immigration reform through pastoral mobilization efforts, such as the Conference of U.S. and Mexican Bishops. At other religious-based and academic binational conferences, I interviewed a selected number of clergy, bishops, and archbishops from Mexico, El Salvador, Honduras, the United States, and the Vatican, who work closely on the issue of transit migration from Central America to the United States. In some cases I traveled to their home countries where I was invited to conduct follow-up fieldwork. For example, in 2005 Cardinal Oscar Rodríguez Maradiaga hosted me in Honduras, and the vicar of the national basilica, Father Carlo Magno, guided me to migrant shrines and churches in Tegucigalpa and surrounding communities.

Although the majority of interviews with religious leaders I conducted were with Catholic clergy, I also interviewed key mainline Protestant leaders who work on migration and social justice on both sides of the Arizona-Mexico border, the most dangerous crossing area for undocumented migrants today, as well as a setting in which interfaith coalitions are increasingly challenging state-sponsored enforcement efforts. These interviews with institutional leaders allowed me to explore the ways religious institutions, coalitions, organizations, and groups, at regional, national, and international levels, are mobilizing around migration issues and contesting state institutions and their policies. Such issues include the increased policing of traditional crossing points along the southwest border, which leads to greater risk for journeying migrants as they are driven to cross at unpopulated desert areas along the border.

Migration Miracle has been five years in the making. During this period, we interviewed more than 250 undocumented migrants about their journey to the United States; most constitute the migrant sample that provided the baseline data for the book. In addition we conducted interviews with migrants at each stage of the process: in their home communities, along the journey, and after their arrival in Houston, New York, and North Carolina. I kept in close contact with a handful of migrants throughout the life of this project, and their stories are presented here in rich detail. Among them is Cecilia, a young Mexican woman who has been my confidant throughout the life of this project and who asked that her true first name be used in the book. She and four others became my trusted informants and friends who listened to my interpretations and confirmed or clarified some of them, while challenging others. To complement the migrants' interviews, I interviewed ninety-four religious leaders, some of whom also became trusted confidants, such as Rev. Hoover, and read earlier drafts of my work. Many of the interviews with faith workers took place at religious institutions and sacred places where migrants stopped to visit along the journey. Finally, even though this is the story of undocumented migrants, as a baseline we interviewed 110 documented migrants. When useful, I inject their numbers and tales into the narrative for comparative purposes.

Readers will find two strands of narrative here. The first explains how and why individual migrants turn to their culture, faith, trusted clergy, and everyday religious practices for the spiritual and psychological strength to overcome hardship and danger in their undocumented journeys from Mexico and Central America to the United States. The second illustrates how churches and their ministers and faith workers—both Catholic and Protestant—respond to the needs of these migrants, foster their spirituality throughout the journey, and ultimately sustain the migration process. Together, they reveal how both agency and structure interact to influence how and why religion permeates the undocumented migration experience from Latin America, from the moment migrants begin pondering their departure, until their safe arrival in a new land, and often beyond.

The story is told in six chapters, the first five of which correspond to stages in the migration process. Chapter 1, "Decision Making and Leave-Taking," describes the hardships and decisions that many migrants face when considering migration north. The chapter moves beyond the perspective of migrants as solitary or exclusively rational decision makers to analyze the different ways in which departing migrants seek religious counsel—divine and human—to help with their decision. The chapter also focuses on the role that religious leaders and local institutions play in helping to prepare the migrant and his or her family for the arduous journey ahead and in promoting emigration devotion in their home communities. Chapter 1 also identifies a number of religious practices that migrants undertake before departing, including pilgrimages to religious shrines and sacred places for final blessings.

Chapter 2, "The Dangerous Journey," analyzes the larger empirical context of danger, tracing the obstacles and dangers that migrants encounter along the way. It provides an overview of state policies to curb undocumented migration from Latin America and the human costs associated with these efforts. It provides the context for understanding why, in the contemporary world of militarized borders, migrants on the undocumented trail turn to faith, familiar cultural practices, and the church for assistance and comfort. The chapter also focuses on the social process of crossing and shows how the dangers of the journey vary depending on place of departure, time on the road, mode of crossing, and gender.

Chapter 3, "Churches Crossing Borders," focuses on the role of religious institutions in supporting undocumented migration. The chapter focuses on the various types of support and services provided to migrants, describing humanitarian and social justice efforts of churches and interfaith organizations in Central America, Mexico, and the United States. The chapter also documents the numerous ways in which small Protestant churches and larger Catholic churches have come together and organized under a banner of providing services for the journeying migrant, and maps out the recent construction of a network of migrant shelters and programs established by the Scalabrinian missionaries, an Italian religious congregation with a long-standing tradition of providing for the immigrant. In addition, it traces the public and advocacy role of the church concerning issues of migrant human rights and militarized borders, a development facilitated through the acceleration of cross-border ties across religious organizations, from local parishes to binational bishop conferences.

Chapter 4, "Miracles in the Desert," tells the story of migrants' everyday religious and cultural practices along the journey, emphasizing the symbiotic relationship between the two. The chapter moves beyond the institutional context of religion and migration and explores the different ways in which migrants draw on and create their relationships with God and their revered holy images to muster the strength to cope with the journey. Moving away from the perspective of religious leaders, this chapter focuses on religion as a lived experience during the isolated journey. The chapter describes the construction, adoption, and transformation of the familiar as coping strategies.

Chapter 5, "La Promesa" (The Promise), describes the multiple ways in which migrants fulfill their vows of reciprocity in return for a safe passage to the United States. The chapter highlights the theme of fulfilling the promise, a process that transcends borders and manifests itself over years and through numerous formal, informal, institutional, and private religious and cultural practices. Chapter 6, "Conclusions," moves beyond the book narrative to discuss the wider implications of this study for migration theory and research.

This book is a study of faith, hope, and meaning on the migration journey. In the pages of research and analysis that follow, I have tried to humanize the data. Too often we cast the immigration experience solely in economic or deviant terms, dehumanizing these desperate and dignified people, making it easier to attack and criminalize them, and to see them as different from and not part of or like us.[31] By exploring migrants' religious and cultural practices and by portraying the harsh realities of their lives and their journeys, I have sought not only to add to the sociological knowledge base, but also to present a fuller, more recognizable human portrait of these newcomers.

CHAPTER 1

Decision Making and Leave-Taking

Hernando was born in Jalisco, Mexico, where many of the residents consider themselves deeply religious, and was raised a Catholic. Unable to locate a full-time job to help support his family, he had long thought about following the footsteps taken by friends and countless young men and women from his village who had migrated to the United States. Hernando longed to move to Houston, Texas, where he had heard that work was plentiful and where he had friends he could count on for initial support. Yet he was reluctant to leave behind all he knew and held dear, and incur the unknown, perhaps dire risks, to reach the land to the north. To help him with this undertaking, he turned to God, La Virgen de San Juan de los Lagos, and to the patron saint of lost causes, San Judas Tadeo (St. Jude), for advice and waited for a sign. "I begged them to open paths for me and I told them that whatever decision they made would be right," he said. "I waited for a sign. I believe that they sent me a message saying it was okay to go to Houston because I finally received a blessing from my mother and grandmother who had prayed to God for advice."

Armed with their blessing, which he believed God had sanctioned, Hernando began to prepare for his journey, which he planned to undertake with several other young men from his hometown, but without the guidance of a coyote. He and his family prayed for safety on the migrant trail, a journey that had taken the lives of other unsuccessful migrants from his community. Before leaving his hometown, he and his mother visited their local priest who counseled Hernando on his migration and urged him to remain faithful to the church while in the United States and to keep in close contact with his mother and grandmother. Before leaving, Hernando, his mother, and grandmother made the pilgrimage to the shrine of La Virgen de San Juan de los Lagos. At the shrine the trio prayed for Hernando's safety and success, and Hernando vowed to La Virgen that if she permitted him a safe journey he would honor her for the rest of his life.

At critical moments in most people's lives, in the face of competing options and uncertain consequences, believers and nonbelievers alike often turn to religion to help them make the right decision and to cope with uncertainty. At times believers cope by turning to revered saints, trusted clergy, and religious groups for counsel, guidance, and support.[1] It comes as no great surprise, then, to confirm that undocumented migrants from Mexico and Central America also draw on their religious resources when planning to migrate. They seek religious counsel while considering whether to migrate to the United States, and religious support when preparing to leave. Vital considerations weigh into their decision: Who will care for or support the family left behind? How will the trip be financed? Will the migrant be able to count on family and friends for support on arrival in the United States? What job opportunities, if any, exist in labor markets there? For undocumented migrants, these concerns escalate and multiply: What life-threatening risks will they encounter on the journey? What will happen if border officials apprehend them?

Making the Decision

Hernando wrestled with his decision by turning to his faith and to those both divine and human who represent the power of that faith. He was not alone in this undertaking. Among the sample of undocumented migrants, four out of every five—Catholics and Protestants, frequent and infrequent churchgoers alike—sought counsel from God, a saint, or a member of the clergy when deciding to migrate to the United States. So powerful was religion in the process that most migrants turned first to holy icons and trusted clergy for counsel before consulting with immediate family members (71 percent) or friends (19 percent). And as the migrants' comments reveal, much of this counsel was in the form of private prayer to God and in consultation with clergy, dialogues that have gone virtually unrecognized in the scholarship on migration and decision making, perhaps because they verge on humanistic orientations that are difficult to conceptualize or document. Instead, the standard literature relies almost exclusively on a rational model of economic factors to explain the decision to migrate.

In general, theories explaining international migration single out some combination of economic models operating at different levels of analysis to predict migration flows. Two of these frameworks—neoclassical economic theory and the new economics of labor migration model—focus on the microlevel decision-making processes of individuals and the households in which they are embedded. According to the first of these models, individuals make a cost-benefit analysis between the places of origin and potential destinations, including an assessment of intervening factors, the psychological costs of leaving family and community, and the difficulty of the trip; they migrate if the net benefit anticipated—usually higher wages—is greater at the destination. This neoclassical explanation of why people move remains anchored in a rational-choice model that assumes individuals weigh these considerations and then they alone make the decision to migrate. Recognizing that individual migrants may rely on nonimmigrants in the decision-making process, the "new economics of migration" broadens the unit of analysis but posits that households, too, make decisions to maximize the economic benefits from migration and minimize market risks in home communities.[2]

Scholarship also recognizes that migration is not just an economic process, but also a social one. Network theory complements economic models of decision making and broadens the social actors involved in decision making and leave-taking. Since the 1920s, social scientists have acknowledged the importance of migrants' social relationships in organizing and encouraging international migration. Social networks, comprised of friends and family with a migration history, provide prospective migrants with assistance to facilitate movement.[3] The concept resurfaced and gained widespread popularity among academics beginning in the 1980s when Doug Massey and his colleagues explained international migration from Mexico as a social process, highlighting migrant networks as a form of social capital.[4] According to network theory, when migrants are all set to move, they will, if they can, activate their personal networks at areas of destination. That is, once the network connections that link sending and receiving communities reach a critical level, prospective departing migrants draw on the assistance provided by friends and family in the United States, which reduces the costs of migration.[5] Scholarship further recognizes that in well-established migrant sending communities, a "culture of migration" can develop. As migratory experience and migrant stories spread throughout a community, aspirations to migrate increase among youth. As Kandel and Massey found in their analysis of migratory behavior in Mexican communities, many youth expect to migrate to the United States when they reach adulthood, and thus, the event becomes a "rite of passage."[6]

This chapter will show that what and who makes migration happen is a much more complex process than portrayed in prevailing scholarship.[7] While economic considerations may trigger the motivation to migrate, and family, trusted friends, and a community tradition of migration may contribute to the decision, often religious factors, embedded in strong cultural and local practices, ultimately guide and support decision-making and leave-taking. For many migrants contemplating leave-taking, religion and faith assists them with their decision to migrate and fortifies them psychologically to prepare for the hardships of the journey. At some stage the decision making moves from a rational, real-world level to a very private, religious, even mystical plane. Moreover, individuals do not make these decisions in isolation or only in consultation with family and friends in sending and receiving communities. Prospective migrants reach this religious space through prayer and consultation with trusted clergy who provide for their spiritual needs. Decisions to migrate are often sanctioned by religious institutions that support the undertaking. By tapping into these dialogues and institutional arrangements we can identify migrants' deepest concerns and understand how they marshal the necessary religious and spiritual resources to make this monumental decision.

Religious resources support and guide the migration undertaking in several ways. Early on in the decision-making process, these resources manifest themselves in the appearance of what migrants often refer to as "signs" or "messages from God," indicating that their migration plans may move forward. Almost three out of four migrants interviewed mentioned waiting for a sign from God before making the final decision to migrate; in some cases, the lack of a sign convinced potential migrants to postpone the trip. These signs or messages took many forms, ranging from confirmation through reading the Scriptures, to approval by a local pastor, to securing a coyote (guide), and even borrowing a visa. In this context, signs or messages from God emerge under particular conditions and represent religious events or occurrences that impact people and propel action. Because signs or messages are not easily quantifiable, however, they are rarely acknowledged or documented by scholars; yet, they remain important, not only because people believe in them but also because they are powerful agents of action. In other words, signs are real in their consequences.[8]

María, an evangelical who migrated without papers from Monterrey, Mexico, to Houston, Texas in 1996, discovered her sign of approval while reading the Bible. She believes that all her successes, including her migration to the United States, came about because God has been with her. Lacking the financial resources to feed and educate her four children, she "had no choice but to leave," she said. Yet, she was frightened about traveling alone without papers with her oldest daughter and had misgivings about leaving her three younger children in her sister's care. And so María waited for a message from God. After months of prayer, God's "sign of approval" came to her when she read "for the first time and with my eyes open" Joshua 1:9, in which God says, "Have I not commanded you? Be strong and courageous. Do not be terrified; do not be discouraged, for the Lord your God will be with you wherever you go."[9] Taking the advice of the biblical verse, María said she "had the strength to make the decision to come, to travel by bus with my daughter, and to pursue an uncertain future in this country for me and my family." Her move to Houston has been a success story; her daughter attends a local community college and María has secured a job as a caregiver for a handicapped woman, earning $3,000 a month.

Another evangelical, Margot, also looked for a sign before migrating from Guatemala to the United States in 1998. Margot was born and raised a Catholic, and joined a Pentecostal church before leaving Guatemala. A number of personal problems at home triggered Margot's desire to migrate to the United States, but she wrestled with the decision for some time because she lacked the funds to secure a coyote and feared for her safety on the journey. Like so many of the evangelical migrants, she fasted for several days and in the solitude of her bedroom read her bible and asked God for advice and strength. "I told God that if it was his will, then he would give me a sign," she explained. "I also challenged God and told him that if Doña Isabela [a local woman who arranged transportation for undocumented migrants] agreed to help me without me giving her the $1,500 she charges to get people from Guatemala to Mexico, then I would accept this as a sign. When I went to see Doña Isabela, she agreed to help me and I promised to send her the money once I was in the United States." Still undecided about the journey, she approached her pastor, who, in the past, had dissuaded some parishioners from migrating. "I told him of the sign that I received and he also thought it was a sign, so he supported my decision. He then asked the church to accept my decision. So you see, I received two signs from God before leaving," Margot said.

It is worth noting that this desire for divine sanction before emigration is not confined to the undocumented; migrants who obtained legal travel papers also interpreted their good fortune as a message of approval from God. Gabriela, a Catholic and mother of two, said that she had no choice but to move to the United States. "There was no hope that things would improve for us in Guatemala. We either had to leave or we would starve. I knew it was God's will when the American Embassy gave us our visas very quickly and without all the trouble that they usually give people," she said. "Everyone I know always has to go back several times before they get their visa and we got ours in one try." Even if receiving travel authorization involved the use of falsified papers, individuals interpreted obtaining these documents as God's will and justifiably legitimate. One young woman, a longtime practicing evangelical from Mexico who read her Bible daily and fasted for several days, said that "God presented a way of getting to the United States. He allowed me to use my cousin's tourist visa. Immigration did not notice this at the border because God wanted me to come here."

When plans did not fall into place, migrants often understood these misfortunes as God's message that it was not a time to travel north, at which point they postponed the journey until a more favorable time. Signs or messages are often transmitted through local clergy who hold enormous prophetic power over their flocks, often encouraging or constraining their actions. A number of migrants, for example, spoke of relatives or friends who had changed their plans after speaking to a local religious figure who advised against the migration. Lucía, a fifty-two-year-old charismatic Catholic from Mexico, spoke at length about her niece's original plans to come to the United States to join her fiancée in Los Angeles. After conferring with a priest in Mexico, however, Lucía's niece postponed her plans indefinitely. According to Lucía, the priest counseled against the journey, telling her niece that if she went to Los Angeles, she would lack the family support to endure the fragility of a new marriage in a foreign land. Lucía's niece stayed in Mexico. In other cases, ministers actually influenced the timing of migration by imploring migrants to postpone trips, saying it was not yet God's will. In initial consultation with her pastor, Carmen, an Episcopalian from El Salvador, was advised to delay her trip until conditions along the Mexico-U.S. border improved. Some months later, the pastor told her, "It is now time to leave," and so she did. While signs took many forms and were transmitted by various mediums, what is important is that migrants in the study interpreted them as divine interventions that enabled them to justify the final decision to migrate on moral grounds, under the banner of God's will.

While nine out of ten Protestants and Catholics who sought religious counsel did so by turning to God for spiritual guidance, their choice of how to pray or if an icon was involved varied by religious affiliation and national origin. Central American and Mexican Catholics primarily seek guidance from the Virgin Mary and other holy images, some of which are popular in their home communities.[10] Roughly a quarter of all the Catholic migrants from Central America we interviewed said they called on the Virgin Mary during the decision-making process. Migrants from Mexico, with their long tradition of venerating sacred images of Christ and the Virgin, said they turned to a litany of holy icons as they contemplated the decision;[11] 25 percent of Catholic migrants from Mexico sought religious counsel through private prayer to the Virgin of Guadalupe, the patroness of Mexico.

Because each region in Mexico has its own venerated religious figure and most of these are sacred images of Christ and the Virgin, migrants often draw on the familiar, that is, an icon to which they have prayed time and again for spiritual support and sustenance. We found, for example, that migrants from the well-established sending communities of western Mexico—a region long recognized for its people's faith and devotion—called on that area's many religious images for spiritual guidance in decision making, among them the Virgin of San Juan of los Lagos, the Virgin of Zapopan, and the Baby Christ (El Niño de Atacho), which is recognized for miraculous rescues of people in danger, especially travelers.[12] Similarly, Catholics from Central America called on their popular images of Christ and the Virgin when contemplating the decision to migrate, although they turned to these religious icons less frequently than did their Mexican counterparts. A number of Catholic Hondurans and Guatemalans, for example, prayed to the Black Christ (El Cristo Negro), an image with which many indigenous Maya Catholics identify. Images of the Black Christ are scattered in sanctuaries throughout Mexico and Central America, and even in the United States. The earliest and most famous Black Christ is located in the sanctuary of Nuestro Señor de Esquipulas in eastern Guatemala, just a few miles from the Honduran border. Honduran and Guatemalan migrants reported making the pilgrimage to the shrine and praying to this image during the decision-making stage of their migration; several of the Hondurans said they also prayed to the patroness of their country, the Virgin of Suyapa (Nuestra Señora de Suyapa). Among the Salvadoran migrants, that country's spiritual protector, Our Lady of Peace (Nuestra Señora de la Paz), provided a major source of guidance.

After calling on a sacred image for spiritual guidance, one in every five migrants in the sample turned to their clergy for additional advice about the decision to migrate. These individuals, most of whom were regular churchgoers, sought confirmation for their decisions. Interestingly, this practice did not vary significantly with the legal status or religious affiliation of the migrant. Trepidation among Catholics and Protestants, documented and undocumented alike, compelled them to turn to religious leaders for guidance. In most cases, the consultation was a relatively informal process, with the migrant visiting a familiar clergy member and asking his or her advice about the trip. Occasionally, other church members were also consulted about their views on the migration. Miguel, a twenty-one-year-old practicing Catholic from Monterrey, Mexico, arrived in Houston in 2000. For several months before leaving, he had agonized over the decision to migrate. Like so many of those who left before and after him, Miguel dreaded the hardships of the journey and feared for the well-being of the family he would leave behind. Even if he arrived safely in the United States, he worried about locating a job. "I prayed day and night for several months," Miguel explained. "I fasted. I grew so anxious that I finally went to see our priest and asked him what I should do." The priest did not want to bless Miguel's decision because the move would involve leaving Miguel's wife and children behind. But the priest also knew the truth of Miguel's statement: "I had no choice. I had to work." The priest asked the whole church to pray over Miguel's dilemma, and he mentioned Miguel's name in several masses, one of which commemorated all the migrant parishioners. After some time, the priest asked Miguel to come see him. "He told me it was okay to leave, but told me not to stray from my family or from the path of God." The priest then concluded by instructing him "to keep in touch with him and to go to church every week." Miguel made it safely to the United States, found a job as a house painter, and is in regular contact with his family and the priest. "I owe all my good fortune to God, the priest, and the church in Monterrey," Miguel said. "I would not be here if it were not for them." Miguel credits his safe journey, arrival, and immigration success to religion.

Guatemalan, Mexican, and Costa Rican clergy all confirmed an increase in migration counseling in recent years and explained this elevated demand as a function of an increase in emigration and the heightened risks run by migrants. Clergy referred to these consultations as migration counseling or migration ministry work. In many sending communities throughout Mexico and Central America, migration ministry work has become integrated into more general ministry work. Through counseling, local clergy provide two types of social support to potential migrants: emotional and instrumental. More specifically, during migration ministering clergy provide spiritual counsel, including blessings; advice on the social and economic consequences of their migration undertaking; and more practical advice about the journey, such as safe crossing routes, their rights if apprehended by officials, and verbal or written documentation about the location of legal aid services and migrant shelters along the migrant trail. Migration ministering sanctions what is otherwise an unauthorized journey.

Father Eduardo Quintero's migration ministry work illustrates the multiple types of emotional and instrumental support provided to migrants by local clergy. Father Eduardo is a young Catholic priest who counsels Guatemalan youth and prospective migrants from Central America. He was ordained in 2001 as a Scalabrinian priest, part of an Italian Catholic order founded in 1886 with the primary mission of providing pastoral care to migrants. Father Eduardo began his training for the priesthood in his native country of Colombia and continued it in Mexico. After completing his studies in the Scalabrini Seminary in Chicago, he settled in Guatemala City. Fluent in three languages (Italian, Spanish, and English) and in the academic literature and religious teachings on the subject of migration, he is most at home fulfilling his missionary goals by working with the poor and the displaced, especially migrants, because, he said, "I have been invited to know Jesus as a migrant."

With meager funds, Father Eduardo runs Casa del Migrante, a modest shelter for migrants in Guatemala City. Since his arrival there, his pastoral work with migrants has been focused in the area of "counseling and educating persons on the migration phenomenon." He estimates that in his community as many as half of all prospective migrants seek counseling. He prepares lectures on migration to present at local schools, community centers, and churches. He has also edited an hour-long educational video that focuses on migrant rights, migration dangers, and the social consequences of journeying north, which he has shown to about seven hundred young people "in the hopes of educating them early on and perhaps discouraging them from making the decision to go north to fulfill what many in Central America now call the American dream," he said. In addition to educating the larger community on migration, Father Eduardo also advises about a dozen prospective migrants a day, some making their first attempt, others more seasoned, having attempted the trip before.

Father Eduardo wrestles with his position on migration, which in turn influences how he counsels migrants. On the one hand, in part because of his theological training as a Catholic priest and as a Scalabrinian, a congregation that emphasizes social justice, Father Eduardo embraces the Catholic Church's doctrine on emigration, which recognizes that migration is a fundamental human right for those who cannot find employment in their own country to support themselves and their families.[13] On the other hand, he knows that today, more than ever before, undocumented migration is a risky route to economic opportunity. Most in his community who venture north without papers have no choice but to traverse the notoriously dangerous six-hundred-mile-long Mexico-Guatemala border where hundreds of migrant lives are claimed every year. Along this border, migrants fall prey to bandits, drown in rivers, and suffer in train and automobile accidents and at the hands of corrupt officials.[14] Indeed, while visiting the shelter I met an uncle and nephew from Honduras who in their recent attempt to cross through Mexico had endured severe psychological trauma and physical injuries after being robbed and thrown from a railway car; nonetheless, they were considering another attempt. Consequently, like many other clergy in Central America and Mexico who provide pastoral care for migrants, Father Eduardo finds that he is advising first-time migrants primarily on the dangers of the journey, and secondly, on the importance of remaining close to the church and home community.

When pressed, Father Eduardo declined to take a definitive position on whether he believes he should encourage or discourage migration in his counseling. "We must respect their own personal decision," he said. "We can only provide information to educate them." Occasionally, however, prospective migrants are so unprepared for the uncertainty that faces them that Father Eduardo admits that he "has no choice" but to discourage the decision to journey north. He gave as an example the case of a group of young men from Honduras who had meager funds, knew little of the terrain they would travel, and had no Mexican or U.S. contacts on which to rely. "When I talk to poor, simple and uneducated people who paint a heavenly story of migration, I feel compelled to balance things by painting a bleak picture of the journey," he said. "In this sense, there are times when I do discourage or invite people to think more before making their decision."

In a perfect world, most clergy agreed, they would probably discourage the flight of their parishioners. This is especially true of the religious leaders of small, independent Pentecostal ministries who depend on every individual for the survival of their churches and who place strong emphasis on family unity. But with declining economic opportunities in Mexico and Central America, Catholic and evangelical clergy alike are unwilling to take a definitive position. Although reluctant to encourage the departure of one of their flock, clergy of the poor are sympathetic to the economic plight within their communities. Plainly, people need jobs to feed their families. Yet priests and ministers are troubled about the dangers of the trip and its consequences. Clergy know they are more than simply spiritual leaders for their parishioners; they understand that their advice may have serious repercussions, not just for the migrants but also for the families left behind.

Father Rigoberto España, a soft-spoken Catholic priest who counsels prospective migrants at the Basílica del Señor de Esquipulas in Esquipulas, Guatemala, summed up the quandary that many clergy, especially Catholic priests trained in the tradition of liberation theology, face when advising migrants about their decision: "Migration is a fundamental part of the way of life here. It is part of our culture. The motivations behind the decision to migrate are economic. Today the economic rationale is the declining price of coffee in Honduras and Guatemala, which makes the need for the American dream stronger than ever before." Many in his homeland amassed hefty loans to support small-scale coffee production, but with the declining price of coffee they have since slipped into tremendous debt. Others have lost their jobs as laborers in the coffee fields. "If they do not go to the United States to work, the banks will take their land, their homes, anything they may own," Father Rigoberto said.

Counseling prospective migrants on the decision to migrate thus involves both acknowledging the hoped-for positives while presenting the negatives, which, according to Father Rigoberto, increasingly means "alerting them to the dangers that await them on the route north and letting them know that migration is fundamentally destructive to the family because it separates it." But, as he pointed out, "They are not naïve. They know of the dangers; they have lost friends to the journey." Moreover, he remarked, "It is not the Catholic way to tell them not to go. We support migration as a human right. We can't stand in their way. These are not all young men; some are forty or fifty years of age. They have established families here. They own land, cars." He summed up the dilemma that he and other clergy face by emphasizing that "in a better world, they would never leave their communities. So, when they say, 'Father, please advise me, please let me go,' what can I say? I must let them go. I must bless their decision."

Preparing for the Journey

The decision to migrate is only the beginning of the struggle for individuals who face uprooting themselves from family and community and bracing for a journey of hardship and a stay of indefinite length in a new land.

Myriad practical preparations, some of which have huge financial, psychological, and physical ramifications for migrants and their families, must be undertaken. Not surprisingly, most migrants have to seek additional funds to support their journey and the initial costs of settlement in the United States. Many have saved their earnings to lessen the debt while others borrow heavily from family and friends. In the absence of regular earnings and family resources, migrants are forced to make enormous sacrifices and take large financial risks. Jaime's experience, sadly, is not unusual. He is a thirty-six-year-old Charismatic Catholic and farmer from Veracruz, Mexico, who arrived in the United States in 1999. To pay the coyote who guided him across the Mexico-U.S. border, he had to sell his land. When he had almost reached the border, he was assaulted and robbed of his money. After seeking temporary shelter in a Catholic Church on the outskirts of Matamoros, a border town in Mexico, he wandered north through the brush and desolation of south Texas ranchland and finally made his way to Houston. By the summer of 2002, Jaime was earning only $800 a month working part time as a house painter and had been unable to recoup his losses or gain a legal foothold in the United States, despite his years of hard work. As Jaime explained, "I expected to send home money to my parents and my sister within months of arriving in the United States, but I have still sent nothing back. I still don't have working papers. I have nothing to return to either."

Another migrant, Navarro, a thirty-year-old Catholic who left his home in Guatemala City in 1991 with his wife and three children, also faced a grim outcome. Anticipating a permanent move, he sold his truck and his furniture, and signed the deed of his house over to his father. The money he earned from these sales covered the cost of securing a coyote to take his family across the Rio Grande. For several weeks they traveled by bus and train and on foot, nearly drowning in the Rio Grande before arriving at Navarro's brother's home in Houston. Navarro found a job at a local newspaper company and worked his way up the ladder. By the summer of 2002, he was earning $5,000 a month, but despite this financial success, his future was bleak. He was arrested in 2002 and faced deportation orders and the inevitable: permanent separation from his family, since "they have no desire to go back to Guatemala." Moreover, Navarro's prospects were equally bleak back home. Having sold off his assets, he would have to return at the mercy of his parents' generosity.

With limited financial resources and lacking travel authorization, many of the poor rely on the assistance of family in the United States to support their migration.[15] Among the migrants in this study, social support proved crucial. Indeed, one out of every five migrants drew on financial or social support from family members in the United States to help with their preparations. Of these, more women than men received assistance from family who had made the trip before, especially from spouses and brothers.[16] Typical is Carmen, a twenty-five-year-old single woman from Honduras, who avoided many of the uncertainties because she traveled with her brother who had "already made the trip, so he knew the way, but we had to pay off, give *mordidas* [bribes] to bus drivers, police, and border people to help get us through." María, a thirty-six-year-old woman who traveled on foot and by bus from her hometown of Asunción, El Salvador, to Houston, Texas, in 1996, also received help from her family in the United States. "My husband sent me the money and I paid the coyote half of the thirty-five thousand dollars to bring me here. My husband paid the other half when we arrived."

In addition to securing the costs of travel and settlement, prospective migrants must locate family and friends to take care of loved ones while they are away, not knowing how long the separation might last. Many of the young mothers in the study sample who traveled to the United States to join family or to seek work left one or more of their children behind. One whose story illustrates these mothers' desperation is Daniela, a Pentecostal who left her home in Oaxaca, Mexico, for the United States in 1997. For some time she struggled with the decision to join her husband in Houston because it meant leaving her children behind. "I didn't want to come here. My husband sent money to my nephew to get a coyote to take me to him," she said. As much as she wanted to see her husband, she refused to leave her three young daughters. Only when her husband sent her enough money to give to her mother for the long-term care of her children did she decide to leave; even then, she was tormented and turned to her religion for comfort. "I prayed and I fasted and asked God to give me the strength and peace I needed to leave my children. I prayed that my children would not cry when I left. They didn't. That was a sign from God that I could go." Once in the United States, Daniela found work cleaning houses, and in less than a year she and her husband had saved enough money to bring their children to the United States. She agonized over how to do this. Would the couple risk their children's safety and hire a coyote, or would they risk their children's apprehension and rely on the papers offered by mothers of other migrant children? To help make this painful decision, she consulted with her pastor and her fellow parishioners. Ultimately, Daniela accepted the papers from other mothers.

The story has a happy ending: the three daughters were able to join their parents in Texas.

Such family separations brought about by labor migration from Latin America are not a new phenomenon: the practice was commonplace during the 1942–1964 Bracero Program, when many Mexican fathers left their children behind in the care of their mothers as they journeyed north to labor as temporary guest workers. However, in recent years, as more women have migrated to the United States to join spouses, work, or leave oppressive family relationships, they, too, are entrusting their children to alternative caregivers.[17] Fearful of taking their children with them on the dangerous journey north (especially the young and the female), they have no choice but to entrust the children to the care of female relatives. Concern for the well-being of their children dominates the prayers of many departing mothers and fathers.

Private Prayer, Family and Community Rituals, and Clergy Blessings

Once the decision to migrate was made, the departing migrants and their families who were interviewed reported continuing to pray in solitude or with family members around home altars adorned with images of revered icons and pictures of departing loved ones. Some sought final blessings from family, clergy, and fellow parishioners. Others purchased religious items and had them blessed to carry with them on the journey for protection. Still others visited well known local regional shrines and other sacred places where they left migration petitions or made promises to religious images in exchange for a successful migration experience.

Once having decided to leave home, migrants become more specific in their prayers and reflect on the precise concerns of those leaving behind the only life they have known to embark on a journey of uncertainty. When praying to God, a Virgin, or a religious image, individuals said they request guidance and help in one or more of four matters: 1) completing travel arrangements; 2) caring for family members left behind; 3) protection on the journey; and 4) assistance during initial settlement in the United States. Most migrants voiced these concerns in a general petition to God within days of the pending departure. Carlos's plea to God was similar to that of many departing migrants. Several days before leaving his hometown of Morelia, in Michoacán, Mexico, he began to pray in earnest. "I prayed many times each day. I prayed for protection from evil forces I might see on the journey north, I prayed for the protection of my wife and children who stayed home, and I prayed to God to let me enter safely into the United States so that I could find work to feed and house my family." Some migrants, seeking strength and guidance to endure the hardships awaiting them, recounted being so desperate that they exhausted their religious repertoire of holy icons during prayer. Miguel, a young Catholic from Guatemala City, prayed to universal, national, and regional icons several days before leaving. "I prayed to Dios, la Virgen de Guadalupe, San Juan Santiago, San Lucas, San Pedro, la Virgen del Rosario, San Miguel and San Rafael. I asked them to give me what I needed for my family, a better economic situation. I felt in my heart that they would allow me to cross safely into the United States."

The most important concern migrants in the study expressed through private prayer was protection on the journey. This was especially true among those who planned to travel without legal papers. More than half the sample (57 percent), legal and undocumented alike, prayed for protection on the journey; however, among those traveling without papers, the proportion climbed to 78 percent, almost twice as many as those who traveled with authorizations (35 percent). Nonetheless, migrants who were fortunate enough to secure documentation expressed the fear that they would not be allowed into the United States, even though their papers were in order. One young woman from Mexico was so anxious that she "said the rosary over and over throughout the plane ride from Guadalajara to Houston" to prepare her for the encounter with U.S. immigration officials at the Houston airport. Persons traveling without papers reported praying for their personal safety and security during the long and dangerous journey. Carla, a Catholic, prayed constantly to the Virgin Mary before leaving her home in La Unión, El Salvador, with her two-year-old daughter. "My husband sent us six thousand dollars to get a coyote, and a letter with instructions for traveling, but I was scared. I went to church the day before we left and prayed to God and to the Virgin Mary," Carla said. "I said the rosary and I fasted for twenty-four hours. I prayed to the Virgin Mary to protect me and my daughter on the trip and to let us arrive safely to the home of my husband."

The finding that documented migrants prayed deeply and almost as frequently as the undocumented and took the same religious steps to prepare for their journeys should not be surprising. Both documented and undocumented migrants come from the same culture, one imbued with deep religious beliefs. The difference lies in what they pray for. Documented migrants avoid the hazardous journey, and so their trip to the United States is an easy one, sometimes made by air. They told me they prayed for a new and better life in the United States. Undocumented migrants said they sought God's help in securing such happiness as well, but with the dangers of the journey confronting them, they prayed first for safe passage.

In well-established sending areas throughout Mexico and Central America, prospective migrants and their families, sometimes with the aid and blessing of trusted local clergy, perform a variety of cultural and religious rituals prior to departure. Almost half (42 percent) the entire sample—Catholics and Protestants, legal and undocumented—performed one or more religious rituals before leaving their hometowns, ranging from home-centered devotional practices to receiving blessings from local clergy to visiting sacred shrines. The most widespread religious practice that departing migrants and their families undertook was additional migration counseling. Not surprisingly, practicing members of particular churches were especially likely to reach out to their priests and pastors with whom they had an established history of prayer and counsel. During these private consultations and public prayer services, migrants continued to present and discuss their hopes and fears, but most of all they sought final blessings from their spiritual leaders, blessings that provided comfort both to the migrants and to the families who would be left behind. Often these blessings were sought in conjunction with a series of home-devotional practices prepared by mothers, sisters, and brothers of departing migrants. The types of practices reported varied by community, reflecting different regional and ethnic cultural practices, as well as the importance of regional and national patron saints, as the following migrant narratives illustrate:

Cecilia was nineteen years old the first time she traveled to the United States from her hometown of Puebla, Mexico. She and her sister Margot and her husband, Juan, flew to Tijuana, where they met a coyote they knew who took them across the border into California for $500 per person. Prior to departing on what she suspected would be a life-threatening journey, Cecilia, Margot, and their mother went to their priest to ask his blessing. Before visiting the priest, however, the three women performed a series of rituals in her home, which Cecilia explained are common Mexican practices developed by mothers and sisters and observed by departing migrants and their families. Cecilia's mother purchased flowers and two *veladoras* (a large candle in a glass container that is adorned with an image) of the Virgin of Guadalupe, which she "cleaned" (rubbed) over her daughters' bodies.

Together, they then went to the church and asked their priest to bless Cecilia and her sister, the flowers, and the candles. The priest anointed the two sisters with holy water while performing his blessing, gave them a holy card of the Virgin of Guadalupe to accompany them, and wished them good fortune and safety on their trip. He also told them "to make the Mexican people proud," and warned them not "to do drugs or join gangs but to become a good person in the United States." He urged Cecilia and Margot to "work hard and to send money home to their parents and sisters." The day of their departure, Cecilia's mother commenced a candle-light vigil. She lit a white candle for each of her daughters to provide light in the dark and placed the candles, along with the flowers, next to a statue of the Virgin of Guadalupe on a homemade altar in the front room of their home. "My mother kept candles lit until we called my mother from California, to let her know that we had arrived safely. She then blew out the candles," Cecilia said. Recalling the crossing brought Cecilia to tears.

A similar domestic ritual was performed by the parents of Marissa, a young Catholic woman from a rural community in Oaxaca, who traveled without authorization to California in 1994. "A shrine in honor of La Virgen de Guadalupe was made by my parents and they prayed to her daily to protect me during my travels," she said. Marissa said that other migrants from Mexico, from areas as distant as her hometown in central Mexico to Monterrey in northern Mexico, routinely undergo these popular devotional practices when preparing to leave their homes for the United States. Several departing migrants in Guanajuato, for example, reported being given a special soap by their local priest and told to scrub the body well before embarking on their journey. The soap, they explained, was to protect them from harm during the journey.

In the highlands of Guatemala, Amelia and her family made several devotional preparations before she left home. A month before her departure, Amelia's father began his nightly vigils. "He would wake up in all hours of the night to pray," she said. "He wanted to pray in silence so that he could concentrate more and God would be sure to hear him. It is our custom to be alone, to pray in the silence of our homes. After many days he told me, '*Yo sé que va a pasar*,' I know that it will happen." The day before Amelia left, at the insistence of her mother and the local priest, her children were baptized. After the ceremony her mother went into town and purchased a white *vela* (candle) of the town's patron saint, San Antonio de Huista. Before Amelia's early-morning departure, her mother crossed Amelia's entire body with the candle, then lit it and placed it on the makeshift altar in her home, alongside an image of El Cristo Negro de Esquipulas, the patron saint of Guatemala, and an arrangement of white flowers. Like Cecilia's mother and as is the custom in many Catholic homes in Mexico and Guatemala, Amelia's mother kept the vigil of the lighted white candle until Amelia arrived safely. When I asked Amelia about the symbolism of white, she told me, "Green is for peace, red is for love, and white is to illuminate. It illuminated the way for me in the dark journey north." Aleksy, who departed from the nearby town of Chiantla in the same highland area of Huehuetenango, experienced the same ritual, though her mother crossed her with a vela adorned with the image of her town saint, La Virgen de Candelaria.

Lighting candles adorned with the image of local saints is a common ritual practiced by Catholic families to commemorate the departure of family members. It is also a ritual practiced by Catholics in unfortunate situations throughout the world. In his analysis of Catholic American devotional practices of the Shrine of St. Jude, Robert Orsi explains that the lighting of vigil candles over the course of a crisis can be best understood as "temporalized spatial symbols, signifying presence by the duration of the flame." In the case of migration, the lighting of the vigil candles before a migrant's departure and keeping the flame burning throughout the journey and until safe arrival provide markers of hope, presence, and finality for the journeying migrant. The departure ritual also enables the family to remain spiritually connected to the migrant throughout the journey, thereby overcoming the barriers of time and space.[18]

Local clergy also have rituals to mark the departure of one of their flock. Clergy in Mexico and Central America repeatedly commented to me on the frequency and importance of blessings and other last-minute religious preparations for departing migrants. Sister Maria Gemma, a Brazilian woman of the Scalabrini congregation who runs Centro Madre Assunta shelter for displaced women in Tijuana, Mexico, described how departing migrants often visit her requesting a blessing before crossing the border. Although she feels awkward about granting their requests because she is not an ordained priest, she complies. As she explained, "How can I refuse them? Their faith is too strong to resist. They truly believe that God will help them endure the migration. Without God they have nothing." These blessings transcend religious affiliation. Lydia Ramírez, an evangelical lay worker who ministers with her father, the pastor of an evangelical church and director of a Salvation Army shelter in Tijuana, voiced the same sentiments. "We always bless them," she explained. "Although we do strongly discourage their departure, we recognize how important a blessing is for them on the long and hard journey."

Even when the blessings fail to protect the travelers on their journeys, their belief in the blessings does not waiver. Father Pellizzari, a Scalabrini priest in Ciudad Juárez, Mexico, who has provided pastoral care to migrants for many years in various countries, reported that it was not uncommon for him to provide blessings to several departing migrants a day. On one occasion, a group of prospective migrants whom he had counseled in the past approached him for a blessing and several rosaries. He complied with their requests. Several weeks later, they called him from Ojinaga, Chihuahua, a Mexican border city that is situated on the Rio Grande, on the other side of the U.S.-Mexico border from Presidio, Texas. The group explained that they had been apprehended by U.S. Border Patrol officials and sent back to Mexico. They now wanted to come to see the priest, rest a few days, and receive another blessing before attempting the trip again. Once the migrants arrived, Father Pellizzari asked them, with a touch of irony, "So the blessing didn't help you that much, did it? Why would you want another one?" One of the young men responded with pure faith and conviction: "Father, forgive me if I contradict you, but with that blessing we arrived as far as Houston. If we had not had your blessing, who knows how far we might have gone? Probably not even to the border."

This steadfast belief and confidence in the power of these blessings, even in numerous examples of failed migrations, sometimes to the annoyance and even amusement of clergy, was a constant theme I found. One young Mexican priest from Tijuana, who juggled the responsibilities of his parish while also directing a migrant shelter, had grown weary of the requests. As he explained, "I always bless migrants in mass, but most migrants ask for an additional blessing before leaving for the United States, which I usually refuse to do, and I tell them, you have already been blessed." One time, he continued, "I had a group of migrants here who asked for a special blessing before leaving, which I refused them; they were caught and sent back. When I asked what happened, they replied that they were caught because they were refused a special blessing."

Holy Shrines, Sacred Places, and Departing Migrants

The sacred geography of Mexico and Central America includes numerous shrines and sacred places that attract hundreds and thousands of pilgrims each year who come to venerate popular saints or to seek an audience with the supernatural. They come with the humble requests of the poor: a cure for a chronic ailment, a job for an out-of-work spouse. They come to give thanks for a prosperous year. And they come in search of final blessings, confessionals, and prayer services before leaving for the United States.[19] In Mexico, the Catholic Church controls most of the shrines, which house icons of Christ, the Virgin, and, increasingly, images of saints. The most popular pilgrimage site in the country, the Basílica de Guadalupe in Mexico City, is home to Mexico's most revered religious image, the Virgin of Guadalupe, the patroness of the country and, to many, the Queen of the Americas. Place is central to many devotional practices and shrines in Latin America. Many regions and localities in Mexico have their own venerated images; the states of Jalisco, San Luis Potosí, and Guanajuato, for example, house their own images of the Virgin and Christ, each of which is located in shrines and popular pilgrimage sites bearing the name of the honored images. Mexico's northern border region, however, houses a number of shrines that people have constructed outside of the control of church authorities. These sites, often homes to popular folk images that have suffered at the hands of the larger society, draw tens of thousands of pilgrims, including migrants, each year. The most famous of these folk icons is Juan Soldado (Juan Castillo Morales), whose colorful image sits in a run-down but heavily visited shrine in a public cemetery in the border city of Tijuana, Mexico.

The Catholic Church also controls the bulk of the shrines in Central America, but in contrast to Mexico, where shrines mainly feature Christ and the Virgin, the Central American shrines include numerous images of saints who have attracted popular devotion in the region. The most popular of the religious images of Christ, El Cristo Negro, reclines on a marble altar in the Basilica of Esquipulas in eastern Guatemala. The Iglesia de San Francisco in Antigua, Guatemala, which houses the image of Central America's first saint, Pedro de San José Betancur, draws tens of thousands of pilgrims each year, many of whom travel from as far away as Peru and Ecuador to pay honor to the saint. Evangelical communities in the highlands of Guatemala, where religious practices are a combination of evangelical beliefs and indigenous practices, organize pilgrimage sites in well-known sacred places. Soothsayers, who act as mediators between people and God, control and care for these sacred sites. Other Central American countries have their key pilgrimage settings, all of which house images of the Virgin Mary. Hondurans flock to the Basilica of Nuestra Señora de Suyapa (Our Lady of Suyapa) in Tegucigalpa to pay their respects to the patroness of the country. In El Salvador, pilgrims undertake the annual visit to the shrine of Nuestra Señora de la Paz (Our Lady of Peace) in San Miguel. In Costa Rica, the Basilica of Nuestra Señora de Los Angeles in the old capital of Cartago houses the most venerated image in the country, La Virgen de Los Angeles (the Virgin of Los Angeles), more commonly known as La Virgen Negrita (the Little Black Virgin). In Nicaragua, the patroness of the country, La Purísima Concepción de El Viejo (The Immaculate Conception of El Viejo), is sheltered in a church in the small village of El Viejo in the country's western region.

Each Latin American country has its own image of the Virgin Mary that it venerates as its national patron saint, but Mexico shelters the most revered of all virgins in the region. Multiple images of La Virgen de Guadalupe, whose appeal extends across the Americas, sits in the massive complex of the basilica of the same name on the hill of Tepeyac, just outside Mexico City. This is the largest pilgrimage site in Mexico, and includes an old basilica, which is crumbling through age and neglect; a much larger new basilica, which was erected in 1976; a museum; and several outdoor shrines, including the famed site on which the Virgin was believed to have appeared in 1531 to Juan Diego, a poor Aztec farmer. Within the huge new basilica, twenty chapels form the balcony surrounding the massive main altar. Every year, hundreds of thousands of pilgrims descend on one of several shrines located in the complex. Supplicants venerating the glass-encased statue of La Virgen, which is located in an outdoor shrine, follow a series of rituals that are observed in many Catholic shrines throughout the region and the world. As they do at the popular shrine of the Black Christ, in Esquipulas, Guatemala, or the world-renowned shrine of Our Lady of Fatima, in Fatima, Portugal, supplicants purchase candles that they rub along the heavily marked glass that shields the Virgin, and then leave flowers at the foot of the image or push handwritten petitions through a metal slot that is located under the Virgin's image. In the basilica's interior shrine, a massive framed picture of the Virgin looms over an extensive two-way camarín (moving sidewalk), which carries the crowds of pilgrims past the image. As is custom, along the way pilgrims leave petitions for favors or notes of thanks in a metal box, labeled *Deposite sus milagros* (Deposit your miracles).

Among the many pilgrims who throng the basilica are departing or journeying migrants. Some come to be blessed by the priest who holds court in a small glass room just outside the church store and the depository for flowers, fruit, and other gifts left by pilgrims in gratitude for favors received. The priest, who blesses hundreds of pilgrims a day, explained to me that many of the pilgrims who come to him request general blessings and do not mention a specific intention. In the months of May and June, however, he often hears requests for final blessings from young men and women who are preparing for the journey to the United States. The basilica has traditionally opened its doors to migrants and celebrated the migration experience, he explained. During the celebration of the "Day of the Migrant," which is held September 7 at the basilica, migrants from all over Latin America come to celebrate and be blessed at the shrine, he said. The celebration primarily honors Mexicans abroad, but draws migrants from all over Latin America. Departing migrants also visit the basilica's retail store, which makes a handsome profit from devotional promotion. The store is stocked with many religious items commemorating the Queen of Mexico, ranging from prayer books to medallions to T-shirts. According to one of the store's staff, an item commonly purchased by departing migrants is the *Devocionario del Migrante* (Migrants' Prayer Book), which is published by the Italian Scalabrini congregation and the Catholic Diocese of Mexico City. The devotional, modeled on the 1960s Manual for Braceros, was first published by the diocese of Zamora in 1989. Since then other dioceses in Mexico and Guatemala have published variations of the prayer book with Scalabrinian assistance.[20] The fifty-six-page devotional provides companionship on the road through the numerous prayers it contains for migrants to recite.

Pilgrims also flock to numerous shrines in the Catholic Mexican states of Jalisco, San Luis Potosí, and Guanajuato, which are home to some of the most revered holy images in the regions, including La Virgen de San Juan de los Lagos, La Virgen de Zapopan, and El Señor de la Misericordia. Since many established sending communities in Mexico are located in these states, it is not surprising to learn that among the pilgrims at these shrines are many departing migrants who have come to seek blessings and spiritual comfort before embarking on the dangerous trip north.

One of the most popular shrines in the region today is the Shrine of St. Toribio, located in what was once the desolate farming village of Santa Ana de Guadalupe in Jalisco, Mexico. Each day hundreds of pilgrims, many of whom are prospective migrants, pass through the huge imposing stone gates and along the "causeway of martyrs" that the local diocese has carved out of the cornfields. The five-minute journey down the causeway is dramatized by the sound of symphonic music blaring from enormous speakers. The local diocese has invested heavily in devotional promotion; in addition to the causeway, the compound includes several churches, a retreat center, a room of miracles, and a thriving retail store crammed with religious artifacts of St. Toribio, the construction of which largely comes from tithes and profits from the retail store.[21]

Pilgrims enter the Chapel of St. Toribio to request favors or give thanks to the legendary priest St. Toribio Romo, one of twenty-four martyrs of the 1927–1929 Cristero Wars between the Mexican revolutionary government and the Catholic Church. In the early twentieth century, Father Toribio and the Catholic Church in Mexico were outspoken critics of emigration to the United States.[22] Today, the priest is revered among clergy and devotees alike as the patron saint of migrants, and the Mexican Catholic Church has embraced this new identity. Saint Toribio was virtually unheard of as recently as 1990. His current fame rests on his canonization by Pope John Paul II in 2000 and on a series of miracles that many claim he has performed, the most legendary of which was granted to a group of journeying migrants.

The "keeper of the miracles" at the Chapel of St. Toribio is Josefina, a lifelong resident of the local community. For years she has worked at the chapel recording the miracles and collecting, organizing, and caring for all the petitions and offerings that pilgrims leave at the shrine. Josefina recounted to me the miracle of St. Toribio, a narrative that most of his believers can recite by heart. One hot, summer day in 1990 or 1991, three migrants left their hometowns in Michoacán to journey to the United States. Lost in the Mexican desert just south of the Mexico-California border, they fell prey to the harsh elements. "They were dying from hunger and thirst," Josefina said. One of the young men, feeling he could endure no more, urged the other two to go on without him, but his companions refused to leave him behind to die alone in the desert. With nowhere else to turn, they dropped to their knees and prayed for their lives to the Virgin of Guadalupe. After some time, a man shrouded in a long, black cloak approached the young men. "What is happening with you?" the stranger asked. The young migrants responded that they were dying from thirst. The stranger told them, "Come with me and I will give you water." The mysterious man led them to a fountain in the desert from which they drank their fill. Then the stranger asked the migrants where they were headed. "To Los Angeles," one responded. The stranger told the three journeying men that he would take them to the City of Angels. Under his care the migrants traveled unnoticed across the border to a U.S. highway. While walking on the side of the highway, a U.S. Border Patrol car sped by. The men were invisible to the U.S. officials. The stranger took the men to a bus station and waited until the three migrants were safely on board, bound for Los Angeles. Thinking that the mysterious man in black was a

coyote, the trio offered to pay him for his services. "You don't owe me anything," the stranger responded. "But when you return to Mexico, come visit
me. My name is Romo and I live in Santa Ana de Guadalupe. I will always
be there. Today I came to do a mission for *su señora*." According to Josefina,
the young men mistakenly interpreted *su señora* in its literal translation of
"your wife." According to the legend, however, the stranger was referring to
La Virgen de Guadalupe to whom the journeying migrants had earlier
prayed in despair. The young men never forgot the kindness of the stranger,
and so when they returned to Mexico four years later, they traveled to Santa
Ana de Guadalupe to express their gratitude. After an exhaustive and fruit-
less search going door-to-door looking for the man (many in the town carry
the Romo surname), Josefina concluded, "They found themselves at the
Chapel of St. Toribio, where the surprised group saw the face of the mysterious man who had helped them in a photograph above the altar."

Since the recording of this miracle in the mid-1990s St. Toribio has become the legendary companion of journeying migrants, many of whom
claim that he helps them under the guise of a coyote. By framing St. Toribio
as a coyote saint, the Catholic Church in Mexico provides a compelling spiritual and moral narrative for undocumented migrants. Each year migrants
in the thousands flock to his shrine and ask the saint to accompany them
on their travels to the United States. According to Father Gabriel González,
a local priest who has discarded traditional priestly black for a bright tur-
quoise shirt and dark sunglasses, a quarter of the pilgrims who come to pay
homage to the saint are migrants, some of whom come to seek guidance and
blessings before departing. The priest has developed the narrative of the migrant as a victim of state policy: "Saint Toribio was persecuted. He experienced all that migrants do. He can understand the pain of family separation,
of not being respected by the state." With reservation, but after some prodding, Father Gabriel later admitted to me that in his early writing Toribio also
acknowledged some of the negative consequences of emigration, including
the "harmful values and behavior" that returning migrants brought to their
home communities.

On a Sunday in early January 2002, several hundred people squeezed into
the chapel of St. Toribio to attend the 10:30 A.M. mass, while an additional
hundred waited patiently outside the chapel doors.[23] Some of the pilgrims
crawled on their knees to the altar on which rests the tomb of Romo Toribio.
They ran their hands over the glass case holding the martyr's blood-stained
clothing. Others attended the 10:30 A.M. mass Father Gabriel celebrated in a

larger church adjoining the Chapel of St. Toribio. Several times during the mass, the priest invoked the name of St. Toribio. A weekly ritual followed the mass: Attendees lined up to speak with the priest or request a blessing from him. Some pleaded with him to listen to the miracles St. Toribio had performed for them or their family members. Josefina, the keeper of the miracles, recorded their accounts.

In conversations with thirteen people approached at the shrine, nine of the men said they were there for migration-related concerns. Twelve of the thirteen were practicing Catholics and all shared a history of migration to the United States. Some had returned to their home communities over the Christmas holidays to visit family and planned to return shortly to the United States. Most would be venturing north without documentation. On this particular Sunday morning, they had traveled from villages and cities located in the region's principal sending states of Jalisco, Michoacán, and Guanajuato.

About half the men had visited the shrine of St. Toribio before. They had learned of the saint and his miraculous powers on behalf of migrants through a variety of sources, including friends and family who had visited the shrine or experienced a miracle, and from television icons. Two of the migrants had made the trip to the shrine after hearing of the saints' divine powers on Spanish network television in the United States. Some of the migrants had visited other shrines in the country such as the Basilica of the Virgin of Guadalupe in Mexico City, but had come to St. Toribio specifically because he "cared for migrants." They were all well versed in the narrative of St. Toribio as a coyote saint.

The young men requested that St. Toribio accompany them on a future journey to ensure themselves a safe passage. One elderly man who visited the shrine commented on the importance of St. Toribio to families and communities who share a tradition of northbound migration: "Almost my entire town goes to live in the United States at some point. So we pray for those who leave, neighbors pray for one another, to St. Toribio, to God, and to La Virgen de Guadalupe." He went on to explain, "I have four sons in the United States and three of them are *mojados* [wetbacks or undocumented migrants]. They go about every other year. I always pray for them, when they leave and once they are there. I am here today praying for their departure."

The most popular Christian shrine in Central America is in the Basílica del Cristo Negro de Esquipulas, which shelters Guatemala's Black Christ, a reclining wooden image that people revere for its miraculous powers. The basilica is referred to by scholars of Latin American religion as the "center of Central American popular religiosity" and was proclaimed the "spiritual center of Central America" by Pope John XXIII. Each year throngs of pilgrims from Guatemala and other Central American countries descend on the grand white basilica in the normally quiet and desolate town of Esquipulas to worship the original image of the Black Christ and hear testimony of the miracles it has bestowed on his worshippers.[24] During the two-week period leading up to the icon's feast day on January 15, Esquipulas attracts more than 100,000 visitors. As they do at other Christian shrines, supplicants with petitions for favors crawl their way to the altar on their knees. This painful journey can take several hours from the starting point at the shrine of Esquipulas, which is the central plaza in front of the church. Each shrine has its own particular rituals once the supplicant reaches the altar; at the Basilica of Esquipulas, supplicants wind around the glass-enclosed altar on the camarín, a plywood walkway on which the pilgrims wait for their time with the venerated Cristo Negro. Once at the altar, worshippers rub candle figurines of specific body parts along the glass, leave handwritten petitions requesting favors from the miraculous Christ, and place at the foot of the icon a variety of ex-voto offerings such as flowers, drawings, handwritten cards, and *milagros* (small silver medallions) in gratitude for a miracle they have received.

Situated more than a hundred miles from Guatemala City, in a mountain valley in the far Eastern corner of Guatemala, Esquipulas serves as a principal border town to Honduras and a crossing corridor to many central Americans. Its proximity to two loosely regulated international borders draws scores of migrants for religious counsel and material assistance. According to Father Rigoberto, one of several priests at the basilica, about forty to fifty migrants visit the shrine each day. The overwhelming majority have no travel authorization. They come from as far away as Ecuador and Peru, but most travel to the shrine from Honduras and from other locations in Guatemala. Some stop at the basilica for material assistance such as a hot meal and a change of clothes. Most are Hondurans who have left their homes only a day or so before and have come to request a blessing as they set off on the two-thousand-mile trek to the United States. "They come to be blessed . . . to gather the spiritual nourishment to travel what will be the most dangerous segment of the journey," Father Rigoberto explained. "Some pass by the feet of El Cristo and pray; others leave petitions to request safe passage on their journey, but most go to the confessionary or the atrium where we bless them. At these blessings, which are often group blessings, we anoint them with holy water, pray together for their safety, and counsel them on the family they are leaving behind."

He explained, "The blessings are very important to them. Sometimes, if time allows, they also share the Eucharist with us, but since many who stop here are not practicing Catholics, all they really want is a final blessing to protect them before they go on their way." When I asked Father Rigoberto about the many non-Catholics who visit the basilica, he said, "Coming to the basilica is not only a Catholic tradition; it is a cultural tradition that transcends any one religious belief system." Sometimes at their request Father Rigoberto provides the departing migrants with a cross or prayer book to take with them on their travels. "It is very important for the migrants to have something religious to carry with them," he said. "You see, it represents the *presence* of God with them, which they never seem to doubt. The presence of God is certain with the migrants compared to the way many of us think, which in contrast is, 'Is God with me?'"

As is the case with popular pilgrimage sites throughout Mexico and Central America, the parish of Esquipulas runs a thriving business selling religious items commemorating the Black Christ. Books about the history of Esquipulas and religious items of the Black Christ along with other well-known holy images crowd a glass counter's shelves. According to the store's staff and the attending vicar, migrants regularly purchase religious items there to accompany them on their trip.

A second popular Catholic shrine is housed in the old colonial city of Antigua, in the western highlands of Guatemala. Resting in the city's Iglesia de San Francisco is the tomb of Guatemala's first saint, San José de Betancur, which draws upwards of tens of thousands of pilgrims a year. Located in a large colonial-style compound and surrounding a central courtyard dating back to 1545 are the imposing white cathedral of San Francisco, the ruins of the convent of San Francisco, and the church's museum where pilgrims have given thanks to Hermano Pedro for miracles received by leaving thousands of ex-votos such as drawings, framed letters, milagros, and crutches. On any given day, but especially on his feast day, April 25, scores of tour buses from all over Central America make their way to the shrine of Brother Pedro, as his followers refer to him. Revered for his work as a Franciscan missionary among the poor, the sick, and the less fortunate, Hermano Pedro is especially popular among the indigent. Following the Catholic ritual of pilgrims seeking favors, supplicants approach the grill-encased tomb on their knees. Once at the altar showcasing the tomb, they observe several rituals particular to the shrine, each depending in part on the favors they are requesting. Most supplicants knock on the side of the tomb, a symbolic gesture requesting an audience with the saint. If the pilgrim seeks a cure for a physical ailment, he or she typically ties small wax figures of the body part that is ailing, such as a limb or a head, to the grillwork surrounding the tomb. Supplicants also leave their written petitions in a *canasta* (basket) at the foot of the tomb, and still others rub a candle alongside the tomb after which they light and place it among hundreds of other burning candles in a makeshift altar outside the side entrance to the church.

Until 2002, the caretaker of the shrine routinely collected and discarded the handwritten petitions left in the canasta. Beginning in the spring of 2003, however, a *cofradría* (a voluntary religious cofraternity associated with the worship of a saint), called the International Brotherhood of Saint Pedro, initiated a project to collect and organize the petitions for additional prayer among its members. The architect behind the project is a practicing psychologist and Catholic, and leads the local chapter of the Cofradría de Hermano Pedro, which has spawned similar chapters in more than fifteen countries throughout the world and thousands of members comprising communities of St. Pedro's followers. The Guatemalan representative, a young woman who lives in Guatemala City but attends mass at the Church of San Pedro, explained the project. First, she developed a petition form on which petitioners fill out their names, country of origin, the date, and their requests. She collects the completed petitions on a monthly basis and scans them into her home computer, after which she sends them as e-mail attachments in bunches of several dozen each to the different chapters of the brotherhood throughout the world. On any given day, she said, six or seven members will be praying over a group of a hundred or so petitions. Faith in Hermano Pedro's miraculous powers is at the core of the project. "There are followers of Hermano Pedro all over the world," she told me, "and since Pope John Paul II canonized Hermano Pedro in July of 2003, the number of his followers has grown. As devout believers of what Hermano Pedro can do, we believe that the petitions have a greater possibility of being heard by him if more people pray over them."

Cofradrías, which often acted as mutual aid societies, assumed an important role in the social and economic life of colonial Latin America.[25] Their popularity declined in the nineteenth century, but has resurfaced in part through the Latin American diaspora. The development of the International Brotherhood of Hermano Pedro shows how devotion for contemporary saints can and does extend beyond the local boundaries of the shrine. In many ways, St. Pedro has become a transnational patron saint. With the advances in technology and communication, his faithful are no longer completely dependent on his presence through physical pilgrimages to the shrine. His followers can also experience his presence and remain connected to one another through their membership in a virtual worldwide community.

The petitions left for Hermano Pedro disclose much about the people. An analysis of eight hundred petitions that the brotherhood at the Church of San Francisco collected during a two-month period (March and April 2003) indicates that most of the pilgrims who visited the shrine were the less fortunate from Guatemala, Honduras, and El Salvador. Viewed in the original handwriting with spelling and grammatical errors unchanged, these petitions exude a heart-warming earnestness. The requests are humble and basic, asking for such things as a blessing for a good year, a stable family, or modest prosperity. A Salvadoran pilgrim placed the following petition in the canasta at the foot of Hermano Pedro:

> Grant us lord, by virtue of Hermano Pedro, what I ask you. To be with you in the kingdom, not to step in jail, to love God and have my loved ones together, peace and protection for me and my house, that I may never take what is mine.

Many of the requests in our analysis were for multiple basic goods and services that North Americans assume will be provided to the poor through tax-supported social agencies. But here in Central America, the less fortunate who have fallen on hard times have nowhere to turn but to a saint for divine intervention. In general, five overlapping areas of concern draw pilgrims to the shrine to seek favors from Hermano Pedro: health crises, financial distress, education issues, family interpersonal relations, and migration related worries. Those with migration petitions came seeking help from Hermano Pedro on a variety of migration matters ranging from family reunification with loved ones to protection for migrant children in the United States. A handful of pilgrims came to the shrine specifically seeking Hermano Pedro's help with decision making, journey preparations, and protection on the trip. The consequences of migration for family members, either left behind or in the United States, worried all the petitioners. A wife and mother who does not mention her age or country of origin visited the Church of San Francisco in March 2003 with a desperate plea to Hermano Pedro to help her migrate so that her family could be reunited:

> Hermano Pedro, I ask you with all my heart that my son and I may go to a foreign land to be with my husband. With all my heart, intercede before our

father so that He may grant us that miracle. We've been struggling for 3 years, please help us. I also ask you, don't take away my health, for me and for my son, so that all three of us may be together, I beg you with all my heart. Hermano Pedro, please listen to a mother and a desperate wife, I want to give my son the chance to be in a stable home. Father, please, hear me out.

Others voiced concern for safety on the journey north. A departing migrant who did not identify his home country pleaded for protection:

I ask you, Hermano Pedro, to watch over me and to protect my trip north with permission from God and from you.

A young Guatemalan woman expressed similar trepidation and anxiety over her pending trip:

Watch over and protect my family, to be good children to our parents. Our trip to Chicago we leave in your hands.

Another young woman from Guatemala requested Hermano Pedro to help her fulfill her dream to migrate to the "promised land" so that she could help her family:

With God's will, may I travel to the United States to be with my grandmother and may God open doors for success for my family.

A young man from Guatemala who left his petition at the saint's tomb in early April 2003 expressed similar sentiments:

Please give me peace in my heart, let me get closer to you. Help me go to the United States to get a job to help my parents, and so I can pay for my car.

A petitioner with little education asked Hermano Pedro for help in preparing his travels while at the same time thanking the saint for the migrant favor granted to his child:

I went to five times masses that the Mexican visas be a success for me and him. I thank you because my son arrive well. My son, my wife, please work for my children.

The importance of national shrines to Central Americans and thus to migrants is evidenced by the grandeur of the structures housing them and the numbers of the devout who attend. Looming over one of the poorest neighborhoods in the outskirts of Tegucigalpa, Honduras, sits the enormous, imposing white basilica that houses the tiny, dark, six-and-a-half-centimeter image of Nuestra Señora de Suyapa, Our Lady of Suyapa, the patroness of Honduras.[26] On the day that I accompanied Father Carlo Magno, the vicar of the Cathedral of Tegucigalpa, to see Suyapa, the complex housing the old and new shrines was fairly quiet. Seeing that I was shocked by the enormous size of the cathedral, Father Carlo explained that each year on February 3, the Virgin's Feast Day, thousands of visitors from all over Central America fill the enormous cathedral to seek favors or give thanks to their beloved patroness. During the Week of the Migrant, in August, the cathedral draws scores of departing and returning migrants. Pilgrims make their way to the image on the camarín, which winds upstairs and around the back of the glass-encased image of the Virgin. Once at the altar, supplicants touch, pray, rub their hands along the worn glass, and place at the foot of the altar a variety of ex-votos, including flowers and milagros, which fill Catholic shrines throughout Central America and Mexico. Many of the Hondurans in the study reported visiting the Virgin of Suyapa to request protection before they embarked on their journey north.

With equal devotion thousands of pilgrims each year visit the Cathedral of Our Lady of Peace (Nuestra Señora de la Paz) in the bustling city of San Miguel, El Salvador.[27] There, flanked by four angels, the life-size wooden statue of the Virgin stands on an impressive pink and white marble altar. Wearing an elaborate gold crown, swathed in a white robe, and covered in the flag of El Salvador, the Virgin holds a gold palm leaf and a dark image of baby Jesus. Pilgrims who visit Nuestra Señora de la Paz are permitted to touch the gown of the Virgin and attach to it their ex-votos. Thus hanging by safety pins from her gown are hundreds of milagros, petitions, and ribbons. The gown, quickly soiled by the hundreds of thousands of hands that stroke it, is changed every month. At the Virgin's feet are mounds of flowers, petitions, and additional ex-votos; supplicants also leave petitions in an offering box that stands next to the image on the main altar.

Because San Miguel is a major migrant-sending region in El Salvador, the shrine of Our Lady of Peace has incorporated migration events into its services, and migrants' petitions have been incorporated into daily services at the cathedral. Before each mass, the attending priest asks the parishioners if they have an intention or petition to share with the group. The priest also reads some of the petitions left in the offering box the day before. According to José, the curator of the church, priests regularly read petitions that request the safe arrival of departing migrants and their families. When asked how many, he estimated that the attending priests read about fifteen migration petitions each week. According to one of the attending priests, Father Chapa, migrants "rarely read their migration intentions and petitions in public, in front of the congregation; rather, we read them for them, usually during the mass and always in services on the Day of the Migrant. Still, after mass they regularly approach the sanctuary for a blessing to protect them on their journey. In many ways, these blessings strengthen their petitions."

Pentecostal Migrants Find Solace at Ayunos

Not all departing migrants in the study called on saints, images of Christ, or traditional clergy at well-established Catholic shrines when making religious preparations for their journey north. Many, in fact, did not. Pentecostals were more likely than Catholics to seek personal counsel instead from their clergy, an event that often took place in the respondent's home and at the request of the family. Before Mario left his hometown in La Unión, his local pastor came to his home to pray with Mario, his wife, and parents. They read from the Bible and he pledged his return. In some Protestant communities, the counseling was described as more public in nature. When María, a Pentecostal, left Tegucigalpa, Honduras, she approached her pastor at weekly services and the whole congregation prayed for her safety, promising to continue their prayers in her name once she left.

As illustrated in the introduction, in the rural highlands of Guatemala where religion is often a combination of evangelical beliefs and practices and local indigenous customs, departing migrants and members of their families from Maya evangelical communities confer with traditional prayer makers and soothsayers at ayunos, or fasting and prayer services, before leaving on their journey north. Maya attend ayunos at sacred sites, including altars in private homes, but especially on hilltops and mountain summits. The attendees of ayunos come to appeal directly to God for numerous needs such as good health, prosperity, and overall spiritual guidance, and they convey their needs through a religious mediator who is often an evangelical pastor with his or her own ministry. Those who attend ayunos believe that if they fast before the service their prayers have a greater chance of being heard. Ayunos take place in the morning for several hours on a weekly basis and generally attract fifty or more participants. At the monthly ayunos, the ceremonies can last up to several days and draw a crowd as large as several hundred. The event begins with a period of devout prayer and a sermon, followed by individual petitions whose contents vary but in general reflect the needs of the poor who remain marginalized by the larger society and have no other recourse than religion for help, guidance, and counsel. Some request recovery from a sickness; for others, work is sorely needed; still others seek reunification with a deserting spouse. Increasingly, persons come to seek protection on the journey north. Presiding pastors of these ayunos say that it is not uncommon to counsel up to ten departing migrants or their family members on any given day.

At the ayuno we attended on the summit of a mountain in western Guatemala, a number of attendees stepped forward with migration requests. At another ayuno held around a makeshift altar in the pastor's home in a small farming settlement outside the town center of San Cristóbal, a group of a hundred or so persons gathered with their petitions. When Pastor Sapon and I arrived, we encountered people of all ages seated and facing the leader who, dressed in the traditional *huipil* and *corte*, stood in front of a crude table propped up by brightly bound bundles of clothes. Pastor Caxaj, an older Maya woman with long gray braids running down the length of her back, has led an independent ministry in her dirt-floor adobe home for twelve years. Many of the attendees were women, but among them was a group of about a dozen or so men who were preparing for their trip to Texas. Pastor Caxaj delivered her service in a mixture of Spanish and Quiche for the benefit of the older, non-Spanish speakers attending the ayuno. After some time, Pastor Caxaj unwrapped the colorful bundles and showed us the traveling clothes of some of the prospective migrants who were attending the ayuno and were seeking prayer and guidance for their travels to the United States. Having their traveling clothes blessed was a final religious step before embarking on the journey. The men, who were planning to leave within the next few days, were first-time migrants. They had coyotes, but these travelers had no idea what route they would be taking. They feared for their safety on the journey. Word had trickled back to the highlands of the hardships and dangers encountered along the trek, and how sometimes migrants were never heard from again. Pastor Caxaj turned to the young men and, along with her congregation, prayed for their safety. Then she alone spoke to them and encouraged them not to stray from God and their faith once in United States.

Others at the ayuno brought forward migration petitions. Four of the women prayed for brothers or husbands who were living and working without immigration papers in Houston. After the prayer meeting, Pastor Caxaj also shared her migration petition with us. Several years earlier, her son had left for the United States in hopes of securing a job and sending home to her and her disabled husband the money needed to keep her ministry afloat. The prayers of her congregation, she believed, granted her son safe passage and successful employment.

After the initial prayer, the attendees spoke out, several voicing migration concerns and asking favors. Four women, all married and with children, requested protection for either brothers or husbands who were preparing for the journey north, but who did not attend the ayuno themselves. The pastor blessed the young men who were planning to migrate, told them that she anticipated a safe journey for them, and asked them to send pictures to her after they arrived in the United States. Like many Pentecostals, the migrants placed enormous trust in their pastor's prophetic words. Pastor Caxaj explained her views on the role of the ayuno in the migration of those in her ministry: "Their goal is to go, to go and work to feed their families, but it's not good for them to go without God's blessing . . . they will need Him in the days ahead."

Promises and Pledges to God

La promesa is a covenant between the believer and a sacred image.[28] In exchange for divine intervention on an issue of concern or granting of a request, the believer promises to perform certain acts, usually devotional, in gratitude. La promesa is a cultural and religious practice among the people of Central America and Mexico, and it is believed to be a powerful protective force in the migration of many to the United States. Before migrants in our sample embarked on their journeys, they and their families offered pledges to God. That is, in return for protection and a safe passage to the United States, they promised to pay some debt to God, the Virgin, or a saint. Half the sample—Catholics and Protestants, frequent and infrequent churchgoers, men and women alike—made promises in exchange for a successful migration. For those who planned to travel the treacherous course without authorization, promises in exchange for a safe arrival were even more pervasive. Three of every four undocumented migrants vowed promises, compared with one in every four of those who traveled with papers.

Departing migrants offered four types of pledges, some of which they intended to fulfill in the United States and others in their home communities. Many promised to be "better Christians" in return for a successful migration.

Fulfilling this pledge translated into promising to increase religious practices in the United States, such as praying more frequently at home or becoming a more regular churchgoer. For others, becoming a better Christian meant caring more for the well-being of family and friends. For still others, it meant giving up "bad habits" and turning around their lives. José, a twenty-year-old single man and Catholic from Mexico, for example, said that his promise was a simple one that many of his friends made before departing their homes in Mexico: "I promised God and La Virgen de Guadalupe that I would help my family and that I would be more involved in the church. Economic support is what I strive to do for my family. I have my mother, stepfather, aunts, and uncles back home to take care of because they have supported me and helped me come to the United States." Marco left Honduras in 1995. At home he had belonged to a gang and frequently used drugs. Although his family is Catholic, he rarely attended church. When preparing to leave Honduras, he made a pledge to God: "I promised him that if he let me come to the United States that I would change my life."

A second type of pledge departing migrants offered in exchange for safe passage involved performing a series of familiar religious rituals to give thanks upon arrival. Often migrants vowed to attend a church and to give thanks by saying the rosary or lighting candles. In many cases, family members in the home communities also vowed to perform these same rituals. By working from both ends, they believed this offered stronger prayers to God. These transnational rituals also retain a powerful bond between the migrants and the families they left behind. Filamena and her young daughter left La Unión, El Salvador, in 1990 to join her husband in Houston. Before departing, she prayed to God and the Virgin Mary for the safety of herself and her child, and she offered a vow to God and the Virgin of Peace, the patron Virgin of El Salvador. "I promised her that if we arrived without harm, I would visit a church and say the rosary several times," Filamena said. In exchange for safe passage, Filamena's sister Greta promised to follow a custom she performed regularly at shrines in her home community, entering the first church she encountered in the United States on her knees to give thanks to God.

A third type of pledge made by many prospective migrants involved the extraordinary—returning home to give thanks at a familiar shrine of a religious figure to which they had prayed for protection on the journey. If they survived the journey, many planned to acknowledge their success by returning to the familiar, their religion, their customs, and especially their religious icons. By making this pledge to return home, either temporarily or permanently, migrants recognized that "coming home" to give thanks is a central way to remain emotionally and spiritually connected to the home community, and that fulfilling the promise by returning home helps nurture transnational life. Lydia, a devout Catholic, left Honduras with her brother in 1996. Before leaving, she prayed to God and to her personal protector, the Black Christ of Esquipulas. "I wanted to go visit El Señor in Esquipulas for prayer. It was on our way. But my brother is Protestant and didn't believe in going to shrines. So I made a vow, a promise to El Señor that if I made it safely, I would return alone to Esquipulas to give thanks. I would light six candles in gratitude for the miracle only he could perform." Miguel, a thirty-nine-year-old Mexican and devout Catholic, promised that in return for safe passage to the United States he would first visit and pray at the shrine of Santo Niño de Atacho, in Plateros, Mexico.

Other migrants realized that it might be some time before they could fulfill the promise of returning home to visit a shrine to give thanks. Lacking financial resources and travel authorizations to make the pilgrimage home in the near future, some migrants made more modest vows to give thanks to those revered images that they believed would grant them safe passage to the United States. Griselda, a thirty-six-year-old Catholic, left her hometown in La Libertad, El Salvador, in 1997. "I promised La Virgen de la Paz that if I made it to the United States I would send my mother my first earnings so that she could visit the Virgin and give her flowers and say a mass for me." Sylvia migrated from her hometown in Puebla, Mexico, to New York at the age of fourteen. She traveled with several other young companions and a coyote. Fearing for her safety, she prayed and fasted before her departure and promised God that if she and her friends arrived safely, she would send money to her pastor in Puebla to "purchase pews and a stereo for the new church."

José, Marco, Filamena, Greta, Lydia, Miguel, Griselda, and Sylvia all arrived safely in the United States. They were spared the life-threatening dangers that some of their friends and relatives experienced in their quest to reach their "promised land." The migrants who had made pledges in exchange for safe passage did not forsake those saints and icons of the Virgin and the Christ who had protected them on their journey, yet fulfillment of their pledges proved difficult for some. Miguel went to extraordinary lengths to make the pilgrimage to Santo Niño de Atacho during his trek north. Marco struggled for years before leaving gangs and securing a steady job. Sylvia gave more than she promised, continuing for many years to send part of her meager earnings as a domestic to her pastor back home. Lydia has not yet had the opportunity to return home, but she insists that as soon as she gets her "papers" she will make the pilgrimage to Esquipulas.

Summary

How do migrants prepare for and cope with leaving home and loved ones? This study shows that they do so by turning to their faith, both privately and publicly, and to those both divine and human who represent the power of that faith. Prospective migrants turn to God, their revered saints, and trusted clergy to help them make the decision to migrate, often waiting for signs or messages from God before taking action. Once the decision to migrate has been made, prospective migrants and their families perform a number of popular departure rituals, some of which are practiced in conjunction with local clergy. In rural Catholic communities in Mexico and Central America many mothers light candles before a family member's departure and keep the flame burning until their safe arrival. This practice signifies hope and presence for the migrant and serves to keep family and migrant spiritually connected across time and space. In line with popular Catholicism in general, many of the religious rituals of departure are influenced by place and culture and created and reproduced by the people who honor them.[29]

Departing migrants also traverse the sacred geography of the region, making pilgrimages to national and local shrines where they deposit petitions requesting safety during their trip and well-being for their families, and make promises to saints in exchange for safe travel. Recognizing that migration to the United States has become a common household strategy and a way of life in many communities, local dioceses, parishes, and the priests who care for these shrines increasingly accommodate the migrants' needs by providing blessings. Local religious leaders, especially in well-established sending communities, also promote migration devotion by incorporating the plight of migrants into their weekly services and framing local saints as protectors and companions of migrants. In many parishes throughout Mexico and Central America, the Day of the Migrant is celebrated to commemorate in part the hardships endured by the migrant, and the Day of the Absent Sons is celebrated to provide solace to parents and to encourage a homecoming.[30] Churches and shrines also promote migration devotion through framing migration miracles and profit from its material aspects by selling to migrants physical mementos—medals, devotionals, scapulars—to comfort them on their long trek north. Devotion to saints, however, is not always bounded by place and in the control of the church. Hermano Pedro, for example, has been taken out of the local shrine by his followers and transformed into a transnational saint, worshipped by members of a global brotherhood.

Migrants also rely heavily on counsel from those they know and trust, local clergy, the revered anchors of their communities, who provide emotional and instrumental support through migration ministering. The functions of these priests, pastors, and in some cases soothsayers, are twofold. The first way in which pastors play a role and provide support is a pragmatic one. Many clergy, especially young ministers who keep up with events beyond their communities and are socially progressive, provide important sources of information to prospective migrants. From these trusted clerics, migrants learn about the dangers of crossing international borders and, in some cases, are directed to alternative and safer routes than they would otherwise adopt. Catholic priests involve themselves far more in providing information to potential migrants than do their Protestant counterparts, a difference that relates both to the former's investment in promoting migration devotion and to the more hierarchical and centralized character of the Catholic Church, which disseminates information across a network of parishes. For example, priests in many churches provide prospective migrants with prayer books to accompany them on the trip. These devotionals, which are published and distributed by the various dioceses in Mexico, also include a directory of shelters and legal services that migrants may draw on if necessary during their journey. These sanctuary and activist aspects of the clergy's pastoral care of migrants is explored in more detail in later chapters.

Clergy also provide religious sanction for the migration, a kind of spiritual travel permit that in most poor and marginalized communities has great symbolic value. So strong is the migrants' steadfast belief in these official blessings and so powerful is the psychological benefit of them in the minds of migrants and their families, they may, in fact, exceed the value of a legitimate visa or passport issued by the state. The degree to which clergy sanction migration, however, varies some by religion. Most ministers of small and often independent churches in Guatemala, El Salvador, and Honduras reluctantly endorse the migration of their own. Recognizing the devastating effects migration can have on family left behind and also the financial loss to an entrepreneurial church itself, evangelical pastors often attempt to discourage the migration of their members before granting approval and providing a blessing. In contrast, most Catholic priests, while counseling the

CHAPTER 2

The Dangerous Journey

The first time Cecilia traveled to the United States, she and her husband, Juan, along with her sister Margot flew from their home town of Puebla, Mexico, to the northern border city of Tijuana where they were met at the airport by a friend and trusted coyote. From the airport their guide drove them to an undisclosed area in the desert where they joined a group of undocumented travelers and another coyote. Strategically, the coyotes separated the women and children from the men. Cecilia, Margot, and several of the other women bid tearful farewells to their husbands or loved ones with whom they planned to reunite the following day at a Days Inn in San Isidro, California. Led by the younger and stronger of the two coyotes—Cecilia's friend—the men headed out on foot toward the border. The women, who paid higher fees than the men for "additional" protection, were crammed into the back of a sealed van.

With tears in her eyes, Cecilia recounted the horrors of the ride: "We were squeezed into the back of a truck like sardines. There were more than a dozen of us, women and children." They drove for several hours in the dark confines of the truck. "We were suffocating from the heat. There were no windows, no ventilation. The driver said that *la migra* [immigration officials] were following us so we kept quiet and still and endured the sweltering trip." Fearful that they would exhaust the meager supply of oxygen remaining in the truck, no one spoke. "I prayed in silence to God and pleaded with him to let me live." After several hours, the truck came to a sudden stop and the driver opened the doors and released the women to the blistering hot but fresh desert air. The coyote gave them water and cookies to replenish their exhausted bodies and told them they could rest for a few hours while waiting to be transferred to a second vehicle that was on the way. Before their second ride arrived, a group of dark SUVs approached from the distance.

When the coyote saw the vehicles, he quickly rounded up the women and rushed them to an area several hundred feet from where the SUVs had stopped.

"We were told that these were 'Mafia,' and that they were smuggling drugs and that they were very dangerous," Cecilia said. "You see, the coyote was paying them to use the area. We were told to form a line and turn our backs to the trucks. He then warned us that if we dared to turn around to look, we would probably be shot." The women followed the instructions. Under the glaring heat of the desert sun, they stood and waited for several hours. "We could hear the men talking and laughing among themselves." The women endured the ordeal through prayer. "Most of us had brought with us holy cards of La Virgen de Guadalupe and very softly—through tears of fear—we recited the prayers that were written on the back of the cards. The woman standing next to me dared to turn around to look at the men. She later told the rest of us that they were carrying bazookas."

Cecilia's narrative tells of the multiple dangers that undocumented migrants confront in their attempts to cross international borders. Since the 1980s, efforts to control undocumented migration have escalated in most developed countries, including the United States.[1] Despite the growth in flows of trade, goods, and services across international borders, managing the flow of labor remains one of the most important issues in many industrialized states. After the September 11, 2001, terrorist attacks in New York City and Washington, D.C., concern over controlling the borders intensified throughout the world, especially in the Untied States where immigration policy is increasingly linked to issues of national security.

Cecilia's harrowing story also reminds us of how those most affected by intensified border policies—poor and powerless migrants—turn to the culturally familiar—their religion and companion saints—in time of crisis. In this sense, the dangerous journey is a powerful social context in which religious practices and experiences make their appearances. In this chapter, I describe the dangerous journey from Central America to the United States, an ordeal that has been chronicled in journalistic accounts of undocumented migration but virtually ignored in analyses by scholars, who have largely been concerned with the economic, social, and policy dimensions of the process. The journey sets the stage for chapters 3 and 4, which focus on the ways in which the experience of danger provokes religious coping strategies by migrants and institutional support from religious institutions. Placing the undocumented journey in policy context, and highlighting the multitudes of different social and physical dangers experienced by Central American and Mexican migrants, will show that the human costs of undocumented travel are substantial.[2] Of course, not all groups experience similar levels or types of danger; a host of geographical and social factors influence the nature and magnitude of the dangers experienced by migrants, including gender of the traveler, the composition of the migrant's travel companions, time on the road, and mode of crossing.

The Journey in Policy Context

In their desperate attempts to reach the United States, unauthorized migrants from Central America and Mexico must overcome a host of legal, social, and physical problems.[3] They are forced to travel by foot and in poorly ventilated and sealed vehicles over thousands of miles across deserts, mountains, rivers, and several guarded international borders to reach the United States. To be sure, unauthorized entry from Mexico into the United States has long been dangerous, at times even fatal. As far back as the 1880s, Chinese migrants perished in the southwest while trying to avoid border enforcement operations stemming from the Chinese Exclusion Act of 1882.[4] In 1953, between three hundred and four hundred crossers died in the swift moving currents of the Rio Grande after a flood.[5] The blistering heat and parched terrain of the southwest have long claimed dozens of lives each year.[6] However, beginning in the mid-1990s, labor migrants traversing Central America and Mexico increasingly have had to endure physical and psychological abuse and take ever more risks in their attempts to reach the United States. This is in large part because of the border enforcement campaigns by both the U.S and Mexican governments to curtail undocumented labor migration from Latin America.[7]

The U.S. campaign, which is officially known as Prevention through Deterrence, was initiated under the Clinton administration in the early 1990s in response to the failure of the Immigration Reform and Control Act of 1986 to curtail undocumented migration.[8] Under Prevention through Deterrence, resources devoted to the southwest border increased dramatically as agents and new technology were funneled to the area at the cost of roughly $2 billion a year throughout the 1990s, increasing to $6 billion a year by 2005.[9] The policy initiative included an influx of new technological equipment, including night-vision cameras, ground sensors, and the construction of new physical barriers along the two-thousand-mile border. The campaign also increased staffing along the border; the number of U.S. Border Patrol agents working along the southwest border doubled between 1993 and 1999, from roughly 3,400 to 7,200.[10] By 2006, 11,500 U.S. Border Patrol agents guarded the U.S. southern border.[11] The United States has spent more than $20 billion on the border campaign and continues to spend at a rate of more than $6 billion a year.

The Prevention through Deterrence campaign deployed these new resources to the border in historical urban crossing areas: Operation Blockade near El Paso in 1993, followed by Operation Gatekeeper in the San Diego area in 1994, and Operation Rio Grande in the Brownsville area in 1997.[12] Collectively, these operations prevent migrants from crossing in well-established urban corridors where they have historically relied on familiar networks for assistance, and deflect them to more remote areas where they are exposed to greater dangers and the risk of death, especially in the harsher environments of deserts and mountains. From the 1960s through the early 1990s, the majority of unauthorized migrants from Latin America entered through San Diego and, to a lesser extent, through the El Paso and Brownsville crossing corridors. Since then, however, migrants have been increasingly squeezed into the Border Patrol sector in Tucson, Arizona, where apprehensions have increased more than 300 percent since 2000, and yearly migrant deaths in the southwest desert have tripled, soaring to the hundreds in the summer months.[13]

The logic behind the U.S. border campaign is to move unauthorized migration to rural terrain where the Border Patrol believes it has the tactical advantage. During the early stages of the campaign, the U.S. Immigration and Naturalization Service (INS) believed that the increased costs to migrants in terms of financial resources and personal safety would inhibit many from crossing.[14] But desperate for work, the migrants have continued to come. Forced to circumvent well-known crossing areas, would-be border crossers are exposed to the extreme elements, suffering dehydration, hypothermia, and drowning. In the late 1980s, the number of migrant crossing deaths exceeded 300 a year, peaking in 1988 at 355. The number of deaths started to decrease, getting as low as 180 in 1993 and 1994. The U.S. government lauched its border enfocement campaign in 1993, and since 1995 deaths along the U.S.-Mexico border have increased steadily, averaging more than 300 per year and peaking at 472 deaths in 2005, when the restructuring of border flows sent migrants through the Sonoran Desert in the scorching summer heat.[15] The U.S. Border Patrol registered 400 crossing deaths in FY 2007. By some estimates as many as 5,000 women, men, and children have died in their attempts to cross the U.S.-Mexico border.[16] The bodies of these unidentified migrants (also referred to as *no identificados*) are found in remote spots throughout the southwest, and were buried in pauper cemeteries along the border. Father Daniel Groody, a theologian who has lived and worked among undocumented migrants along the U.S.-Mexico border, compared the journey to the Way of the Cross.

Despite the billions of dollars that have been invested in curbing undocumented migration across the U.S.-Mexico border, most observers agree that the operation has failed to substantially curb the numbers of migrants entering the country.[17] Nonetheless, the strategy has been politically successful in terms of its symbolic effects—the border appears to be under control.[18] The increasing financial costs of crossing has also had the unintended consequence of encouraging unauthorized migrants to stay longer on each trip or to settle permanently in the United States. Ironically, burgeoning enforcement has transformed a temporary and circular labor supply into a permanent settled population.[19] Even the Government Accounting Office (GAO), the investigative arm of Congress, questions the efficacy of a costly border policy.[20] Yet despite these continued criticisms, Congress and the White House have largely refused to question their own failed policy, let alone take any responsibility for the mounting death toll. Along with most media, they blame professional smugglers and coyotes for the rising number of fatalities, pointing to the dangerous crossing tactics they use, although it is well known among migrants and scholars alike that the crossers would experience similar if not greater levels of danger in these remote areas without professional guides.[21] Nonetheless, official accounts deflect responsibility for the dangers of crossing from government enforcement policies to all coyotes, who are labeled by officials as criminals and have become scapegoats for the deadly conditions of the migrant trail.[22] Redirecting the problem of migrant deaths to coyotes has proven to be a successful political strategy as the public has come increasingly to view the migration phenomenon as criminal activity.

There is every reason to suspect that the U.S.-Mexico border will become an even more deadly crossing terrain in the near future, given that in the post-9/11 era immigration has become increasingly linked to national security concerns. In 2006, after several years of simmering, the immigration issue came to a boil in a divided Congress, with the House urging tougher enforcement and the Senate calling for more effective workplace and border enforcement in conjunction with guest-worker and legalization programs, in the image of the Immigration Reform and Control Act of 1986 (IRCA). Bowing to midterm election-year politics and responding to pressures from the right-wing faction of the Republican Party, the Bush administration in 2006 dropped consideration of a legalization program and employer sanctions and deployed six thousand National Guard troops to the southwest border on a temporary basis and agreed to create a virtual border with Mexico, which would include the installation of unmanned aerial vehicles, ground surveillance satellites, and motion-detector vehicles, along with a commitment to add to the existing seventy-four miles of fencing an additional seven hundred miles of new barriers along the Arizona-Mexico portion of the border at a total cost of $1.2 billion.[23] Called the Secure Border Initiative (SBI), the multi-year campaign and brainchild of the Department of Homeland Security (DHS) aims to reduce unauthorized migration primarily by increasing interior border enforcement activities and securing U.S. borders. SBI will augment funds and staffing for the Border Patrol and Immigration and Customs Enforcement (ICE), the DHS arm charged with enforcement of the nation's interior, including deportation initiatives. The plan also includes deployment of an additional seven thousand agents before Bush leaves office, which would bring the total number of agents to 18,500.[24] In 2007, a year in which the issue of immigration reform resurfaced but did not lead to legislative reform, increased border enforcement operations preceded any discussion of a pathway to citizenship for undocumented workers.

The next chapter in the story of U.S. border enforcement policies is predictable: increased deportations will lead to further undocumented migration as persons sent home return to join family left behind in the United States.[25] Expanded operations along the U.S.-Mexico border will raise the human costs for all crossing migrants as tighter security forces migrants and their coyotes to take even more dangerous routes, ultimately leading to more risks and deaths.

Ironically, these initiatives may backfire even further as spouses and children left behind in Mexico and Central America rush to reunite with family in the United States before the border becomes more dangerous to cross. Marta, a single mother and undocumented immigrant from Guatemala, has been separated from her son since she left Guatemala in 2000. When we spoke in 2006, she had no plans to bring her son to the United States to join her. Rather, she planned to wait until she could get her papers and then return to Guatemala to visit him. When I spoke to her later, she had changed her mind, in large part because of increased enforcement along the border. "Jaime leaves Guatemala next week to join me," Marta said. "It is clear that there will be no amnesty for us here and that the border is becoming more dangerous. He has to get here before it becomes too difficult to cross." The cost for hiring two coyotes and securing falsified papers to cross the U.S.-Mexico border is $9,000. Eduardo, a young Salvadoran migrant, was undecided about returning to the United States and joining his wife in Houston after being deported for the fourth time to El Salvador in 2003. He joined her in 2006. At first he considered waiting to return to the United States to see if he could locate work and hope that his wife would join him, but his plans have had to change: "The border will only become harder to cross and I can't afford a coyote. I took my chances."

Central American migrants, along with transit migrants from South America, face even more dangers than Mexicans in their quest to reach the United States as they must cross thousands of miles and several international borders, some of which are more tightly regulated than others. Central American governments have historically been open to migration across borders, especially to interregional seasonal labor migration. In recent years, however, under pressure from Mexico and with financial backing from the United States, these governments have also launched interior and border enforcement campaigns to restrict the movement of undocumented labor throughout the region. These efforts include transportation of illegal migrants to homelands, installation of monitoring equipment, training and deployment of border personnel, and requiring nationals to carry passports. In the process, thousands of Central Americans have been apprehended, detained, and deported.

Despite these mounting barriers, most migrants from Central and South America report that the real dangers emerge when leaving Guatemala and crossing the thousand-mile length of Mexico.[26] The first step in this arduous trip involves crossing the notorious Mexico-Guatemala border towns of Tapachula, Tecún Umán, El Carmen, and La Mesilla, areas that in recent years have been characterized by criminal activities ranging from drug trafficking to human smuggling, to corruption by border officials. Tecún Umán, the most infamous of the border towns, is referred to by journalists as "Little Tijuana" because of the hundreds of *polleros* (local coyotes) and other industries that have exploded in recent years to provide services for transit migrants.[27] If and when migrants manage to pass through the chaos of these bustling and booming border towns, they then must overcome the fortified border and interior enforcement efforts of the Mexican government.[28]

By the late 1990s, regaining control of its southern border had developed into a top priority for the Mexican government. The Central American refugee crisis of the 1980s, which displaced scores of Guatemalans to the southern part of the country, is etched deep in the memories of the Mexican people. The economic and political instability of southeastern Mexico resulting from the 1994 Zapatista rebellion dominated nationalist concerns. As widespread poverty, market failure, civil strife, and natural disasters (the worst of which were Hurricane Mitch in 1998 and the 2001 Salvadoran earthquakes) continued to plague the region, migration from Central America increased dramatically in the 1990s.[29]

In the mid- to late 1980s, the U.S. government responded by funding interdiction efforts along Mexico's southern border in an attempt to keep Central American refugees from reaching the United States.[30] Then in 2001, under additional urging from the United States, the Mexican government launched its border campaign, Plan Sur, to curtail transit migration through Mexico and to control drug trafficking. Hoping to gain legalization for Mexican residents in the United States, and under pressure from the Bush administration to fortify its border with Guatemala, the Mexican government strengthened its border enforcement campaign by increasing inspection activities and fortifying immigration control along land and coastal borders, and increasing its detention and deportation.[31] With partial U.S.-financing, two border enforcement operations were established at historic crossing points. The first barrier, which is manned by police and the army, was established along the jungle frontier with Belize and Guatemala; the other is further north across the Isthmus of Tehuatepec. To police these barriers the government deployed thousands of army troops to the southern states of Chiapas and Oaxaca to conduct border patrols and install checkpoints along established crossing corridors.[32] Indeed, the execution of Plan Sur relied heavily on the increased collaboration and coordinated efforts of various national, state, and local government agencies, including the Secretariat for International Relations, the Secretariat of the Interior, the Office of the Attorney General, the Secretariat of Public Security, and state and local governments of border states and their municipalities.[33]

After 9/11, the United States placed further pressure on Mexico to curtail transit migration from Central America, resulting in reinforced measures of detection, detention, and deportation, and an increase in apprehensions of Central Americans, thousands of whom were deported in 2001.[34] These measures are directed at curbing transit migration to the United States, and the human consequences, not surprisingly, match those on the U.S.-Mexico border as the Mexican campaign is largely based on the Prevention through Deterrence model developed by the United States.[35]

In their attempts to evade police and army controls, many migrants travel through the remote and harsh jungle areas of southern Mexico, where they fall prey not only to physical dangers such as exhaustion, but also to violent members of numerous rival gangs, the most notorious of which is the Mara Salvatrucha, or MS13,[36] members of which may rob and assault them. Once reaching more populated areas, the migrants face shakedowns by border officials and local police who force them to pay bribes to pass further. The human toll from enforcement efforts and the resulting chaos along the Guatemala-Mexico border is staggering. In 2000, 120 migrants died at or near the six-hundred-mile Guatemala-Mexico border. By 2001, this number had almost tripled, to 355. The most recent figures indicate another increase: in 2003, Mexican authorities reported 371 migrant crossing deaths along or near the Mexican-Guatemalan border.[37] As a young Scalabrini priest and director of a migrant shelter in Chiapas reported in 1998, "For those people who pass through Chiapas, the route is not the Way of the Cross, but a hellish crucifixion."[38] Several years later when I interviewed Father Flor in 2003, he said that the state of Chiapas has become a "cemetery without a cross."[39]

Migrant Dangers along the Journey

In this context of border and crossing danger, it is not surprising that more than three out of every four undocumented migrants in the study sample (78 percent) reported having undergone at least one type of dangerous circumstance, with half of them experiencing at least two different dangerous situations, and almost a third reporting three.[40]

Table 2 shows that the types of dangers that migrants experienced on the journey north fall into two broad categories. First are the physical dangers that can result from crossing harsh terrain and from concealment, including dehydration and heat stroke (in the desert or the back of an enclosed vehicle); accidental injury (e.g., being struck running across a highway, injured jumping on or off a train); illness; hunger; and drowning. The most common physical problems reported by far were those resulting from exposure to extreme temperatures or natural elements without adequate protection and sustenance, for example, dehydration and heat stroke. One young man complained about "coming close to suffocation after three days in a truck without food or water," with only a hole in the side of the truck through which to breathe. Others spoke about "walking days and nights in the desert without food and water." Second are the dangers created by other people—social dangers including rape and other assaults, robbery, theft, murder, and

Table 2. Number of different types of dangerous problems experienced by undocumented migrant men and women in transit to the United States

Problem Category	Total (199) In percent	Women (76) In percent	Men (123) In percent
Number of different problems			
At least one type of problem	78	74	80
At least two types of problems	50	50	49
At least three types of problems	30	32	31
At least four types of problems	14	15	13
Mean number of different problems	1.7	1.7	1.7
Physical Problems			
Extreme hunger/thirst	53	47	57
Injury	13	13	13
Extreme temperature	29	36	25
Sickness	11	11	11
Social Problems			
Assault	7	7	7
Robbery	16	15	16
Law enforcement encounter	28	24	31

Note: None of the observed differences between men and women were found to be statistically significant.

other mistreatment at the hands of unscrupulous coyotes, vigilantes, and bandits who prey on migrants, as well as mistreatment and extortion by police and border officials. Various social problems overlap considerably. One young Honduran was assaulted and robbed by the coyote who was guiding him across the border, only to be abandoned later by the same coyote in the desert. Moreover, various physical dangers often resulted from human mistreatment, even if only indirectly, so that the division between social and physical danger is only an approximate one. Juanita, a Mexican woman, reported being "assaulted and abandoned by gang members [social danger]. I was alone with no money . . . [and] I spent a lot of time hiding from *la migra*. . . . I hid in a garbage can and felt so sick . . . [and] hungry [physical danger]."

Ten percent of those interviewed (twenty) reported near-death experiences (e.g., almost drowning, barely surviving the journey across the desert) and five respondents reported witnessing eight deaths of fellow travelers. One young traveler who was part of a group of several migrants led across the Sonoran Desert by a coyote, relayed a heart-wrenching story. After several days in the desert without sufficient provisions, a baby in the group died and another traveler—a young woman—was left behind to fend for herself because she could not keep up with the group. The respondent, who barely made it out of the desert himself, assured me that there was no way that the woman could have survived on her own. In another tragic case, a young Guatemalan woman reported that the group she was traveling with walked around the body of a young girl. Several in the group wanted to provide a burial but their coyote pushed them on. In another case, a young Salvadoran man who set off with a group of friends from his hometown in Santa Ana recounted the tragic tale of their fatal Rio Grande crossing. No one in the group knew how to swim; they were clinging to a make-shift rope that extended the width of the river: "The waters looked still and shallow so we didn't really hang on to the rope like we should have. Once we were halfway across the river, the waters rose. Three of my friends were swept away. I never saw them again." In yet another case, a Mexican woman reported the drowning of a fourteen-year-old girl who had been traveling with her group. This girl, too, was swept away by the unpredictable waters of the Rio Grande. In a final tragedy, a respondent reported that *la bestia* (the beast, as migrants refer to the freight trains that run the length of southern Mexico) had taken a fellow traveler.

Looking more closely at the types of dangers listed in the table, one can see that the most striking finding is how little difference there is between men and women. Reports of physical injury, sickness, assault (including rape), and robbery/theft are virtually identical for women and men. There are some slight gender differences, however. Women were 10 percent more likely to report facing extreme temperatures, while women were about 11 percent less likely to report hunger/thirst, a variance that could possibly be explained by the alternate crossing strategies that coyotes adopt when guiding women and men across the U.S.-Mexico border. Men were also somewhat more likely than women to report problems at the hands of law enforcement officials (31 percent compared to 24 percent), a difference associated with the greater use of coyotes by women than by men (60 percent verses 53 percent) as coyotes shield migrants from encounters with law enforcement. But the overall picture seems to be that undocumented men and women are about equally exposed to various physical dangers on the journey, and men are slightly—but only slightly—more exposed to social dangers.

Migrants, moreover, tend to underreport the magnitude of the danger. Given the passage of time, they may simply forget some incidents, while other experiences may have been so harrowing that the victims are reluctant to dredge up the memories or to share them with a stranger, a problem perhaps more likely in cases of female victims of rape or other assaults. Only after knowing me for almost a year did one female respondent, a young woman from Honduras, tell of her near-death experience of being robbed and raped by a group of bandits while the coyote and the rest of the party stood by and watched. It is also impossible to measure how many times a migrant experienced any one type of problem since the questionnaire asked respondents only about the number of different types of problems experienced, not their total number of adverse experiences. Information from open-ended questions and reports by a host of civil society organizations in the region provide additional data attesting to the magnitude of the dangers to which migrants are exposed, as does widespread word-of-mouth reports among migrants.

Danger and Crossing Strategies

Not all migrants are at equal risk for the same level or types of danger; a host of factors influences the nature and magnitude of hazardous experiences along the journey. Distance traveled and length of time spent on the road, geography, and the different ways in which migrant men, women, and their families plan those journeys and organize the crossings affect exposure to danger. Those traveling from Central America, for example, must cross several guarded international borders and traverse thousands of miles to reach the United States; it is not surprising then that many of them would experience more dangers than their Mexican counterparts who travel a shorter distance and cross only one international boundary.

Central Americans in the study confirmed this assumption, reporting on average almost twice as many different types of problems as their Mexican counterparts (2.05 versus 1.27), a difference largely explained by their relatively longer trips. Most Central American migrants were on the road for more than a week (81 percent) and over a quarter (27 percent) reported that it took more than a month to reach the United States. Some Hondurans reported traveling more than three thousand miles and spending almost two months on the road before reaching the U.S.-Mexico border. In contrast, 70 percent of Mexicans interviewed arrived in the United States within a week of departure. Time on the road does indeed relate directly to dangers encountered, translating into a much more problematic journey for Central Americans.

The dangers of the journey are so well known that they have become the basis for a popular ballad sung by groups of migrants as they make their way north. Many migrants I spoke with knew at least one of the verses by heart and said they learned them from more seasoned migrants they met at shelters and hospitality houses along the way. Paul Jeffrey has compared these songs to the ballads of Woody Guthrie, who wrote about the abuse and discrimination suffered by dust-bowl migrants in the United States during the Great Depression.[41] Written and recorded by a Mexican group, Los Tigres del Norte, and titled "Tres Veces Mojado" ("Three Times a Wetback"), many of the song's verses, such as the one below, narrate the harsh realities of the migrant journey:

"Tres Veces Mojado"

"Mexico is nice but how I suffered
To cross over without papers is difficult
Those five thousand kilometers that I traveled
I can say that I remember each one"

"I knew that I would need more than courage
I knew that at best I would perish on the road
There are three borders that I had to cross
Through three countries I went without documents
Three times I had to risk my life
That's why they say I'm three times a wetback"

"In Guatemala and Mexico when I crossed
Two times they threw me in jail
The same language and skin color we share
How is it possible to call me a foreigner?"

The migratory route Central Americans adopt in their attempt to cross an additional international boundary, the Mexican-Guatemalan border, determines the nature and magnitude of the problems they experience. Those who cross in remote jungles face greater danger from border bandits than do those who sail for northern Mexico in the coastal waters near the Mexico-Guatemala border. But they, too, are taking dangerous chances, as this route can lead to shipwreck and drowning.[42] Most Central Americans launch their trip through Mexico from Tecún Umán, the lawless Guatemalan border town and dumping ground for persons who are deported on a daily basis from cities in southern Mexico. To elude Mexican border guards at the official Tecún Umán-Ciudad Hidalgo crossing point, most migrants try to pass as locals who daily transport goods and people via *balsas* (rafts made of inner tubes) across the River Suchiate, the natural boundary between Mexico and Guatemala, evading bandits who control the area at night. Migrants have no choice but to float across this river during the day, under the watchful eye of Mexican authorities. Many migrants cross early in the morning to blend in with the hundreds of labor migrants from the local Guatemala border region who, as border area residents, have visas that allow them to cross to and from work to farms in southern Mexico. Migrants who succeed in passing as locals continue on the migrant trail. Many, however, are apprehended by Mexican officials and forced to pay a bribe to pass further or are transported to Tecún Umán on one of the many buses that leave Tapachula on a daily basis.[43]

The study sample provides confirmation of the social dangers associated with crossing the Guatemala-Mexico frontier, especially the rampant corruption and arbitrary treatment migrants receive in the hands of officials. Central American migrants were almost three times as likely as their Mexican counterparts to experience robbery and theft (26 percent versus 9 percent) and more than half of these victimizations involved bribing a Mexican official to either cross the border or pass through an official checkpoint. One young Guatemalan reported being robbed by the coyote who took him across the border. He was then forced to pay a bribe to a Mexican official, only later to be deported back to Guatemala. The man bribed eight officials and attempted three crossings before succeeding in 2005.

Some Central American migrants never make it beyond the Tecún Umán-Cuidad Hidalgo crossing point. Financially destitute as a result of robbery or bribes, they are trapped in the unruly but bustling Guatemalan frontier post and forced to become prostitutes or petty criminals until they can save up enough money to attempt the journey again.[44] Tragically, an increasing number of young women who have been robbed or raped on their journey north have turned to prostitution, a bourgeoning business that caters to officials and commercial truckers. According to a recent report by the Organization of International Migration (OIM), many of the women and girls in prostitution in southern Mexico are Central Americans from Guatemala (68 percent), El Salvador (20 percent), and Honduras (12 percent).[45]

Various religious groups, human rights organizations, and governmental agencies have documented similar migrant dangers along the Guatemala-Mexico border area. In 2000, more than three of every four migrants staying at the Casa Albergue de Migrante in Tapachula reported that they had been robbed by gangs or Mexican police. Among the 2,685 migrants who stayed at the Casa Albergue a year later, 1,256 reported abuses. Four of every five of these offenses occurred in Mexico (81 percent), the remaining fifth (19 percent) in Guatemala. Most abuses (61 percent) involved robbery, rape, and assaults by bandits,[46] but abuses by Mexican and Guatemalan officials were also substantial, comprising 39 percent of all reported abuses. These criminal acts by officials usually involved bribes, but assaults and rapes were also reported. Other sources further corroborate the nature and extent of migrant abuses, particularly those inflicted by Mexican authorities along the Mexico-Guatemala border.[47] Respondents in this study reported repeated abuse at the hands of officials, from bribes to assaults to rape. Bribes were commonplace and expected. Francisco, a young Salvadoran man and recent arrival in the United States, told me of the multiple bribes he paid to Mexican officials. "I paid at least five bribes, when I entered and at each checkpoint. One time in Mexico City I was approached by a policeman who told me to go over to a nearby phone booth and leave there everything I had in my pocket."

To avoid detection by border patrol agents and other government officials, migrants use different modes of transportation and adopt several crossing strategies. These transportation methods vary by geography, country of origin, and financial resources, exposing migrants to various forms of danger. Some migrants travel on foot, others by boat; some swim in unsafe waters or ride in a van, truck, or car that may be totally enclosed, leading to dehydration. Some use public transportation, especially buses, and in Mexico, trains. Collectively, the sample of migrants adopted sixteen combinations of transportation on their journey.

Some of the more financially fortunate minimized the risks by flying to a large interior city in Mexico, and more often than not, this strategy paid off, resulting in a less dangerous trip. Salvadorans were more likely than their Honduran and Guatemalan neighbors to adopt this strategy, in part because of the greater distance they must travel to reach the United States, as well as the relative ease at which Salvadorans can leave their country.[48] One out of every five Salvadorans in the study sample flew to either Mexico City or Guadalajara, and then embarked on their overland journey north.[49] From these large Mexican cities where transit migrants easily blend into the local resident population, they can arrange for the overland segment of the journey. One of every twelve Mexicans also adopted the strategy of flying to a

Mexican border city such as Tijuana, where they then made arrangements to cross the border overland with a coyote.

Those lacking the money to travel by air must rely on inexpensive public transportation such as buses or trains. Indeed, almost half the sample (45 percent) relied on the bus and on walking at some point in their journey. Central Americans traveling through Guatemala reported that they avoided isolated areas where they would fall prey to bandits and officials familiar with the migratory rural routes. Instead, they favored public buses, which are not subject to random stops by officials. But not even these are always an option for the impoverished; some had no choice but to walk a large part of the distance and turn over their meager resources to bandits and Guatemalan officials at checkpoints, a practice that has also been documented by area human rights organizations.[50]

Once in Mexico, many Central Americans make the twenty-kilometer jungle trek to Tapachula to one of the growing number of shelters that church and nongovernmental organizations (NGOs) have erected in recent years to protect and provide services to transit migrants. Because buses are now officially searched, many migrants must make the twenty-kilometer trip by foot. Along the way, migrants fall prey to *maras*, as the gangs and bandits are known, who regularly rob and assault transit migrants. For this reason, many migrants try their best to blend in with streams of daily laborers who work on the farms in southern Chiapas.

Crossing the Mexico-U.S. border by foot is also dangerous but the problems are usually physical in nature and related to exposure to the elements. Migrants crossing the southwest border of the United States risk drowning, dehydration in the southwest desert, and hypothermia in the California mountains. In this study, crossing borders on foot and walking long distances to populated areas exposed migrants, especially women, to twice as many dangers than those who were able to avoid this mode of transportation.

From all migrant accounts, the most deadly way to reach the United States is to travel the freight trains that run the length of Mexico.[51] Riding the trains to the United States can take up to several weeks and involve changing multiple trains along the way. Because the trains have no fixed schedule, large numbers of migrants accumulate along the tracks, sometimes reaching as high as five hundred.[52] Riding the trains of Mexico, reminiscent of but far more dangerous than the train hopping of Americans during the Great Depression, is a route adopted only by the most desperate: those who lack the resources to hire a coyote or to pay for public transportation. Migrants refer to the train as "la bestia" or as the "death express" because of the lives it claims.[53] Migrants in the study who rode the trains in Mexico reported experiencing more than twice as many problems as those who did not. A young Honduran told of how he and his fellow traveler were hiding underneath a freight car for a day and a half, waiting for its departure. His friend fell asleep and, according to the young respondent, "was torn to bits" by the moving train. Clinging to the train, the respondent rode the remainder of the trip in tears and prayer.

Well aware of the risks of train travel, women generally avoid la bestia, with twice as many men as women in the sample traveling that way (17 percent of men versus 9 percent of women). Migrants regularly run for their lives as they attempt to jump on the freight train as it leaves the train yards. To catch a train they must run at a quick pace of ten to fifteen kilometers until they can grab a ladder hanging from the back of the cars and can pull themselves up onto the "iron worm," as it is also referred to by residents in the region. Between Tapachula and Mexico City, a distance of roughly seven hundred miles, riders must evade twelve migration checkpoints. Each time the train approaches a checkpoint, the migrants jump off and run for cover; then they try to remount as the train pulls away. In these life-threatening moves, they lose arms, limbs, and even their lives.[54]

Once aboard the train, other dangers emerge. In the dark freight compartments robberies and rapes by gang members—some of whom claim the train as their turf—are commonplace. Once abused, the young victims are often thrown from the train, penniless and severely injured. Some do not survive the ordeal. Migrants have also suffocated to death in the confines of the closed cars.[55] According to the Mexican National Institute of Migration, hundreds of migrants suffer train injuries each year. In 2004, Grupo Beta, a task force established by the Mexican government to help migrants in need, assisted 188 injured migrants and 34 amputees.[56]

There are occasional bright moments on the train ride. In some towns and villages along the train route, most notable in the states Oaxaca and Veracruz, area residents rush the passing trains and throw food to the destitute migrants. These "food throwers" number in the dozens and live in some of the poorest Mexican villages. Despite their own meager circumstances, they are known for their generosity to the migrants, throwing precious items such as bananas, tortillas, and bags of juice and water.[57]

To evade detection by border patrol agents and migration officials, migrants also rely on crossing networks. Inexperienced crossers and women do not travel alone; rather, they rely on coyotes and the social support and knowledge of more seasoned family and friends.[58] More than half the sample (56 percent) traveled at least some portion if not all of the journey with a coyote or family member and friends, or both. This is not an unexpected finding; a number of studies have shown that those entering the United States for the first time are more likely to use a coyote than are those who have more experience crossing the border.[59] Many, however, did not have access to personal social networks or to coyotes to assist them. Usually unfamiliar with the migratory routes, they relied on crossing information provided by fellow travelers or religious and social service workers they met on the road.

Crossing strategies vary for Central Americans and Mexicans and for men and women. These different approaches ultimately influence the type and level of danger each group endures. Central Americans were almost twice as likely to cross alone or with persons they met on the road as were Mexicans (57 percent versus 37 percent). Moreover, the group most at risk to traveling without the protection and guidance of a coyote or family and friends were Hondurans: four out of every five did not have access to personal networks to assist them during the crossing. Hondurans migrants are often young and poor, and many are inexperienced. Devastated by the long-term economic consequences of Hurricane Mitch, these migrants are among the poorest and most recent of the undocumented northbound migration streams; as such, they have neither the financial means to hire a coyote nor an established network to assist in the crossing process. These group differences suggest that there is far more variation in network structure and the social capital derived from it than is commonly assumed in the literature on migrant crossing, which largely examines only Mexicans who, as a group, have a long history of undocumented migration.[60] These different crossing strategies also help to explain why Central Americans, but especially Hondurans, reported experiencing more problems than Mexicans on the journey and relying more on religious groups and organizations along the trail for assistance.

Tightened border security has elevated the demand for coyotes, who have developed more complex crossing strategies to circumvent border enforcement operations, and migrants and their families, of course, must bear the economic and human costs of these strategies in the context of a militarized border.[61] Depending on service and distance, the migrants in this study paid fees ranging from $500 to $8,000 with no guarantee of success; the large majority had to rely on family in both the United States and their home communities to fund their travel.

Traveling under the guidance of a coyote can be a risky venture; indeed, except for traveling alone, no other arrangement (friends on the road, family only, family and friends) presents as many different types of problems for the transit migrant. However, traveling with a coyote, regardless of whether family members or friends are also companions, appears to protect the migrant from social dangers (such as official detection and border bandits), although in the process of evading official detection, migrants face adverse physical situations, such as exposure to harsh natural elements. Most of the migrants in the sample who traveled with a coyote crossed through the Texas-Mexico border, as their destination was Houston. More migrants than before, however, are crossing the Mexico-Arizona border, where they face dangers posed by the isolation and heat of the desert terrain. The Texas-Mexico route subjects travelers to two types of physical hardship: crossing the "Rio Bravo" (as the Rio Grande is often referred to) and crossing the desert and arid ranchland area of the southwest. Many travelers surveyed did not know how to swim so that traversing the unpredictable and cold waters of the Rio Grande at night while carrying belongings posed enormous challenges. Many lost all they owned in the crossing. Tragically, one respondent lost her baby to the river, and several others came close to drowning. The greatest danger posed in the desert is dehydration and it was a common experience for migrants in the study who had crossed on foot. They commonly ran out of food (e.g., crackers and sardines) and water, and some resorted to drinking their own urine to survive. Clearly, some of the coyotes were inexperienced and unprepared for the traumas of a desert crossing. It is pretty clear, however, that many more migrants could face life-threatening situations if they ventured across the southwest border without the aid of coyotes. In other words, coyotes cannot protect migrants entirely from the physical elements.

The relationship between using a coyote and experiencing danger is inherently difficult to disentangle. Migrants employ many different crossing strategies during a single journey of which securing a coyote is but one. Furthermore, migrants often travel with several people, including friends and family who are seasoned travelers, along with a coyote, who could be a trusted guide from home, a well-established border crosser, or an unscrupulous border transporter who preys on migrants.[62] Indeed, migrants readily distinguish between good and bad coyotes, a difference that has largely been ignored by the media and government officials. Migrants thus can experience danger under myriad situations during different stages of the journey and in the company of various traveling companions, including differentially motivated coyotes.

While there were numerous reports in the study of unscrupulous coyotes preying on their cargo, there were just as many stories of heroic ones. In more than a few cases, women were spared rape by fellow travelers because of the intervention of a coyote. In other cases, coyotes made sure that women were safely under the care of family, friends, or church before leaving them in the United States. In still other cases, coyotes prayed with their human cargo and asked for their forgiveness for the unexpected hardships they had endured in their care. In one instance, a coyote actually took a woman to an Arizona hospital emergency room to be treated for dehydration before handing her over to another coyote, who then drove her to her final destination in North Carolina.

Gender further complicates the relationship between the use of a coyote and danger. Recognizing the different risks facing men and women on the journey, Latin American families make every effort to shield and protect daughters and wives more so than they do sons and husbands. Reluctant to travel without trusted men, these women welcome their families' efforts, which may include placing women and girls under the protection of male relatives who have experience crossing the borders or hiring smugglers who provide extra protective services for women. Family members may pay the cost of a coyote to protect the women in the group and provide important information as to where to seek assistance and shelter during the journey. Not surprisingly, women were more likely to travel with a coyote than were men (60 percent verses 53 percent), but the difference is small. Men were more likely than women to travel alone or with companions they met on the road (27 percent versus 12 percent) during their first trip to the United States, although the high number of women who do so is surprising. While few migrants of either sex traveled with a spouse, women were nonetheless three times more likely to do so than men (10 percent versus 3 percent). Half of all women traveled with one or more family members, compared to less than a quarter (23 percent) of their male counterparts. Men rarely traveled with children (3 percent), while 15 percent of women did so, and almost all of those children were younger than sixteen. All together, women were accompanied by friends and/or family members considerably more often than were men—59 percent verses 42 percent.

In all eleven cases in which women traveled with children, they were under the careful guidance of family members and/or coyotes, and thus were largely spared dangerous situations. They also avoided deadly crossing stretches, such as deserts. In other words, migrants are less willing to put their mothers and children in dangerous situations to reach the United States. One young Guatemalan woman who traveled with her five-year-old daughter to join her husband in North Carolina, made the entire trip in less than four days under the guidance of a coyote and in the confines of a closed vehicle. As the husband of the young woman reported, she paid extra ($8,000) to evade the grueling and dangerous desert trek across the Mexico-Arizona border; she and her daughter waded the Rio Grande into southern Texas, where they were then transported by van to North Carolina.

For those women who do migrate, especially the married ones and those traveling with children, the safest possible journey is planned, whether that be at the expense of coyotes for two border crossings for Central American women, higher smuggling fees for especially trustworthy coyotes, or being met by husbands or other trusted male relatives or friends to be escorted across the border. For women, the price of reduced risk is more planning before the trip, more expense on the trip, and often more danger of apprehension by border officials for male relatives who had migrated earlier.[63]

Maricela, an established migrant from Guatemala and resident of North Carolina at the time, was anxiously awaiting the arrival of her sister. According to Maricela, a trusted female coyote from her western highland hometown organized her sister's journey. She hired three sets of coyotes—all Guatemalan—to transport Maricela's sister to North Carolina. The first coyote is well known to Maricela and her family and so Maricela's sister and several other migrants were entrusted to his care for the two-week overland segment of the journey (from Guatemala to Altar, Mexico, just south of the Arizona-Mexico desert). Maricela's family in Guatemala paid the coyote an advance fee of $2,000. Once in Altar, Maricela's sister and her companions were handed over to a second group of coyotes, who led them through the twenty-five-mile desert hike into southern Arizona (Maricela had wired the $2,000 fee to the border crossing coyotes). In the final leg of the trek, Maricela's sister was transported to North Carolina at an additional cost of $1,000, wired to the final set of coyotes in Arizona. Although Maricela's sister reported that her journey through the desert was exhausting and physically demanding, lasting a week and resulting in hospitalization upon her arrival in North Carolina, she says that she was spared any social dangers because she "was entrusted to a coyote for the entire voyage."

The gendered nature of the travel, then, influences the type and degree of danger men and women experience, yet undocumented travel remains an unsafe venture for both men and women. Central American women appear to endure a wider range of problems than do their Mexican sisters, reflecting the greater physical hardships they encounter on their longer journey to the United States. Interestingly, while traveling with any combination of coyote, spouses, and friends presents comparable dangers to both men and women, traveling with children dramatically reduces the likelihood of experiencing danger due to the precautions adopted. Migrants, especially mothers, are reluctant to place their children in harm's way, so if they must migrate, they take every precaution to assure their safety.[64]

Summary

Despite all the precautions that migrants take to make it safely to the United States, the dangers remain formidable. In recent years, as both Mexico and the United States have built up military operations on their southern borders, migrant risks have escalated dramatically. Central American migrants, who must travel longer distances, traverse multiple international borders, and thus spend substantial time on the road, experience more danger than their Mexican counterparts. They are exposed to mounting social dangers as they travel through Mexico, including robbery, bribery, rape, and assaults from gangs and Mexican officials who prey on the undocumented. Crossing the U.S.-Mexico border also poses enormous challenges; the dangers both Central American and Mexican migrants experience here are primarily physical and associated with exposure to natural elements. As migrants circumvent intensified enforcement activities in established cities and settlements along the border, they are pushed further into desolate areas where they are exposed to long stretches of cold and heat. Migrants have attempted to circumvent these dangers by increasingly relying on multiple crossing strategies and different social networks, each of which varies by country of origin and by gender. When financially feasible, migrants avoid traveling alone or by foot or train; they prefer to travel with family and/or coyotes, who appear to protect the migrant from social dangers but not physical ones.

Current migration policies that rely solely on enforcement operations, such as apprehension, detention, and deportation, are likely to yield far-reaching and unintended consequences. Militarizing the southern borders of the United States and Mexico has so far done little if anything to stem the flow of unauthorized migrants, despite astronomical sums spent by taxpayers in both countries and the human costs to migrants who attempt to circumvent the barriers. Yet both countries continue this policy approach. These billion-dollar operations serve only to deflect migrants from established urban crossing areas to more remote, often harsh rural areas of deserts and mountains where they are exposed to great physical and social dangers and risk of death. There is no quick fix when it comes to immigration reform; the United States and Mexico must develop a cohesive and reasonable balance among civil liberties, law enforcement, and societal benefits. As this study shows and other research has documented, enforcement policies alone do not end undocumented migration; they simply raise the human and economic costs.

The tragic situation in which transit migrants find themselves begs answers to a host of questions: How do migrants cope with the threat of impending danger? How do they cope with the experience of danger? To whom do they turn in times of need? How do they muster up the physical and psychological strength to continue on the journey after experiencing hardship? To answer these questions, we now turn to the central role of religion and faith in the undocumented journey.

CHAPTER 3

Churches Crossing Borders

Ernesto was twenty-five years old when he migrated to the United States in the summer of 1999. Before leaving his hometown just north of Veracruz, Mexico, he sold his horse and his land, and crammed all his personal belongings into a suitcase. After receiving a blessing from his priest and bidding farewell to his parents, brothers, and sisters, he set out alone on the long journey north. He possessed little knowledge about the migratory route, and so relied on information he solicited from strangers along the way. He traveled most of the journey to the border by foot and on public buses, riding by day and sleeping on the floors of bus depots at night. On his second night, not far from the border, he was assaulted and robbed. "I cried for the first time in many years," he admitted. "I cried and prayed myself to sleep. I had no one to help me. When I woke, I walked to the first church I could find. The priest opened his door to me; he bandaged my wounds, fed me, and then together we prayed. This is how I found the strength to continue my trip."

Ernesto is one of many transit migrants who seek assistance, refuge, and spiritual nourishment from the church, an institution long recognized for providing sanctuary to those in need. With the increase in Central American and Mexican unauthorized migration to the United States and the continued militarization of Mexico's northern and southern borders, the church, both Catholic and Protestant, has resurrected its public face in regional migration matters to a level not seen since the 1980s, when large numbers of Central Americans fled the political turmoil in their homelands in search of refuge and political asylum in Mexico and the United States. During that period, with no official Mexican recognition of refugee status under the Mexican constitution, tens of thousands of Guatemalan and Salvadoran refugees found themselves separated from their families and trapped in limbo for indefinite periods of time in the southernmost Mexican state of Chiapas, where they resided in camps run by the Mexican government and the UN High Commissioner for Refugees (UNHCR).[1] In response, the Catholic Church in Chiapas, which defended the right of the refugees to seek safe haven outside the camps, began to provide refuge to Central Americans and sometimes arranged for their transportation to safer places. By 1981 a sanctuary network had developed throughout the country to help unauthorized Central Americans avoid official detection and locate housing and employment. In the same year, U.S. religious and faith workers formed the U.S. Sanctuary Movement, a faith-based political movement founded in support of Central American refugees. During the ensuing years, religious workers in Mexico and the United States coordinated efforts to assure the safe passage of Central American refugees through Mexico to the United States and as far north as Canada.[2]

More than twenty years later, the public role of churches and religious groups in the region has resurfaced in matters of Latin American migration to the United States. Although the original political and military conflicts that gave rise to refugee and migration flows from Central America in the 1980s have abated, their effects on the economic and civil bases of society have been devastating, giving rise to large displaced populations that have fled their homelands for a better life in Mexico and the United States.[3]

Today's sanctuary efforts are directed toward protecting the economic and human rights of migrants and are sanctioned by multiple levels of church hierarchy, from the Vatican to transnational congregations to binational Episcopal leaders, from cross-border diocesan efforts to local clergy and lay religious workers throughout the region. At a humanitarian level, religious groups (often in coalitions with NGOs) compensate for the lack of public institutional mechanisms to protect the human rights and care for the well-being of unauthorized journeying migrants. In the larger public sphere, however, where the church is increasingly an advocate for the rights of migrants, the expanded presence of churches and religious groups in regional migration matters reflects not only their historical role in refugee advocacy specifically but also a more recent and broader development in what has been referred to as the widespread deprivatization of religion—that is, the increasingly pubic and active role played by churches and religious groups throughout the world in ways that sometimes challenge state institutions and their regulatory activities.[4]

Yet today's religious groups in the region do more than provide for the material needs of migrants and advocate on their behalf. As Ernesto's experience reveals, faith workers offer counsel and spiritual nourishment to journeying migrants, a resource so powerful that it can inspire the believer into action. For Ernesto, prayer and consultation with a priest he sought out along the migrant trail gave meaning to Ernesto's suffering and the strength to continue on his journey.

In this chapter I return to the theme of institutional support for migration, but move from the local clergy and churches in the sending communities to the supporting clergy, congregations, and religious and humanitarian organizations along the migrant trail from Central America to the United States. I emphasize the ways in which faith workers, institutional arrangements, and transnational congregational and organizational practices provide transit migrants with the social, spiritual, and psychological capital to cope with hardship and continue on their journeys and reach the United States. I show that the religious actors that work the migrant trail today foster spirituality and play an important role in sustaining the migration process. In the face of governmental border enforcement and a quasi-criminal underground railroad, they have become guardians of migrant rights and dignity, a role they maintain in part through migration counseling, and are part of the ever-expansive and complex social infrastructure that supports migrants in their travels. Accounting for these religious actors and the social capital they provide expands the scholarship on the social dimension of unauthorized migration, which has focused almost exclusively on migrants' personal networks and the for-profit migration industry to understand how migrants navigate the journey and crossing experiences.

International, Governmental, and Civil Society Organizations Respond

The organizations that work with or advocate on behalf of transit migrants from Central America and Mexico can be sorted into three groups: international, governmental, and a collection of civil society organizations (CSOs) that mediate between the state and the migrants.[5] The CSOs include secular and faith-based NGOs as well as other faith-based organizations, churches, and community groups, some of which are local while others are part of national, regional, and transnational organizations and advocacy networks.[6] The large majority of these institutions and organizations have mandates to monitor state migration activities and disseminate information that often challenges states' debates. Others work on behalf of the state to monitor official migration activities. Collectively, they are committed to protecting and enforcing the rights and treatment of migrants who are increasingly prey to conditions of exploitation and victimization in their attempts to gain access to economic opportunities in the United States. Some international organization and faith-based groups, such as the International Organization for Migration (IOM) and Catholic Charities, work closely with local groups in the resettlement of persons deported from the United States.[7] The numbers of organizations in the region working with or on behalf of transit migrants are numerous and a discussion of them is beyond the goals of this chapter, which primarily focuses on religious and faith-based groups that work directly to support, provide for, and protect migrants on their journeys north.

The UNHCR is one major secular international organization that does provide some indirect assistance to transit migrants traveling through Mexico to the United States. The UNHCR has offices in Mexico City and in the southern Chiapas town of Tapachula, both stopover points for migrants on their way to the United States, though for some, like political asylum applicants, Mexico City is a final destination. Most Central Americans who pass through Mexico today are unauthorized, but a small minority file asylum cases with the UNHCR, though their numbers are as few as three hundred per year, and acceptance rates remain low (15 percent). Although the UNHCR's mandate in Mexico is limited to working only with those seeking asylum, it does monitor and report on the detention and deportation of undocumented migrants, especially under conditions of concern, such as the reported widespread arbitrary detention of Central Americans in Mexico resulting from the lack of due process.[8]

Most transit migrants who are apprehended in Mexico are detained in one of Mexico's migrant holding centers (MHC) before being deported. Some migrants, including several in my sample, were apprehended and detained in the MHC in Tapachula for about twenty-four hours before being deported across the border to Tecún-Umán, Guatemala. The largest MHC in Mexico is located in the poor barrio of Iztapala, in Mexico City. On September 8, 2003, the day I accompanied a binational delegation from the Episcopal Conference for the Pastoral Care of Migrants on their visit to the center, it held roughly three hundred migrants, all men. Most hailed from Central and South America, but we also spoke with Nigerians, Bangladeshis, Canadians, Chinese, and nationals of Balkan countries, all of whom were using Mexico as a launching point to reach the United States. The binational delegation, composed of Mexican and U.S. religious leaders, had come to observe the conditions in the center; most detainees reported bearable conditions but lengthy detentions, ranging from two days to eight months.

The delegation and the detainees met in the center's large common courtyard. Several U.S. bishops among the Episcopal Commission stepped forward and explained to the detainees the commission's ongoing efforts to convince the Mexican government to reconsider the expedited removal of unauthorized persons in the country without a fair hearing. Six migrants stood up to speak and they relied on religious discourse to communicate their concerns. Among them was a young man who recited by heart the Parable of the Last Judgment, a biblical verse often quoted by religious workers who provide for migrants because of its fundamental emphasis on the vulnerabilities and conditions of the unauthorized journeying migrant. The passage, Matthew 25:35–40, reads in part, "For I was hungry and you gave me something to eat, I was thirsty and you gave me something to drink, I was a stranger and you invited me in, I needed clothes and you clothed me, I was sick and you looked after me, I was in prison and you came to visit me." Bishop Renato of Mexico responded by reminding the detainees, "You are all human beings in the eyes of God, regardless of religion and legal status." Within minutes, the crowd, led by a young migrant from Ghana, burst into a spontaneous chorus, singing each in his own language Bob Marley's "Redemption Song."

Both the U.S. and Mexican governments have established special patrol forces to assist and rescue migrants in dangerous situations. When some of the predictions about the dangers (including death) to migrants who tried to cross the heavily fortified U.S.-Mexico border proved true, the U.S. Border Patrol implemented the Border Safety Initiative (BSI) in 1998 in cooperation with the Mexican government. The search-and-rescue aspect of the BSI employs BORSTAR (Border Search Trauma and Rescue) teams and includes deployment of emergency medical services (EMS) units, increased EMS training for agents, increased life-saving equipment, and emphasis on patrolling-for-rescue, especially during the summer months when the hot weather places migrants in elevated danger. The initiative also includes an advertising campaign in Mexico and Central America warning potential migrants of border dangers. According to BORSTAR, since 2002 it has performed more than a thousand missions and saved more than 2,500 lives along the U.S.-Mexico border.[9]

On the recommendation of its Comisión Nacional de Derechos Humanos (National Commission of Human Rights), in 1996 the Mexican government established Grupo Beta, a police force to provide human rights protection and assistance to migrants. Although Grupo Beta claims to work outside the reach of the government, it is derived from the National Institute of Migration and is funded by state, municipal, and federal funds. Grupo Beta launched its first operations in populated settlement areas along the Mexico-U.S. border, where it assists lost or stranded migrants, some of whom have been abandoned by coyotes in the desert or in vast ranchlands. Its mandate is not to arrest migrants but to assist and protect them. To this end, Beta forces may provide migrants with transportation funds to return to their home communities, or more often than not, direct them to churches and well-known religious shelters in cities and towns on the Mexican side of the U.S.-Mexico border. In recent years the Beta patrols have become more visible in southern areas such as Tapachula, where human rights abuses of migrants have escalated. To protect migrants from abuses by coyotes, bandits, and police, Beta forces comb bus stations, freight cars, and roads that constitute the southern migratory route. Although there have been reports of abuse at the hands of Beta forces, those in my sample reported only their humanitarian acts.

A number of migrants credit Beta troops with saving their lives. At the Albergue San Juan Bosco, a run-down religious shelter for the poor located in the dusty and desolate Mexican border town of Nogales, I met Felipe, an older Mexican who was recovering from severe wounds to his legs and feet resulting from a fifteen-hour hike through the desert. He found refuge at the shelter. When I first saw Felipe, he was sitting on his mattress, hunched over with fatigue; one of his two very swollen and bruised legs was soaking in a medicinal solution. When I asked him about his injury, he proceeded to show me his foot, which was missing the bottom layer of skin, taken, along with the soles of his shoes, by the scorching desert sand. In grief and pain, he explained how he had been abandoned by his coyote and had wandered aimlessly in the desert until he was finally rescued by Beta forces, who brought him to the shelter, not an uncommon practice. Robbed of $1,600 by his coyote, Felipe had no choice but to return home; Grupo Beta provided him with a bus ticket.

The Mexican National Commission for Human Rights also has an office in Tapachula and is charged with protecting, observing, promoting, and investigating information about human rights. In this capacity it often directly works with migrants in vulnerable situations. It is a major source for the publication and dissemination of reports of human rights abuses in the border regions; unfortunately, few complaints they receive are actually resolved.[10]

A growing number of local NGOs and CSOs along the northern and southern borders of Mexico mediate between the state and the migrants by advocating on behalf of migrants' human and legal rights. Some receive international assistance from Catholic Charities and IOM.[11] Among the more active is El Centro de Derechos Humanos Fray Matías de Córdova (Human Rights Center of Fray Matias de Cordova) in Tapachula. It was founded in 1994 to protect the human rights of the many Central Americans that live and work in the Chiapas area. Since 1997 its activities have expanded to include monitoring reports of human rights violations committed against migrants. Similarly, Sin Fronteras (Without Borders) is an NGO that also works on regional migration issues, but with an interest in Mexico-U.S.-bound migration. Although its work primarily focuses on research, dissemination, and advocacy, in recent years, with funding from Catholic Relief Services, it has expanded its social and legal services provided to newcomer and journeying migrants.

The Role of Religious Institutions, Groups, and Workers in Migration

U.S. and Mexican border enforcement policies since the mid-1990s have come under fire by religious workers in Central America, Mexico, and the U.S. border areas. In contrast to the governments of Mexico and the United States, which claim sovereign rights to protect and seal their borders in the name of national security, many religious institutions, organizations, and workers argue that when the poor in their communities cannot find work to support themselves and their families, a situation in which many Mexican and Central Americans now find themselves, they have a right to cross borders to find work elsewhere. While not explicitly challenging the right of sovereign nations to control their borders, as was the case during the heyday of the U.S. Sanctuary Movement, religious actors and interfaith groups composed of Catholics, mainline Protestants, peace churches, and Jewish organizations have become increasingly critical of current U.S. and Mexico border and interior enforcement policies, because they violate the human rights and human dignity of migrants.

Calling for immigration reform and social justice, a growing number of local, regional, national, and transnational religious workers and coalitions explicitly seek policies that do not exploit migrants, place them in danger, violate their right to due process, or detain them indefinitely. To shield migrants from violations of their human and statutory rights, religious leaders encourage their clergy to provide pastoral and humanitarian care for migrants during the entirety of the migration process, from departure through the journey to arrival. And missionaries and clergy in the region have responded by establishing what now amounts to a loosely organized network of shelters and safe houses for migrants. In the 1980s, political refugees from Central America sought refuge in Catholic and Protestant churches along the northbound migratory route. Today, the motivations that trigger migration from Central America are mostly economic as opposed to political, yet migrants continue to turn to those they know they can trust—religious and faith workers—for temporary shelter and assistance. These religious workers are therefore critical to study when it comes to social action associated with issues of migration, because of the social and political resources they possess and the opportunity structures in which they can wield influence and mobilize their followers to challenge public policy.[12]

The U.S.-Mexico Catholic Bishops Conference and the Right to Migrate

Catholic social teaching has a long tradition of defending the right to migrate, based on the church's view of itself as a "pilgrim people in a pilgrim church,"[13] as well as on principles of Catholic social theology that emphasize that the causes of migration are embedded in structural injustices that must be resolved: poverty, market imbalances, and political strife. Since Vatican II, the Catholic Church has largely shifted its role from being an ally of the state to being an advocate for the poor and disenfranchised.[14] In some dioceses throughout Central America and Mexico, for example, bishops and clergy alike have in recent decades pledged their commitment to liberation theology and the provision of pastoral care for the poor, including the displaced migrant. In matters of migration, this public face of church hierarchy manifests itself in Vatican documents, social teachings, and pastoral work that incorporate the concept of migration as a fundamental human right.[15] And because most nations, including the United States and Mexico, have rejected this right, historical tension exists between the Catholic Church and nation states.[16]

Catholic social teaching has resurrected the right to migrate in the specific case of unauthorized Latin American migrants and in the context of militarized borders.[17] Responding to the escalation of enforcement activities along the Mexico-U.S. border, Catholic bishops in Central America, Mexico, and the United States have reached across their common borders to express publicly their unified support of the rights of individuals and their families to migrate, as well as opposition to governmental policies that deny this right and border enforcement efforts that place migrants in physical danger. In the post-Vatican II era, the Catholic Church has become more accepting of coordinated migration activities that bypass the Vatican, evidenced in the increasing responsibility for migration matters placed in the hands of national bishops conferences and the bilateral and transnational regional networks they have developed.

In 2003, the Mexican Conference of Catholic Bishops and the U.S. Conferences of Catholic Bishops, which collectively shepherd more than 150 million Catholics, published the first-ever joint pastoral letter on migration, titled "Strangers No Longer: Together on the Journey of Hope."[18] The letter's basic message is that the U.S. immigration system is broken and in need of reform. The Tex-Mex bishops (as they refer to themselves) argue that the consequences of the current immigration system linking the two nations—family separation, increased danger for journeying migrants, and the exploitation of migrant labor—are contrary to Catholic social teachings because they challenge the basic dignity and human rights of migrants.[19] The title of the letter, "Strangers No Longer," reflects the migration theme of the alien in Christian theology, one that is repeated often in the Bible, the most frequently cited of which is the story of Abraham and Sarah extending hospitality to three strangers in a hostile environment (Genesis 18:1–15), who in contemporary reference can be understood as undocumented immigrants.

Fundamental, then, to Catholic social theology is the belief that migrants should be treated with the respect due every human, and the protection of this dignity, a communitarian position, is basic to the political and social agenda of the Catholic social doctrine of migration.[20] The links between theology and migrant well-being is firmly etched into the social doctrine of the Catholic Church and is visible in multiple cross-border religious practices that directly challenge nation state enforcement strategies. In this sense, many Catholic clergy and missionaries are increasingly practicing a theology of migration that links church doctrine directly to social policy.

The church hierarchy in the United States and Mexico practices a theology of migration at three levels: solidarity, advocacy, and hospitality.[21] At the level of solidarity, the U.S. bishops support numerous nonprofit national and international organizations (such as Catholic Relief Services, Catholic Legal Immigration Network, and Catholic Charities) that are active in providing an array of humanitarian, social, civil, and legal services for migrants in Mexico, Central America, and the United States.[22] At the advocacy level, the U.S. bishops in particular are situated in the center of the U.S. immigration debate, regularly challenging the enforcement arm of U.S. immigration policy through their public statements. In the 2003 joint pastoral letter in particular, the bishops called for U.S. and Mexican enforcement authorities to dismantle enforcement strategies that promote smuggling operations and that redirect migrants to routes that place their lives in danger.[23] Similar themes were repeated in May 2005, when the U.S. bishops launched a national effort, "Justice for Immigrants," a nationwide campaign for immigration reform in the United States. The U.S. bishops took their campaign a step further in 2006. On Ash Wednesday, March 1, 2006, Cardinal Roger Mahoney of Los Angeles, California, strategically announced that he would instruct priests and lay Catholics to ignore provisions in a 2005 House of Representatives enforcement-only bill (H.R. 4437) that would make it a crime to aid unauthorized migrants.

The proactive role of the U.S. Conference of Catholic Bishops in defending the rights of individuals to migrate and settle legally in the United States reflects the Catholic Church's legacy of caring for its own, regardless of national origin or legal status, as it cared for the needs of the great waves of immigrants to the United States in the late nineteenth and early twentieth centuries. To meet the integration needs of immigrants during this period (who by 1920 comprised 75 percent of all Catholics in the United States), the church developed or expanded many of its institutions, including parishes, schools, and hospitals.[24] In some ways, then, the Catholic Church's present-day position represents continuity in its historical role of providing and caring for immigrant groups. What stands out today, however, is its central role in the northbound journey from Central America and Mexico and its emphasis on influencing public policy and instructing its followers on the ethics and morality of migration matters.

Today the hierarchy of bishops both in the United States and Mexico also incorporate into their theology of migration a decentralized sanctuary agenda that calls for the greater inclusion of clergy, lay workers, congregations, and parishioners in the everyday lives of migrants. To protect migrants from violation of their rights, the bishops encourage more involvement by clergy and religious workers in providing pastoral and humanitarian care for departing, journeying, and arriving migrants, what I have termed migration counseling or migration ministering.[25] The Catholic Church's tradition of serving the settlement needs of Mexican and other Latin American migrants in the United States has been expanded to include the bishops' call for binational efforts to

coordinate pastoral care and migration counseling for departing and journeying migrants. Further, the growth of relatively autonomous U.S.-Mexico
networks of Catholic bishops over issues concerning human rights and migration reflects a more general development in transnational networks that
circumvent Rome.[26]

Assistance of Diocesan and Parish Networks along the Migratory Route

Solidarity, advocacy, and hospitality are also practiced in the front lines by
pastors, missionaries, and faith workers who coordinate programs and shelters situated along the undocumented migrant corridor from Guatemala
through Mexico to the Mexico side of the Mexico-U.S. border. These shelters
and the programs they provide, which local, regional, national, and international religious (largely Catholic) groups support and coordinate, can be sorted
into three types: origin, transit, and destination. These contrast with the traditional settlement programs—such as education, legal services, and health
access that the Catholic Church provides newcomer immigrant communities throughout the region and especially in the United States—in that origin, transit, and destination programs provide a variety of humanitarian and
social services specifically for the journeying, arriving, and returning migrant.[27] The types of services also reflect the bilateral efforts of the Catholic
Church in Mexico and the United States, efforts that are especially pro-
nounced among border dioceses. No one knows exactly how many churches
and shelters in the region have pastoral programs for migrants, since for obvious reasons their activities are not publicized and so much of the assistance they provide goes unrecorded.

I found, at the very least, forty dioceses stretching the length of the migration journey, from the dioceses of San Marcos, Guatemala, to Tijuana, Mexico, house churches with migrant programs or shelters that serve departing
and journeying migrants. Some dioceses are more involved than others in
providing this support, reflecting both the disproportionate impact of migration in particular dioceses (e.g., dioceses along the Mexico-Guatemala and
Mexico-U.S. borders), the viewpoint of the bishop and support provided by
the country's Episcopal Conference of Bishops.[28] The Diocese of San Marcos,
Guatemala, for example, which is situated along the border with Mexico,
has been affected heavily by emigration, return migration, and transit migration. The bishop of the diocese, the Most Reverend Alvaro Ramazzini, has
been very active in migration and social justice matters and works closely with

the Guatemalan Episcopal Conference, as well as with Mexican and U.S. bishops on the migration question. The diocese has established Human Mobility, a comprehensive program to address the migration issue. Working closely with local municipalities and twenty-nine parishes within the San Marcos diocese, Human Mobility provides training and information workshops for displaced migrant groups (regional labor migrants, as well as transit migrants heading north); disseminates information about migration patterns and dangers through radio programs; organizes activities during the Week of the Migrants each September; documents cases of abuse of migrants; and facilitates institutional coordination among the participating parishes in the diocese.[29]

Although there is a great deal of variation in the level of migrant program support in the region, most dioceses recognize the transit migrants' growing reliance on the church and the need for integrating programs into the dioceses' pastoral activities and coordinating efforts with other parishes in Mexico, the United States, and Central America. To this end, since as early as 2000 the Mexican Episcopal Conference of Bishops has organized an annual workshop on the pastoral care of migrants. During its 2003 meeting, representatives from at thirty-four Mexican and several U.S. dioceses that straddle the northern border of Mexico met to assess the needs and coordinate resolutions to regional migration problems. Many of the bishops refer to themselves as having dioceses without borders and are striving for a borderless church. As the 2003 workshop took place shortly after the publication of "Strangers No Longer," bishops from both sides of the border attended the workshop to promote their position and present it to Mexican President Vicente Fox. Michael Blume, SVD, under secretary of the Pontifical Council for the Pastoral Care of Migrants and Itinerant People, attended the workshop to observe and support what he called "a unique joint endeavor between U.S. and Mexican bishops conferences" that he hoped would spread to other conferences throughout Latin America.[30]

One of the long-term goals of the annual workshop is to coordinate activities and develop among local diocesan churches a network of shelters and assistance along the migrant journey. Participants at the 2003 workshop conducted a self-diagnostic survey to assess how well they were meeting these goals. Workshop attendees included both priests and lay workers who direct or work in parish-level migrant programs and shelters, thus the responses and findings of the survey are probably influenced by the individual provider's experiences and theological and/or social orientation. Nonetheless, the religious workers' responses offer an institutional provider perspective on several dimensions of the migration phenomenon.

Some of the more interesting data focused on different networks through which the migrants learn about the transit shelters, who accompanies them to the shelters, and what the migrants' most pressing needs were on arrival, all aspects of the migration journey about which we know very little. Fifty nine of the faith workers who attended the meeting responded to these survey questions. When asked, "Why do the migrants choose your diocese as a step on their way to their destination?" 43 percent of the faith workers directing diocese transit and destination programs responded that migrants learned of the shelter through various paths of communication among their personal or traveling networks (e.g., fellow travelers, relatives who had made the trip before); 28 percent reported that migrants approached without specific knowledge of the shelter but rather because of its geographical location that crossed their migratory route (e.g., near a border crossing point); and 12 percent reported that migrants selected the route because of the location of a shelter.[31] When asked, "Do the migrants generally arrive individually, in groups (including family members), and/or escorted by coyotes?" 56 percent responded "groups" (usually three to four persons); 31 percent reported "individually"; and 18 percent reported coyotes and either groups or individuals.[32] These findings point to the increasingly important role that religious groups and organizations assume in the social infrastructure of the journey for individuals and groups of migrants and even coyotes who place their cargo in the care of these religious groups.

Not surprisingly, the large majority of religious leaders who participated in the self-diagnostic survey also reported that migrant needs exceeded available services and resources. In other words, there are institutional limits to migrant care. Some parishes have so few resources that their programs include simply farming out traveling migrants to congregant families who provide temporary shelter. Others have erected shelters with the assistance of the Scalabrinian Missionaries, a transnational congregation that serves migrants. And while most of the shelters provide for basic material and spiritual needs, including the provision of food, a place to rest for a few days, and access to religious services and counseling before continuing on the journey, many lacked the resources to provide for the medical, legal, and social service needs of traveling migrants.

The resources available clearly are influenced by the level of support that the various shelters receive; most of the programs and shelters in Mexico are associated with and supported by Catholic dioceses in Mexico, some of which are wealthier than others. Some churches with migrant programs have developed ties with U.S. churches whose congregations provide the funding for programs. Others work closely with their diocese counterparts on opposite sides of the border. In 2002, the bishops of Hermosillo, Mexico and Tucson and Phoenix, Arizona formed Dioceses Without Borders, a cross-border partnership to work on migration issues. Supported by Catholic Relief Services' global partnership initiative, Dioceses Without Borders seeks to develop a spiritual community without borders. To this end, Bishop Gerald Kincanas of Tucson regularly makes trips to northern Mexico to support migrant ministry work and to draw attention to the suffering of those that must migrate across the area's deadly desert. The partnership regularly organizes cross border youth retreats to reflect on migration themes.

Still other programs in the region are funded by international congregations that support mission work in Mexico and Central America, such as the Maryknolls, Jesuits, and St. Charles or Scalabrinian Missionaries. In 2007, for example, Jesuits began discussions with the archdiocese of Hermosillo to coordinate and establish a shelter in the Mexican city of Nogales, Sonora, for women and children deported to Mexico from the United States.[33] On occasion, these congregation-based programs receive additional financial support from churches in other countries, especially from the United States and Europe.

The Scalabrini Regional Sanctuary Network

The most well-established and far-reaching program for migrants in the region, Red Casas del Migrante (Network of Migrant Houses), is designed and directed by the Missionaries of Saint Charles, also known as the Congregation of the Scalabrinian Missionaries and the Congregation of St. Charles. Since its founding in 1887 by the Bishop Giovanni Battista Scalabrini of Piacenza, Italy—apostle to the migrants, as he is often called by his followers—this Roman Catholic order of priests and sisters remains the sole transnational religious congregation with the mission of providing pastoral care to migrants and refugees. Its pastoral territory includes missions in twenty-four countries in Asia, Australia, Africa, Europe and the Americas.[34]

The Scalabrini congregation was originally founded to minister to the needs of Italian immigrants in North and South America, and established churches, hospitals, and other institutions to assist in the settlement of Italian migrants. But by the 1930s, according to Peter D'Agostino, a scholar on the Italian Emigrant Church, the congregation had undergone a process of internationalization. By World War II, Scalabrinians were serving Italian migrant workers in Germany and France. During the post–World War II period the congregation expanded its presence to Australia, Venezuela, and Canada, and began to minister also to migrants who were not Italian. With the August 1, 1952, publication of the apostolic constitution Exsul Familia (On the Spiritual Care for Migrants), the Scalabrini presence was expanded to Latino Catholics in the Americas. In the Exsul Familia, the first modern Vatican document to acknowledge the right to migrate, Pope Pius XII authorized the Pontifical College to begin selecting priests to form Scalabrini congregations in Latin America. In 1966, the congregation's mission was formally expanded beyond providing for Italian nationals and was redefined as one providing for all refugees, migrants, and seamen around the globe.[35]

It was in this second mission that the Scalabrinians began to increasingly oversee the migration process. In this expanded role, the missionaries were called on to work with local dioceses to develop pastoral plans for migrants, counsel the departing migrants, and, if necessary, direct them toward safe passage and monitor those officials who regulate the process to assure that they did not violate the law or exploit migrants.[36] It is this pastoral challenge—the care of the journeying migrants—that largely constitutes the border ministry work of the Scalabrinians in Mexico and Central America in the twenty-first century.

The Scalabrinian presence in the region flourished in the 1980s, under the direction of Father Corbellini, who in 1980 founded a seminary in the outskirts of Guadalajara, Mexico, to train priests and missionaries for ministry work and to encourage the Mexican church to advance a more consistent policy toward internal and international migrants. Shortly after the seminarians began publishing a magazine, *Migrante,* which chronicles their services, documents migration trends and human rights abuses, and publishes migration stories that illustrate the moral and social theological bases for their work. The weekly also includes messages that emphasize the need to provide for the religious, humanitarian, and legal needs of journeying migrants. Indeed, in a 1988 publication, a message urged each Mexican diocese to establish a Day of the Emigrants.[37]

The Scalabrinians were also instrumental in developing the pocket-size devotional that accompanies many Mexican and Central American migrants. First published in 1989 by the diocese of Zamora, Mexico, and Guatemala with the help of a Scalabrini priest, the devotional has since been published by interior and border dioceses throughout Mexico and Guatemala with the assistance of the Scalabrini congregation.[38] The number of prayers and versions of the devotional have expanded over the years, reflecting the concerns and customs of the parishes and dioceses that publish it. In September 2003 the Mexican Episcopal Conference published its own version, titled *Adoración al Santísimo por la Intención de los Migrantes,* which includes in its introduction mention of the joint pastoral letters drafted by the U.S. and Mexico Bishops Conferences.

Beginning in 1987 the Scalabrinians, with the cooperation of local parishes and dioceses, begun to build their regional network of migrant shelters called Casas del Migrante (Migrant Homes or safe houses) that are situated adjacent to the most dangerous crossing corridors along the Guatemala-Mexico and Mexico-U.S. borders. The casas provide pastoral and humanitarian care for journeying migrants, as well as resettlement and reintegration programs for the returned migrant who has been deported. The casas primarily provide for male migrants, but in recognizing the growing numbers of female migrants, several have added rooms for traveling women and children, and in 1994 an independent shelter for women was erected in Tijuana.

The casas are funded by the Scalabrinian congregation; the Mexican, U.S., and Guatemalan Episcopal conferences; NGO, dioceses and local parishes with whom they partner; and by individuals. Sometimes the shelters are erected and run solely by the Scalabrinian missionaries; in general, however, the Scalabrinian brothers erect or reorganize shelters according to their mission guidelines at the request of local dioceses and then hand them over to trained local clergy to run, as is the case with the Casas del Migrante in the Mexican northern department of Hermosillo. Their Scalabrinian mission, then, is to encourage dioceses, parishes, churches (of all denominations), and congregants along the migrant trail to maintain humanitarian, public, and moral involvement in migration matters. As Brother Francisco explained, "Not only do we welcome migrants but we must teach members of local churches to welcome migrants as well." Their legacy in the region will be a network of safe houses and institutionalized migrant programs in diocesan churches along the migrant trail.

The mediating role of the casas in the migration journey is multifaceted and fundamental to survival. The transit shelters provide humanitarian, educational, psychological, and spiritual support to literally hundreds of transit migrants each day, as well as temporary relief for those deported across the border to either Mexico or Guatemala. They provide individual and group migration counseling, and companionship and networking resources to departing migrants. In addition to providing food, temporary shelter, and clothing to journeying migrants who, in most cases, are allowed to stay at the shelter for no more than three days, the people who run the shelters also hold instructional classes that prepare migrants for the dangers they may confront on the journey. For example, some casas, like those in Tapachula and Altar, Mexico, offer courses on legal rights, health and infectious diseases, and AIDS. Others, such as the Casa del Migrante in Altar, through their Community Center for Migrants Services, offer classes on dangerous routes to avoid on the journey and instructions on migrants' human and legal rights as undocumented travelers.

Most casas are located alongside parish churches where the Scalabrinian priests provide daily or weekly masses. If requested, services, religious counsel, and final blessings are provided to departing migrants. From these parish pulpits the Scalabrinians also inform parishioners about the migration phenomenon and present to them the human face of the migrants. As one brother has pointed out, the missionaries try to challenge people to see the face of Jesus in the migrant. In their multiple roles of priest, provider, and advocate, they sometimes encourage their congregants to become more publicly involved in migration matters and more sensitive to the needs of the journeying migrants. Often their public positions are symbolically displayed in posters, artifacts, and words that commemorate themes of the stranger and the migrant from the Bible, along with others that illustrate the sufferings and dangers along the migrant trail. Hanging on the walls of most Casas del Migrante are posters warning migrants of the pending dangers, alongside others that include such statements as "Jesus was a Migrant," or "There is no such identity as nationality, only Christianity."

Located next to a casa in the small Mexican border town of Agua Prieta in the northernmost diocese of Hermosillo is a modest Catholic church in which the director of the Agua Prieta Casa, Father Cayetano Cabrera, is also vicar. Hanging adjacent to the altar is a large green banner with the following words embroidered in Spanish: "If the migrant is not your brother then God is not your father." In Altar, Mexico, a launching ground for migrants crossing the Sonoran Desert into southern Arizona, Father René Castaneda, who under the direction of the Mexican Diocese of Hermosillo took over the Casa del Migrante from the Scalabrinian missionaries, exhorts his congregants from his pulpit in the town's Church of Our Lady of Guadalupe. Father René has integrated migrant counseling and a migrant ministry into his church. His parishioners paid in large part for the Casa del Migrante. "I drew them a picture of the casa and asked for help." Father Castaneda integrates into each mass a "prayer for our migrant brothers and sisters," a part of worship that is increasingly common in border churches that have both supportive bishops and Scalabrinian training. Composed by the archbishop of the Hermosillo diocese, the prayer calls both for safe passage north and the eventual return home for the migrant. In this instance Scalabrinian work finds a public face in public prayer and worship.

Collectively, the network of Scalabrinian shelters and the dioceses in which they are located provide true sanctuary for the journeying migrant. Because they are run by religious congregations and sanctioned by the parish and diocese in which they are located, the shelters operate as safe houses within the boundaries of the church and outside the reach of the state. Consequently, the migrants they attend to are protected from apprehension and deportation, if only on a temporary basis. Interestingly and ironically, both the Mexican and Guatemalan governments depend on the casas for humanitarian and material assistance; it is to them that they regularly bring apprehended or deported migrants. Indeed, soon-to-be-deported migrants are often shown videos that direct them to particular casas, and Grupo Beta forces rely heavily on the assistance of migrant shelters.

The first two Casas del Migrante were founded in the late 1980s in Tijuana and Ciudad Juárez, then the major crossing locations for Mexican migrants. As enforcement activities cracked down on established crossing corridors and migrants were redirected to other crossing areas along the border, the Scalabrinian missionaries followed the migrant trail and erected shelters alongside new and often more dangerous crossing locations, including the southern Mexican border town of Tapachula, and the northern crossing towns of Agua Prieta, Altar, and Nuevo Laredo (the casas in Altar and Agua Prieta have since been handed over to and are now run by Mexican dioceses). Casas are also located in Guatemala City and Tecún Umán, which straddles the Mexico-Guatemala border.

In response to the increasing number of women comprising current migration streams, the Scalabrinian sisters erected the first independent shelter for women in the region in Tijuana in 1994. Centro Madre Assunta was built on land purchased by the Scalabrinians, constructed with funding from the Mexican government and bishops conference, and furnished with donations from a church in Germany. It serves about a thousand women a year, some of whom are deportees, others internally displaced, and still others international migrants headed for the United States. The women's casa is run somewhat differently from the shelter for men, which is located down the road; Sister Gemma, a Scalabrinian sister who runs the Centro Madre Assunta, does not impose a strict time limit on her guests. They stay in the shelter while they look for work and earn enough money to continue on their travels or establish their own homes.

Each Casa del Migrante provides services that reflect its geographical location, the different needs of the migrant population it serves, and the level of commitment and support from the diocese in which it operates. The Casa del Migrante in Guatemala City is a small home located in a poor, hard-to-find barrio on the outskirts of the city. It is a modest enterprise that can accommodate about a dozen men at a time.[39] Father Eduardo Quintero, who has been assistant director of the shelter since its founding in 1999, added on a room to house women and their children, but he is forced to keep the room locked at night to protect the women from the men. The casa was originally erected to provide for the internally displaced and international transit migrants, but now largely serves transit Hondurans, although it has provided for transit migrants from other Latin American countries, China, and Africa. Some of the Hondurans Father Eduardo sees are on their way north, but most of those whom he provides for are the unsuccessful: the deported who stop at his casa to rest before returning home or trying again. Father Eduardo has developed a close relationship with the local diocese and area residents, and on occasion he administers mass in the parish church and regularly directs his sermons to the migration phenomenon. He also organizes migration workshops and outreach programs for area youth on a regular basis.

Because migrant traffic is much heavier along or near international borders, casas located in these areas play a more extensive institutional role in the migration journey than do those located in the interior. The Casa del Migrante in Tijuana provides assistance to close to a hundred migrants a day. When the Tijuana casa was erected in the mid-1980s, it provided material, educational, and spiritual services for transit migrants preparing to cross the border. Now about 60 percent of those served are persons deported from the United States. Built into the wall at the entrance of the casa is a tiled figure of Our Lady of Guadalupe. According to Father Luis, the shelter's director, migrants customarily "drop to their knees and pray to the patroness for protection before leaving."

The Casa del Migrante in Tecún Umán is one of two casas with an office for the Human Mobility program mentioned above (the other is in Ciudad Juárez, Mexico). In addition to working with police officers and other officials to assure that migrants who have been arrested receive due process, the office also functions as a clearinghouse for national, regional, and international NGOs and governmental organizations that increasingly depend on it for information. Casa staff are frequent guests and participants in national and regional human rights organizations concerned with the welfare of the transit migrants, including the Mesa Nacional para las Migraciones en Guatemala (MENAMIG, National Roundtable for Migrants in Guatemala), a collaborative national forum for NGOs, government officials, community representatives, and social service providers; the Grupo Regional para la Defensa de los Derechos Humanos de los Migrantes (GREDEMIG, Regional Group for the Defense of Human Rights of Migrants); and the Oficina de Derechos Humanos del Arzobispado de Guatemala (ODHAG, Human Rights Office of the Archdiocese of Guatemala). In recent years, the Tecún Umán Office of Human Mobility has also cooperated with the Comisión Nacional de Derechos Humanos in Mexico (National Commission for Human Rights in Mexico) in assisting with the documentation of migrant deaths and efforts to locate missing family members.[40]

The Casa del Migrante commonly known as Albergue Belén is in Tapachula, Mexico, a border town located some twenty kilometers from the Rio Suchiate, the natural boundary dividing Guatemala and Mexico. It was opened in 1997, and is directed by Father Flor María Rigoni, a Scalabrinian missionary who has directed missions along several borders throughout Latin America, including the Tijuana-California border where, both as a political protest and to provide comfort to the migrants, he raised make-shift altars along the border highway where he provided daily communion and blessings to migrants before they darted across the road to the U.S. side. Affectionately called the prophet by his fellow missionaries because of his long unruly beard and simple white frock held together by rope and cross, Father Flor prefers to think of himself as a "Samaritan of the Street."

The Casa del Migrante in Tapachula is a welcome resting point for those who traverse the Suchiate River and walk the distance to Tapachula and it attends to the material, psychological, and social needs of the migrants. Here, as many as five hundred migrants a day are provided with temporary shelter and food before they embark on the long journey through Mexico, are offered attend classes about such health risks as exposure to HIV, and receive information about dangerous crossings and gangs that prey on migrants. The casa also has a Western Union pickup service where, for thirty pesos, migrants can receive money wired from a U.S. relative, though the amount is capped at $100 to reduce the risk of robbery once a migrant leaves the shelter. This casa, like others along the migrant trail, offers an indirect networking resource as migrants at these shelters connect with one another and exchange ideas and information about the crossing experience. These migrant networks, forged in the shelters, buffer the migrants against disruption and isolation of the journey. First-time emigrants gain access to a host of resources, ranging from simple companionship to vital financial help from their more seasoned fellow travelers.

To welcome the migrants and provide for their spiritual needs, Father Flor built from palms a simple thatched-roof chapel he named the Chapel of Emmaus, after the town where Jesus, having risen from the dead, was welcomed as an unknown stranger by his disciples (Luke 24:13–25). Father Flor cites this reference as a challenge to see the face of Jesus in the migrants. "The migrants are the wandering God," he said. In this humble chapel, Father Flor holds services for both Catholic and Protestant migrants and blesses them before they continue on their journey, provides counseling to them, and furnishes devotionals. These institutional religious practices, which are performed by many casas, sanction the journey and provide spiritual and psychological strength to the journeying migrant.

Like many religious groups who work with the poor in Latin America, Scalabrinian missionaries embrace communitarian social theologies that emphasize the quest for social justice, especially liberation theology that focuses on engaging the world for the sake of transforming it from various forms of oppression. Drawing often on the words of Gustavo Gutiérrez, the father of liberation theology, they believe that they "must be the voice of the voiceless."[41] For the Scalabrinian missionaries working the front lines in Mexico and Central America, being the voice of the voiceless involves speaking out for the hundreds of thousands of undocumented migrants who are most at risk and most vulnerable to exploitation.[42] Consequently, many of the Scalabrini missionaries are more public than other Catholic orders and congregations in migration matters, and often different casas and their directors will come together to protest state migration polices. Their activist orientation and identity result largely from Scalabrini teachings, which emphasize the transformation and liberalization of migrants.[43]

For example, each Christmas Father Flor and Father Eduardo join forces to express the theme of the stranger and guest and protest the social injustice of Mexican border enforcement policies. On one of the days leading up to Christmas, usually Christmas Eve, each missionary travels with several hundred followers (most of whom are migrants staying at the shelters) to the Mexico-Guatemala border to celebrate the Mexican and Catholic posada ritual, a procession that reenacts Joseph and Mary's long and tiring search for shelter in Bethlehem. After traveling from house to house seeking shelter and eventually receiving it, the two groups, each of which is led by a Scalabrinian missionary and sometimes the bishops of the border departments of Tapachula, Mexico, and San Marcos, Guatemala, meet halfway across the bridge in a symbolic demonstration of unity across borders and welcoming of the stranger. Called the Posada of the Migrant, it is one of many posadas organized by transnational religious orders and interfaith groups that have emerged along Mexico's borders in the past decade to illustrate Christian practices of succor and to protest border enforcement policies in the region.[44]

The Scalabrinian missionaries have no fixed pastoral model. As one Scalabrinian brother told me, "We are part of a pilgrim church and we respond to the local pastoral needs of the populations we accompany." In this sense, the Scalabrinian missionaries, who work closely with the church hierarchy, remain an important vehicle for disseminating church migration policies and implementing migrant programs. Because they practice a theology of migration that goes beyond welcoming the stranger on the road to encompass transforming and liberating migrants, the missionaries are also the public voice of the Catholic Church and its social justice work in the region.

Social Justice and Protest Activities and Sanctuary along the U.S.-Mexico Border

The Catholic Church and the Scalabrinian missionaries do not stand alone in their opposition to the U.S. border enforcement campaign that has rechanneled migrant flows from population centers to remote, waterless regions such as the Sonoran Desert (since 2000 the busiest crossing area along the border). Rising deaths in the desert near the Tucson area of the U.S.-Mexico border have galvanized a series of overlapping interfaith groups into greater action on two fronts: services and sanctuary for migrants, and social protest on their behalf. The goals and membership lists of these faith-based organizations have grown in range and size over the years, and some of the founders of these organizations can trace their roots to the U.S. Sanctuary Movement that was founded and flourished in the Tucson area in the 1980s.[45]

Initially organized to provide humanitarian aid to crossing migrants, these present-day interfaith and civil efforts have swelled in number, culminating in recent years in a collective, cross-border social movement with the goals of providing humanitarian assistance to crossing migrants, educating the public about the human costs of U.S. border enforcement campaigns, and ultimately calling for reform in U.S. immigration policy.[46] Their Jewish, Catholic, Quaker, and mainline Protestant members share common meanings of protest. They embrace communitarian social theologies that stress the quest for social justice and civic and political action and share a long and strong history of activism in the United States, ranging from public issues such as homelessness to social welfare to environmental efforts.[47] Some of the present-day faith leaders are new to the immigration scene, while others have remained active in issues of poverty, migration, and social justice since the days of U.S. Sanctuary Movement. None of these groups or their faith-based initiatives represent the Christian right in America, who gained political power and social strength under President George W. Bush but to date have not embraced the immigration issue, avoiding both the restrictionist and inclusive sides of the debate.[48]

The first group to challenge current U.S. border enforcement policy was a peace church that established its presence along the border in 1987 when the Quaker organization, the American Friends Service Committee, founded the Immigration Law Enforcement Monitoring Project (ILEMP). The program was implemented soon after the Immigration Reform and Control Act of 1986 (IRCA) increased enforcement activities along the southwest border. It was charged with monitoring the civil and human rights consequences of U.S. border enforcement policy from 1987 through 2003, when the program was closed. With funding from the Friends, the first systematic study of death at the border was conducted and the problem introduced to the larger American public.[49] The presence of Quakers along the border is consistent with their position that all people are equal and entitled to dignity and respect regardless of nationality or legal status. Implicit in this position is the idea of a global community in which persons are free to choose where they live and work.[50]

In 1999, as the California-based Operation Gatekeeper Campaign continued to push migration flows to the Arizona border, Quaker faith communities joined forces with Catholic and Presbyterian groups in the area to form Healing Our Borders, an international faith-based NGO located in Douglas, Arizona, a small border town separated from its sister city, Agua Prieta in Sonora, Mexico, by a wall erected by the U.S. government. The group, which draws members from both sides of the border, was initially formed to provide humanitarian assistance to journeying migrants and advocate on their behalf. In this capacity, members distribute blankets and provisions to apprehended migrants and since 2000 have been holding a weekly prayer vigil commemorating the dead. During the vigil the group makes crosses for each migrant who has died in Conchise County and places them against the curb along the vigil route. Like many interfaith groups who have witnessed a rise in human rights tragedies resulting from escalating enforcement activities along the border, Healing Our Borders grew to involve advocacy and social protest.[51] As Father Bob Carney, one of the founding members of the interfaith coalition, explained, "The gospel demands that we act. The role of religion in contemporary migration is the role of the prophet and the prophet doesn't predict the future but states what is. We must respond to what we are witnessing along the border. If not, one day our Savior will ask why we didn't do anything in the face of death."[52]

Further west along the border, in San Diego, California, the Interfaith Coalition for Immigrants Rights (ICIR), which draws its membership from religious and NGO participants on both sides of the border, holds similar vigils to protest Operation Gatekeeper. In these efforts, Scalabrinian missionaries regularly travel to the U.S-Mexico border to protest enforcement operations because of the lives they claim. In Ciudad Juárez and Tijuana, the Scalabrinian missionaries have been especially active in promoting peaceful social justice protests. In these cities they have joined forces with sister churches and religious workers on the U.S. side and organized cross-border posadas during Christmas week; services, educational activities, and seminars during the Day of the Migrants in September; and numerous border vigils on the Day of the Dead. Each November 1, the Day of the Dead, a religious service is organized and crosses are placed along the border wall listing the names, ages, and origins of the thousands of migrants who have died in their crossing attempts. Reenacting ancestral traditions and rituals, local residents, many of whom are Latino, also erect traditional Day of the Dead altars adorned with fruit, masks, candles, and *pan de muerto* (bread for the dead) in memory of dead migrants.[53] Since 2001, the parishes of St. Anthony and St. Joseph in Holtville, California, along with California Rural Legal Aid and the Scalabrinian missionaries from Tijuana, have come together each year on November 1 at the Terrace Park Cemetery to remember the several hundred unidentified migrants who lie in what was once called a potter's field, with numbered bricks to mark the graves. The missionaries lead a procession from the local church to a barren lot located behind the main cemetery and then bless the graves, simply marked with John Doe or Jane Doe.[54]

Many of the cross-border ecumenical events are both commemorative and performative in that they are rituals to mourn the dead but also to bring public attention to the larger social and political circumstances under which poor migrants die in their search for a better life.[55] These commemorations sometimes lead to the construction of spontaneous shrines that are then witnessed and visited by the larger public, such as the unmarked crosses along the walls that separate the U.S.-Mexico border, or the simple roadside shrines protesting militarization of the border along well traveled-roads in southern Arizona, or the Shrine of El Tiradito in Tucson, Arizona, where each Wednesday evening at seven o'clock residents can come together to pray and commemorate the dead.

Some of these humanitarian and social justice protests have garnered more public attention than others. In 2000, a year following a record number of migrant deaths in the Tucson area, Reverend Robin Hoover of Tucson's First Christian Church founded Humane Borders, Inc., a binational interfaith organization established to "create a just and more humane border environment."[56] To this end Humane Border volunteers began placing water tanks with thirty-foot flagpole markers along migrant paths across the southern Arizona desert. By 2006 they had erected eighty-five flagpoles and tanks and were dispensing in private, public, and federal lands more than five hundred gallons of water a week. They had also developed working relationships with the Mexican government to distribute maps directing migrants to water stations. By 2006, it had become part of an expansive network of transnational advocacy organizations that have mushroomed along the border and throughout the region.

Humane Borders' members are a diverse coalition of seventy Protestant and Catholic churches from Mexico and the United States and a number of secular NGOs, including human rights organizations and legal advocacy groups. Although the Humane Brothers was initially founded to provide temporary humanitarian relief to journeying migrants, its mission statement has expanded to call for a more equitable immigration policy that would provide legalization and temporary work opportunities for migrants living and working in the United States. To support this goal, members have assumed a mediating role between migrants and government actors, including local and state politicians working in the area of immigration reform. Humane Borders' activities stay well within the limits of the law, a stricture Rev. Hoover believes is crucial if the interfaith organization is to continue its border ministry work. As he said on more than one occasion, "Humane Borders is in the humanitarian business, not the sanctuary business."[57] Motivated by faith, Rev. Hoover regularly draws on biblical interpretation to link faith and activism and rally support of his congregation. During one Sunday sermon we attended, he compared Humane Borders to biblical figures who "crossed the line in faith," including Abraham, the father of faith, who, Rev. Hoover explained to his congregation, "was a border jumper, an alien, an illegal, an undocumented person, a migrant." Abraham was "the other."[58] It is appropriate then that Hoover should draw on Isaiah when inviting persons to volunteer at Humane Borders. "They will neither hunger nor thirst, nor will the desert heat or the sun beat upon them. He who has compassion on them will guide them and lead them beside springs of water" (Isaiah 49:10).[59]

Although the humanitarian and protest activities of the various interfaith groups along the Arizona-Mexico border received considerable national and international media attention, their efforts did not lead to any changes in border policy and the human consequences, in the form of increasing migrant fatalities, continued to escalate in the summer months as the scorching desert heat claimed lives. In escalated protest in 2003, an expanded group of interfaith groups from both sides of the border joined Reverend John Fife of the Southside Presbyterian church in Tucson (one of the founders of the Sanctuary Movement) and took things a step further by creating the Samaritans, a coalition of Quakers, Jews, Disciples of Christ, Methodists, Catholics, and Presbyterians that made regular trips to the desert in all-terrain vehicles equipped with water, food, a medical team, and first-aid supplies.[60] According to Rev. Fife, the group was founded on the principle that it is the "right and responsibility" of civil organizations to aid victims of human rights violations. When migrants in distress are found, the Samaritans either call on the U.S. Border Patrol for helicopter assistance or transport them to a local hospital.[61]

In the spring of 2004, with no hint of a slowdown in migrant deaths in the area, religious-based protest activities began to challenge the law openly. A broader effort developed to work for justice along the border and provide sustained humanitarian relief for journeying migrants, twenty-four hours a day, seven days a week. Titled No More Deaths, its membership includes an expanded binational coalition of individuals, faith communities, religious leaders, and human rights grassroots organizers. Its members refer to No More Deaths as a "movement" and not as an organization. They engage in direct and indirect action to challenge and reform U.S. immigration policy, limit crossing deaths, and raise public awareness. Its members share common

principles regarding pathways to immigration reform.[62] Central in the movement is the biblically inspired Ark of the Covenant effort that involves placing moveable camps in the desert. The camps are named for a wooden Ark
of the Covenant box in the Old Testament that symbolized the presence of
God guiding the people of Israel when they were wandering in the desert.
As Rev. Fife explains, "We took sanctuary of the church to the desert." In the
summer months, volunteers work the desert camps twenty-four hours a
day. The volunteers, many of whom are recruited from churches, colleges,
and universities throughout the United States, number several hundred each
summer. Volunteer training materials begin with a single sentence from the
Torah: "Know the heart of the stranger, for you too were strangers," which
echoes the biblical passage, "Do not oppress an alien; you yourselves know
how it feels to be aliens, because you were aliens in Egypt" (Exodus 23:9,
NIV).[63] The desert camps provide water, food, and medical assistance.

If a serious medical problem arises, volunteers are instructed to "evacu-
ate" (transport) the distressed migrant to a hospital or to call the U.S. Border
Patrol's Search, Trauma and Rescue (BORSTAR) unit. In less severe cases of
dehydration, exhaustion, or minor injuries, volunteers arrange for migrants
to be transported to a Tucson church or clinic. Although the U.S. government has not yet developed a policy regarding humanitarian aid along the
border, No More Death faith workers stated that there was a verbal agreement and guidelines between the U.S. Border Patrol and No More Deaths.
In the month of June 2005 alone, volunteers rescued 175 migrants in distress in the Arizona desert. As Rev. Fife explained, "We have no choice now
but to take Sanctuary out of the church into the desert. State violation of
human rights has been resurrected at the border and we have no recourse
but to act out what Jim Corbett, the founder of Sanctuary, called 'civil initiative,' which refers to peaceful protest within the bounds of the law."[64]

In the summer of 2004, a confrontation between the church and the state
developed when the U.S. government challenged these desert sanctuary
practices. On July 9, 2005, two No More Deaths volunteers, Shanti Selz and
Daniel Strauss, were arrested by U.S. Border Patrol officers while transporting three extremely dehydrated migrants to a Tucson hospital. The two were
charged with transporting illegal migrants, a felony under the Immigration
and Nationality Act. The case gained national and international attention as
religious groups, humanitarian organizations, and thousands of supporters
spoke out against the arrest, under the banner "humanitarian aid is not illegal." In August 2006, supporters' cries of protest were heard when U.S. Dis-

trict Judge Raner Collins dismissed the charges, arguing that the volunteers "had made reasonable efforts to ensure that their actions were not in violation of the law, and that further prosecution would violate the defendants' due process right."[65] Although charges were dropped against the volunteers, the policy regarding humanitarian aid to crossers along the border remains unclear.

This growing opposition to the state and the subsequent activities of church-based groups and religious leaders are reminiscent of the regional Sanctuary Movement of the 1980s, when faith and activism were linked.[66] Migrant conditions and movement goals are different today than they were twenty years ago, however. As Rev. Fife stated:

> The context of migration changed in the 1990s and so has the migrant needs. The context today is not political, as it was in the 1980s, but economic and related to NAFTA, globalization, that is, issues of economic inequalities for migrants today are paramount, e.g., right to cross, work, receive medical treatment. We are trying interim efforts such as humanitarian assistance to migrants like that provided by Humane Borders. However, if militarization of the border continues and escalates and migrants continue to die, we may have no choice but to organize into a movement, one that might ultimately lead to sanctuary.[67]

For now many of the interfaith activities along the border remain peaceful as supporters work primarily within the boundaries of the law. Many of the cross-border ecumenical commemorations—including the Annual Migrant Walk, which since 2002 has taken participants on a weeklong trek across seventy-five miles of desert from Sasabe to the Arizona-Mexico border— express solidarity with the migrants and bring public attention to the human consequences of border enforcement policies.

Sanctuary and Locally Based Churches and Shelters

There are countless churches and shelters along the migratory route that care for journeying migrants but do not specifically have a migrant program, are not part of an interfaith organization or group, and are not part of a religious or congregational order. Consequently, their humanitarian role in providing for migrants goes unrecorded as do their church-level practices of sanctuary. The work of some ministers is sanctioned by church hierarchy, but in other cases these good Samaritans work alone and with meager resources. In small parishes throughout Veracruz, Mexico, priests offer their churches and their homes as temporary refuge to transit migrants from Central America. Motivated by faith and encouraged by their local bishop, Hipólito Reyes Larios, clergy, and residents throughout the state offer food and shelter to migrants who travel Mexico on the freight trains. It is in the small Veracruz towns, such as Fortín de las Flores, Cuichapa, Ecinar, and Presidio that residents rush to meet the trains to offer food to the destitute passengers.[68]

Churches in border crossing towns also regularly provide refuge to transit migrants. Recall the case of Ernesto, who found himself destitute in a small town south of the border city of Matamoros, Mexico. He turned to a Catholic Church and priest for assistance and received shelter for the evening in the home of the priest who prayed with him and gave him breakfast before Ernesto set out on the remainder of his journey. Mario, a young Honduran migrant who ran out of money in Matamoros, turned for help to an evangelical minister, who located temporary work for him. While staying with the pastor and his wife, Mario befriended other migrants, who were also staying there. It was here that Mario recruited companionship for the crossing into the United States.

On the other side of the border, in small towns throughout the southwest United States, dozens upon dozens of churches, temples, and monasteries silently provide sanctuary. In one such Texas town a Catholic Church sits perched on the banks of the Rio Grande, regularly providing refuge to migrants who sprint the short distance to the church from the river, often with the U.S. Border Patrol on their heels. Out of respect for the Catholic doctrine of church sanctuary, U.S. Border Patrol agents do not enter churches to pursue crossing migrants. Although his actions are not sanctioned by the diocese, the priest explains that his "mission is to God, not the diocese." Consequently, without hesitation, and motivated by faith, he regularly provides food, water, and blessings to journeying migrants.

Catholic churches are not the only places of worship that provide unofficial refuge to migrants. In Agua Prieta in northern Mexico, a Presbyterian church with no migrant ministry regularly takes in destitute migrants. On several occasions, members of the church have extended their homes as temporary places of refuge. The Agua Prieta church receives some assistance from Presbyterian churches in the United States that unofficially embrace the concept of sanctuary. Similarly, more than a thousand miles away in Matamoros, Mexico, an evangelical minister regularly houses traveling migrants in the modest home he shares with his wife and children. To cover the costs, he receives donations from a sponsoring church elsewhere in Texas. Across the border in Arizona, sanctuary is practiced at the church level by individual Catholic and Protestant churches alike that are active in family reunification for their members.

Many shelters are organized and run by individuals motivated by faith but loosely affiliated with a congregation. The Casa de Mujer in the Guatemalan border town of Tecún Umán, which was established in 1995 and run by a Spanish religious order, provides temporary refuge for female migrants in transit, many of whom have labored as sex workers to earn the funds to complete their journey north. Across the Suchiate River in the Mexican border town of Tapachula, Olga Sánchez Martínez, a charismatic Catholic and cancer survivor, runs a shelter for migrants who have been injured while riding the trains. Albergue El Buen Pastor del Pobre y el Migrante (Jesus the Good Shepherd for the Poor and Migrant), established in the late 1990s, provides temporary refuge for some twenty-five to thirty amputees on any given day. Martínez receives funding entirely from donations and local fund-raising events.

In the town of Tijuana, an evangelical pastor and his daughter run a Salvation Army Shelter for journeying migrants. Founded more than forty years ago to serve the internally displaced, the Albergue para Migrantes houses a dormitory to accommodate the growing number of international transit migrants and deportees who are brought to the shelter by Grupo Beta officials. On the day we visited in the summer of 2002, eighty migrants filled the shelter. Several dozen were on their knees and deep in prayer in the shelter's chapel. Like many migrant shelters along the border, the Albergue works closely with the Scalabrinian-run shelter in Tijuana. The two shelters exchange migrants, food, and information. Like other evangelical pastors with whom we spoke, Pastor Ramírez and his daughter do not encourage migration because of its disruptive elements for family stability. Nonetheless, motivated by faith, they have little recourse but to provide for the migrants' needs and bless them before they depart on their journey across the border.

Summary

At every level of church hierarchy, from transnational religious groups to binational bishops conferences to interfaith organizations, to local churches and shelters and individual pastors in Central America, Mexico, and along the U.S.-Mexico border, faith workers are increasingly involved in matters of international transit migration. From their perspective, they are putting their faith into action and practicing a theology of migration. The Catholic Church leads regional efforts in providing humanitarian support, spiritual sustenance, and social support to journeying migrants, in addition to advocating on their behalf. The church is able to provide effective and far-reaching service through multiple and overlapping transnational advocacy networks that national Catholic bishops conferences, regional diocesan conferences, and Scalabrinian missionaries have developed to promote regional cooperation among clergy, missionaries, and faithful followers. The public face of these organizations has grown substantially in recent years as they have developed their own migrant programs and human rights offices. As advocates for migrant rights, these religious workers and the hierarchies in which they operate have emerged as important vehicles for monitoring state institutions and policies. Their efforts have not gone unnoticed by the governments of Central America and Mexico, which are increasingly concerned about how to manage the consequences of large-scale transit migration to the United States, especially in the context of tighter borders. Increasingly, links are being forged among state agencies, state human rights organizations, NGOs, church dioceses, and a host of faith-based organizations over the migration issue.

Along the U.S-Mexico border, Protestant, Jewish, peace, and Catholic churches, NGOs, and individual advocates comprise cross-border interfaith coalitions that are instrumental in promoting social justice activities on behalf of the migrant and have acted in direct protest of U.S. military operations that place migrants in harm's way. As advocates who call for social justice and immigration reform, these religious groups and the Catholic and Protestant structures of hierarchy in which they operate have emerged as important vehicles for challenging U.S. border enforcement policy and encouraging social and political protest among followers. In fact, the issue of illegal immigration at the U.S.-Mexico border illustrates how regional and global problems such as transit migration may lead activists to work across state boundaries and form transnational social movements.

Collectively, these religious groups and interfaith coalitions also assume an important responsibility in the organization of unauthorized migration from Central America and Mexico to the United States through coordinated sanctuary opportunities and material and spiritual support for journeying migrants. Their growing institutional presence represents a countervailing force against the expansive smuggling industry and the vast military operations with which they share the migratory route. By providing counseling, religious services, blessings, and devotionals, these institutions support, foster, and ultimately sustain spirituality and religiosity over the course of migration, long after leave-taking from home communities. They provide companionship in grief and offer networking resources to departing migrants, which buffer the migrants against disruption and isolation, offering solidarity and protection on the road. They see the migrant on his or her way with practical, political, and spiritual help; they bind up his or her wounds at journey's end. But what of the middle passage and the resources with which pilgrims sustain themselves through isolation and danger to reach their promised land? The next chapter moves beyond the narratives of institutional informants to those of the migrants to explore the coping strategies—spiritual, psychological, cultural—that they develop during the journey north.

CHAPTER 4

Miracles in the Desert

They reach a point at which they have nothing of their own. They have been robbed, raped, abused, and exploited. Even their dignity has been stolen. The only reality that people cannot steal from them is their faith. For instance, a migrant said to me recently, "Thanks to God I am alive." That is not thanks to my capacity, nor to my intelligence, but thanks to God.

—Scalabrinian missionary

Javier Pérez left Guatemala City in 1999. He traveled most of the journey by public transport and in the company of fellow migrants whom he met on the road. He crossed the Guatemala-Mexico border without incident and went undetected through Mexico. In Agua Prieta, Javier and a group of other first-time crossers hired two coyotes to guide them across the Arizona-Mexico border. Their guides abandoned them a day into the journey. Stranded, lost, and disoriented in the desolate desert terrain of southern Arizona, the men wandered aimlessly before running out of supplies, including their last drop of water. They resigned themselves to death. Huddled in a group, they began to pray for their souls and for those of their families. In low whispering voices—parched from the sun and barely audible from dehydration—they recited familiar prayers and prepared for death. One among the group refused to give up and implored the younger among them to push a little farther in search of help. Javier and another volunteer mustered up what little energy they had remaining and set out.

Several hours later, the scouting duo saw what they first thought was a mirage but then recognized as a miracle: a landing strip, a four-wheel-drive truck, and several men. The strangers immediately came to their rescue and provided the dehydrated travelers with water. They carried the larger group to a highway and gas station where they were eventually picked up by U.S. Border Patrol agents. Javier and his fellow travelers were deported to Agua Prieta in the Mexican province of Sonora. Despite his unsuccessful crossing, Javier, a practicing Catholic, went to an area Presbyterian church to tell his story and to give thanks to God for listening to his prayers and granting the miracle of the men in the desert who had saved his life and the lives of his traveling companions.

In 1951, when chronicling the hardships of the cross-Atlantic journey of the millions of European immigrants who came to the United States in the late nineteenth and early twentieth centuries, Oscar Handlin wrote:

> The conditions of emigration and the hardships of the crossing were immediate sources of confusion. On the way, in the ships, the terrible disorder made troublesome any ritual observance. The prolonged lapse of unsettled time obscured the calendar; on the move, no day was individual from any other. Without the ministrations of a priest, without the sustenance of a whole community, the worshiper was limited to his own humble sources of prayer.[1]

This passage from *The Uprooted* could also describe the psychological experience and the everyday coping strategies of contemporary migrants from Latin America during their overland crossing to the United States. Migrants on the road are separated from their family and church, and far from the reach of organizations that offer help to them. In the isolated and remote stretches of the journey, many migrants rely on religion and spirituality in the form of unfamiliar churches; belief systems and culturally familiar religious activities and transformed practices; and humble prayer to help them make sense of and make bearable the traumas and hardships they encounter and sometimes overcome. While individual and group traumas that migrants from Latin America experience on the road may differ in detail, the study found that the narratives, interpretations, and explanations of their experiences are generally framed in a Christian and popular religious discourse. However, many of the everyday practices on which they rely cannot be fully explained by the different religious orientations or ideologies of the migrant. Often, these everyday coping activities reflect cultural practices and familiar memories unique to their home communities, memories and practices that are often appropriated in times of need and transformed and shaped by the social context of the journey. In this sense, religion is a dynamic process that cannot be separated from the journey or the actions of the traveling migrants.

The migration experience of Javier and others like him compels us to consider religion outside institutional settings and look at the many ways in which migrants practice their faith in their everyday lives to muster the psychological and physical strength to cope with their journey and derive meaning from their experiences. While the perspectives of religious leaders and faith workers help explain the ways in which institutions provide social and spiritual capital to sustain migrants, omitted from these narratives is the individual agency dimension—the rich diversity of cultural practices reproduced, borrowed, transformed, and even created or improvised by journeying migrants, and the way these practices form the context in which migrants express their faith on the road. In this sense, the rituals that migrants practice tell us much about identity and the struggles that shape individual and collective experiences and propel action. These also offer believers explanations and meanings during their period of crisis.[2]

In the pages that follow, I join the company of a number of scholars of religion who study what is termed "everyday religion" by some or "la religion vecue" (lived religion) by others, which puts emphasis on religion as practice, or what David Hall says is "the thinking and doing of lay men and women."[3] As Robert Orsi explains, this perspective constitutes a reorientation of religious scholarship away from static concepts of Catholicism and Protestantism, and from the academy's long-standing fixation on denominations and congregations, toward "a study of how particular people, in particular places and times, live with, through , and against the religious idioms available to them in culture."[4] In this chapter, I take the reader once again along the migrant trail, sometimes returning to shrines and clergy introduced in earlier chapters, but now telling the story of the spiritual and religious journey through the migrants' actions rather than those of institutional actors.

During their long treks across nations, over mountains and rivers, through towns and deserts, in the remote reaches of the migrant trail, nine out of ten migrants in the study practiced religion to help them cope with the journey north and, in some cases, to understand their own survival of near-death experiences. Some, including infrequent churchgoers, practiced what they knew from their tradition in their home communities and stopped at churches along the way to attend a religious service, say a prayer, light a candle, or seek spiritual assistance from clergy. Others strayed from their migratory route to visit a shrine to give thanks for making it as far as they had or to beseech further protection for the days ahead. In the absence of holy places sanctioned by the Catholic Church, some migrants visited shrines housing popular saints that had been erected by local residents. In the absence of these shrines, some migrants improvised and spontaneously erected shrines to revered icons from their home communities in order to reproduce those cultural practices with which they are most familiar and most comfortable and to recreate relations with their sacred icons. Still others called on the companionship and protection of revered local saints and icons in their home communities to whom they had prayed for protection before their journey; in transit they wore medals around their necks depicting these saints and carried holy cards in their pockets. Some, like Javier and his fellow travelers, coped with impending death through group prayer and then interpreted their rescue from death in terms of a miracle from God. These migration miracles provided meaning and hope. They manifested themselves in particular social contexts—during periods of crisis, such as times during the journey when migrants were spared death or capture.

In situations of crisis and loss of hope, migrants turned for succor to the familiar: Christianity, its traditional and more popular belief systems and rituals, and their most revered holy icons. Sometimes, these religious expressions are transformed depending on what resources the migrant trail offers. Unable to control the situations in which they found themselves and stripped of all social and material resources, these people were so desperate to communicate with God that at times they resorted to the most humble expressions of devotion, including drawing with simple stones on rock structures familiar religious images and etchings of pleas for comfort and salvation. The religious artifacts migrants leave along the trail, in desert camps and along frontier highways where they are picked up by coyotes or family, are further testimony to the importance of faith as both resource and identity in the migration process and the fundamental ways that values, belief systems, and everyday cultural practices organize the migration journey.

Churches, Shrines, and Sacred Places along the Way

Reaching out to clergy and revered holy images and saints for counsel and guidance in the preparation and departure stages of migration was a commonly reported practice. Many migrants continued to honor this tradition during the journey. Despite the obvious logistical and legal obstacles, one of every four undocumented migrants, Protestants and Catholics alike, visited a church or shrine or participated in an organized religious event, such as a procession, during the northward trek. Half of those who reported traveling at least some distance alone (individuals who were unable to pay for coyotes or receive help from personal networks) were especially likely to turn to the church and religious workers and clergy for material and spiritual sustenance. The religious orientation of the clergy and church was not a practical consideration when it came to migrants' requesting assistance; Protestants regularly reached out to Catholic clergy in large part because of the Catholic Church's policies of promoting outreach to journeying migrants and establishing migrant programs and centers of refuge along the migratory route.

The churches and shrines where migrants stop are situated primarily in towns and cities along international frontiers, places where provisions are available and where journeying migrants would be most likely to stay for a period of time to rest and gather needed resources such as a *coyote*, traveling companions, and supplies to continue on their northern trek. In the eastern Guatemalan town of Esquipulas, which is located only a few miles from the Honduras-Guatemala border, Honduran migrants regularly navigate the frontier and then blend in with the groups of pilgrims who travel the route to pray to El Cristo Negro at the Shrine of Nuestro Señor de Esquipulas. At the shrine, they receive provisions and blessings and purchase mementos of protection and companionship to carry with them on their journey.

Miguel, a young nonpracticing Catholic from the Honduran coastal city of San Pedro Sula, was one of the fifty or so journeying migrants who stopped by the Basilica in Esquipulas one day. Motivated by the possibility of regular work and adventure, Miguel left his hometown in the fall of 2001. Unable to afford a coyote, he decided to travel the two-thousand-mile distance to Houston by bus, train, and on foot. After leaving his hometown, he boarded a bus to the loosely guarded Guatemala-Honduras border and from there proceeded on foot for six miles before arriving in Esquipulas. At the basilica, he walked the *camarín* (the path that guides pilgrims around the altar) and paid his respects to the Cristo Negro. He then joined a group of migrants who were being shepherded by the attending vicar to the sanctuary for a group blessing. Afterward, Miguel made his way to a little store located next to the church to purchase religious items. Books about the history of Esquipulas line the store walls and the glass counter shelves are crammed with religious images of the venerated Black Christ and other well-known regional icons. Miguel made several purchases, including a glow-in-the-dark medallion of the Black Christ that he has never removed from his neck. As is the custom in many Latin American Catholic communities, the petitioner often promises to wear the holy item for a certain period after the saint or holy icon has answered a prayer.[5] Miguel vowed to wear the medallion until it fell from his neck. He firmly credits his safe arrival to the miraculous powers of El Cristo Negro and La Virgen de Guadalupe.

After crossing the Guatemala-Mexico border, the U.S.-bound migratory route takes Central American migrants to the southern Mexican town of Tapachula, where many rest and recoup for several days in one of the shelters that provide beds, food, and a change of clothing. Here, migrants may exchange coyotes, wait for additional funds to travel further, and seek spiritual nourishment. While in Tapachula, many Protestant and Catholic migrants visit one of three area Catholic churches—El Cristo de Emmaus, the main church in Tapachula, or La Iglesia de Guadalupe—to seek comfort and protection before embarking on their precarious trip through Mexico.

From Tapachula the route forks and the trail migrants follow will depend on the mode of crossing and the resources available. Some will join other migrants and head toward the Texas-Mexico border and either cross the Rio Grande or navigate the waters of the Gulf of Mexico. Others, the less fortunate, will brave the Mexico-Arizona desert crossing. Brianna, a Maya woman from a rural hamlet in the highland department of Totonicapan, Guatemala, crossed the Rio Grande under the guidance of a coyote. Shortly after what she thought was a successful crossing, she found herself stranded on the U.S. side, unable to proceed because of Immigration and Naturalization Service (INS) checkpoints. She turned to the spiritual anchor from her home community, a trusted evangelical pastor who had counseled her before departure. They prayed together over the phone. Similarly, Mauricio, stuck in a detention center in Laredo, Texas, called his pastor back home who prayed with him and then assured him that he would care for Mauricio's family. Later, the pastor led them in prayer as well. On rare occasions, such as a failed trip, pastors told me that they have offered financial support to the family. In both these cases, migrants relied on migration counseling from clerics from home to sustain them in their journey. The familiar spiritual and cultural space transcends national borders.

Independent migrant streams also head north from Mexico's central and western sending provinces toward the California and Arizona borders. By all accounts, one of the busiest but most deadly crossing corridors runs through the Sonoran Desert along the Arizona-Mexico border, where the desert claims hundreds of migrant lives each year. In 2007 it claimed the lives of more than 400 migrants. Most cross-border trips through the desert are launched

from the Sonora town of Altar, where the population of 16,000 faces temperatures near 120 degrees during the summer months. Altar is one of several
major ports of entry along with Agua Prieta, Nogales, and San Luis. All four
towns are included in the Mexican diocese of Hermosillo, which in recent
years has become very involved in promoting migration ministries, especially
in parishes that are situated along the border.

On any given day, hundreds of migrants flock into the dusty and sweltering town of Altar and spend several days preparing for what will be no doubt
the most dangerous segment of the journey; a sixty-three-mile taxi ride to
the border town of Sasabe, followed by a harrowing trek through the Altar
Valley, through the Buenos Aires National Wildlife Refuge, and, depending on
the route, perhaps through the Tohono O'Odham Indian reservation. The trek
takes several days and can encompass more than seventy miles, depending
on the final destination. Along the way, the lucky and fortunate may stum-
ble across a Humane Borders water station. According to Reverend Robin
Hoover, the founder and president of Humane Borders, sometimes the migrants will find antlers atop the water stations, a symbol used by the local
Yaqui Indians to signify "God bless you and your whole lineage." Some migrants are escorted by their coyotes on foot all the way to Tucson; others
walk part of the distance to one of the main Arizona highways where they
then are picked up by coyotes; still others walk a portion of the journey and
stay at safe houses until they are guided to Phoenix.

Like its southern border counterpart, Tapachula, Altar has developed in
recent years a booming migration industry to capitalize on the thousand-plus
transit migrants who are in town on any given day. Altar has attracted scores
of short-distance coyotes and produced all sorts of local entrepreneurs, many
of whom cater to the spiritual needs of journeying migrants. Vendors sell an
array of religious artifacts, such as medallions, devotionals, T-shirts, gallons
of "holy water," and even baseball caps adorned with the image of Our Lady
of Guadalupe to protect them from the sun and other desert dangers.

While in Altar, transit migrants may stay at the Casa del Migrante, where
Father Castaneda provides for their humanitarian needs and offers classes to
educate migrants on crossing perils and their rights if apprehended. If at all
possible, however, coyotes avoid the Casas del Migrante where they are not
welcomed by religious workers, and instead place their human cargo in small
guesthouses or private homes that have sprouted up in recent years to take
advantage of the transit traffic. The coyote who guided Aleksy from her
hometown of Chiantla, Guatemala, to Altar, Mexico, dropped her and the

rest of his cargo off at a private home where the migrants were instructed to remain indoors and wait for another group of coyotes who would take them across the desert to Arizona. Aleksy and her traveling companions spent much of their time "praying before a statue of the Virgin of Guadalupe," which rested on a small altar in the room where the migrants were being held. Aleksy explained to me the importance of the patroness of Mexico in her journey. "Before I left Guatemala, I prayed to my patron Virgin of Candelaria. Many in our group also carried cards of the patron saints of their communities. But in Altar, we turned to the Virgin of Guadalupe, as she takes special care of those crossing Mexico into the United States." Since Aleksy's arrival in the United States, however, she has returned to honoring her patron saint, La Virgin de Candelaria. Interestingly, then, the icon of devotion for Aleksy and other migrants transformed with place along the journey, which is shaped by culture and by situation and influenced by pending danger.

While in Altar migrants flock to the local church, Our Lady of Guadalupe, to seek comfort, protection, and guidance for what will be the most dangerous leg of the trip—the crossing of the Sonoran Desert. The church provides a sacred space where migrants can reproduce their relations with the sacred and create solidarity with other migrants. As is customary when venerating an icon, in a humble act of sacrifice migrants crawl along the marble aisle on their knees to reach the altar. Some fill the church to hear the daily mass by Father Castaneda, who includes in each service a special "Prayer for Our Migrant Brothers and Sisters." Others simply light votive candles to request safe passage and then settle themselves in pews to pray. Melissa, a young Honduran woman and Catholic who traveled alone with her child, prayed to the Virgin of Guadalupe to help her find the companionship of others on the road.

Amelia, a mother who left behind her children in her hometown in Guatemala in 2003 to join her husband in North Carolina, prayed for help with the concerns of any parent who faces an uncertain future, including the possibility of death. Summoning up her memories of the harrowing desert journey she had tried desperately to forget, Amelia told me of how in the Altar church she prayed that she would one day see her four children again (she still hasn't). She prayed that if she did not survive the trip, her children would forgive her and understand why she had done what she did. She prayed that she had done the right thing by not saying good-bye to them the morning she had departed. She prayed that her parents, sister, and brother-in-law would care for her children in her absence. Then she prayed for her safety and beseeched La Virgen to now care for and protect her sister-in-law with whom she traveled, whose health had faltered in recent days and who grew weaker by the hour. Worried that the coyote would leave behind the pair, she also prayed that the coyote would be sympathetic to her sister-in-law's failing condition while crossing the desert. Amelia came to grips with the real possibility of death through private prayer with God. She surrendered to God's will and released control of the situation. "I realized that the decision as to whether we would live or die was in God's hands," she said. Amelia would later tell me that when her sister-in-law became too weak to travel further, the coyote and male fellow travelers took turns carrying the heavyset woman on their backs for several hours until they were picked up by another coyote driving a van along a highway in southern Arizona. She steadfastly credits God, La Virgen de Guadalupe, and her hometown patron, San Antonio, for granting them a trustworthy coyote, honest and respectful travel companions, and a safe arrival.

Although most of the journeying migrants in the study limited their visits to churches in towns they passed through on the migratory route, some took additional steps to visit Catholic and popular shrines of their most revered icons, saints, and *almas* (souls). By far the most visited shrine on the journey was the Basílica of the Virgin of Guadalupe, the national icon of Mexico, which sits in the enormous compound of the same name on the hill of Tepeyac, just outside Mexico City. Some of the migrants who visited La Virgen had flown to Mexico City from their home countries (e.g., El Salvador) and made a point of visiting La Virgen before embarking on the next stage of their journey; others, such as Mexican migrants, had gone out of their way to pay their respects to the Queen of Mexico and most revered icon in all of the Americas. Once at the basilica, visiting migrants followed the customary pilgrim tradition of purchasing and lighting small votive candles in honor of their patroness and leaving handwritten petitions seeking her protection on the journey. They also purchased commemorative artifacts of the Virgin of Guadalupe to carry with them on their journey. It was in the basilica shop that Arturo, a young Honduran, purchased an international phone card with the image of the Virgin of Guadalupe on one side of it.

Not all the established shrines visited by journeying migrants are erected or sanctioned by the Catholic Church. In the northern Mexico border area, a popular cultural tradition practiced by many area residents involves seeking assistance from almas, or victim intercessors who have suffered at the hands of the larger society and are believed to have been judged innocent by God, and thus possess supernatural powers. Although they are not recognized as saints by the Catholic Church, these almas—Pedro Blanco, a gambler;

Jesus Malverde, a bandit; and Juan Soldado, wrongly accused of murder—
are familiar popular saints of the people.[6] In the northern Mexican town of
Tijuana, several popular shrines have been raised in public spaces by area
residents in honor of these almas that protect border crossers. By far the
most revered of these border saints is Juan Soldado (John the Soldier), whose
colorful image sits in one of two rundown but heavily visited shrines in a
public cemetery. Each year on June 24, the cemetery is packed with pilgrims
who come to request petitions or to pay a *manda*—a debt for a favor granted
by their alma. As is tradition, Juan's followers are often accompanied by mu-
sicians who serenade him in thanks for a favor granted.

According to legend, Juan Castillo Morales, a private in the Mexican army,
was wrongly accused of raping and murdering a young girl. The real culprit
was allegedly Juan Soldado's commanding officer who, in order to keep him
from testifying against him, shot him while trying to escape, a common practice at the time also known as *la ley de fuga* (the law of the flight).[7] According
to the legend recounted to me by Rosario, the vendor of religious artifacts at
the cemetery, Juan's commanding officer told Juan that if he could manage
to run the distance across a marked line, he would be set free. Juanito, as he
is affectionately referred to by his followers, managed to cross the line, but
nonetheless he was executed. To many of the faithful, like Jesus, Juanito's
betrayal allowed him to cross the distance from alleged criminal to revered
icon. At the same time, the line that Juan Soldado himself crossed has come
to symbolize the border separating Mexico from the United States. Over the
ensuing years, Juanito came to be known as a source of comfort and hope
among the poor, destitute, and illegal migrants in particular, to whom he com-
forts and protects in their border crossings. Among border residents, from
towns in northern Mexico to Los Angeles, California, he is recognized as the
patron of the migrants. Juan Soldado's well-established popularity equals if
not exceeds his southern counterpart, St. Toribio in Jalisco, and he is revered
as a new and popular coyote saint of migrants. Crowds of people, including
many traveling and returning migrants, flock to the shrine of Juan Soldado,
erected above his gravesite, to leave ex-votos, petitions, and other religious
artifacts.[8]

To Juanito's devotees, he represents a companion on the undocumented
trail, someone to protect the migrants from authorities; the migration miracles
he has granted crossers are legendary. According to Rosario, in 1999 a young
woman left her hometown in El Salvador for California, where she had
family. Under the guidance of a coyote, María and a group of other migrants
traveled across two international borders before arriving without incident in

a small town in southern California. From there she and several of her fellow travelers boarded a bus for Los Angeles, where she had plans to reunite with her sister and brother-in-law. To avoid detection, the migrants strategically separated from one another. María sat in the center of the bus and shortly thereafter fell asleep. She was awakened by the commotion of several persons boarding the bus, and immediately recognized them by their uniforms as U.S. Border Patrol agents. The officials made their way down the aisle, questioning persons and asking some for identification. María closed her eyes and prayed in silence. Just before reaching her seat, the agents stopped abruptly, turned around, and left the bus. Relieved but nonetheless stunned by her good fortune, María turned to her right and was greeted by the gentle and reassuring face of a young soldier. Several days later, in the safety of a Los Angeles apartment, she recounted the miraculous story to her sister who, upon hearing the account, quickly rushed to another room and returned with a card bearing the face and name of Juan Soldado. Some time later, after obtaining legal residency in the United States, María traveled to the shrine of Juan Soldado in Tijuana on June 24, the Day of Juan Soldado, to thank her guardian angel for the migration miracle he had granted her, a safe and successful crossing.

Located on the side of the main road to Tecate, some ten kilometers outside the city of Tijuana, sits the crude and neglected shrine of Jesus Malverde, the Mexican Robin Hood, an alleged bandit from Sinaola who, on May 5, 1909, was hanged for his crimes. The small, rundown shed in which the frame of Jesus Malverde hangs is chock-full of candles, pictures, and handwritten petitions. Two of his devotees we interviewed at the shrine had come to beseech their alma for good fortune on their jobs, but the shrine is also a frequent stopping point, we were assured, for migrants, coyotes, and drug smugglers. As one of the men told us, "For many he was a thief, but for the poor he is a saint. He robbed from the rich and gave to the poor." Because Juan Soldado and Jesus Malverde are seen by supplicants as poor victims of an unjust society, these almas provide a persuasive spiritual and moral narrative for undocumented crossers.

Commemoration, Companionship, Solidarity, and Prayer on the Journey

Journeying migrants not only visit but also create shrines. They erect them to remember and honor companions who have died along the trail and to provide for themselves and those who come after a sacred place to rest and nourish their bodies and souls during times of desperation. Sometimes the shrines are erected spontaneously and with religious artifacts the migrants carry with them, such as hand-size crosses and *veladoras* (glass-encased candles with images of saints). Other times, the migrants rely on the objects available to them along the trail, such as stones and rocks. In migrant campsites in southern Arizona, desert areas where migrants wait to be picked up by coyotes for the last or next-to-last leg of the trip, weary travelers are often forced to abandon the many supplies and artifacts they have brought with them. At these sites alongside empty water jugs, cans of sardines, and baby carriages, they leave prayer books, Bibles, candles, crosses, scapulars hanging from tree branches—ample materials to spontaneously create, when necessary, makeshift shrines along the way. A number of migrants also reported coming across small shrines made of stones memorializing those that died on the trail, usually crosses adorned with the remaining belongings of the victim and sometimes a holy artifact. Some of the deceased had been buried; all that remained of others were skeletons. It is customary for traveling migrants to stop and pay their respects to the dead who have gone before them.[9]

It is also customary to stop and pay respects to shrines of revered icons migrants encounter along the journey. Carved into the exterior wall of a migrant shelter in Altar is a mosaic of Our Lady of Guadalupe. Below it stands a small altar made of stones and crosses in memory of people who died in the desert trying to reach the United States. Migrants regularly pay their respects to those who have perished before them before continuing on their journey. On the road from Altar to Sasabe in the Sonoran Desert sits a small shrine that houses a concrete altar, a wrought-iron cross, statues of La Virgen de Guadalupe and St. Jude, and dozens of small votive candles, some lit, some long melted. Nobody knows who erected the simple shrine—perhaps a devout area resident, a religious worker, or family member of a migrant whose life was claimed in that desert spot—but it is visited by hundreds of migrants each day as they make their way to Sasabe. From here they will begin their dangerous trek through the desert. By all accounts it is now customary for the van taking the migrants from Altar to Sasabe to stop at the five-foot-high makeshift shrine, perhaps the last place migrants worship before they attempt to cross the border, and for riders to descend to say a prayer for the miracle of a safe crossing and pay their respects to the patroness of Mexico and the Saint of Lost Causes before heading north.

In the absence of religious artifacts with which to erect shrines to communicate with God and their saints, migrants seeking guidance, protection, and respite transform their surroundings into shrines of worship and comfort. Under several trestles along a southern highway of Arizona, migrants regularly make camp after the long desert trek from Sasabe, and wait for coyotes and transportation to take them to an interior urban city such as Phoenix or Tucson. Here, with the sharp edges of rocks and stones, the migrants have engraved their pleas for help from the divine. Worn and shadowy from wind and weather, some images and words are too faint to make out; other messages are clear, and their themes and images are powerful reminders of the fundamental presence of faith among those who journey north. As we traced migrant art and shrines along the Arizona-Mexico border, on one trestle we came across crude life-size engravings of the image of Jesus. Carved with stones into the concrete wall under and alongside the images are messages of hope, pleas for help, and calls of desperation: *"Fey"* (misspelled faith); "I am in your hands Lord"; *"Paz en Cristo"* (Peace in Christ); and in English, "God is Love."

Migrants also find comfort and safety in the religious artifacts they carry with them on the journey. One young missionary who directs a shelter for migrants along the Mexico-California border, emphasized the regularity of this custom and explained the crucial role that these sacred objects play in the dangerous migration journey: "Migrants always carry something with them. It is God on the road. A religious artifact represents companionship. It keeps them close to God on the road, especially in times of despair, when they are lost or stranded."

We recall how Cecilia and her travel companions relied on their holy cards and the prayers written on the back of them to cope with and endure the psychological and physical trauma they underwent in their crossing. The symbols of divine companionship are numerous and include rosaries, crosses, holy cards, medallions, scapulars, amulets, devotionals, Bibles, candles, and statues. Sometimes family members provide migrants with the artifacts before their departure, such as personalized scapulars. Other times the journeyers purchase them during visits to pilgrimage sites. More often, however, religious leaders from the migrants' home communities provide departing migrants with artifacts commemorating familiar patron saints and icons, in part as protection and companionship and in part to encourage the migrant to remain spiritually and materially connected to his or her hometown long after departure. Sometimes the religious artifacts ward off dangerous situations. One young Mexican man who was stopped by INS in southern Arizona reported that he was being repeatedly kicked by his apprehender and attacked by the agents' dog until the migrant turned over and revealed a Bible pressed closely to his chest. The agent immediately called off the dog and stopped the beating.

The objects that Catholics and Protestants carry with them differ, reflecting their distinctive religious traditions, though exceptions to this rule were abundant in the study. While evangelical Protestants simply wore crosses and carried Bibles with them on the journey, Catholics carried a litany of sacred objects—crosses, rosaries, devotionals, scapulars, and holy cards. A number of migrants who were raised Catholic and later joined Pentecostal churches reported that they, too, carried medallions of saints and revered Catholic images with them, revealing the lasting cultural influence of local religion as well as their need to exhaust all sources of strength and comfort, regardless of religious identity. On the dangerous journey, it was not uncommon for Protestant and Catholic devotional cultures and practices to converge.

Sometimes indigenous culture trumps religious identity. Maya Guatemalans followed traditional cultural customs and often wore homemade amulets containing special herbs believed to protect them on the journey. As one young Maya woman from the western highlands of Guatemala explained, "This practice is part of our culture. I know that our local priest wouldn't approve of it, so we didn't tell him. But my mother made it for me and I wore it. It was a comfort during the long train ride in Mexico, when I was forced to hide for many hours in a large spool in a train boxcar." Another Maya woman, from southern Mexico, reported that before she left her mother placed around her neck an elaborate coral and glass-beaded necklace interlaced with *dijes* or *pixcoy* (detailed silver miniature objects such as bells or coins) to keep her from harm. Like Miguel, who promised to wear his medallion of the Black Christ until it fell from his neck, Marta promised to wear her necklace until she returned home and could give it back to her mother.

When visiting the Centro Madre Assunta, a Scalabrinian shelter for female migrants in Tijuana, Mexico, I interviewed eight women who had sought temporary refuge there while working to earn enough money either to hire a coyote to cross into the United States or return to their home communities. The traveling companions of some had sought refuge in the adjacent shelter for men; others, however, had traveled in groups formed on the journey or with their children, who sought temporary refuge with them at the shelter. The women identified themselves as practicing Catholics and hailed from different countries, including Venezuela, Colombia, El Salvador, and Mexico. Their reasons for migration varied as did their future plans.

What bound the women together in solidarity on the trail, however, was their reliance on shared Christian belief systems and cultural customs in preparing for and coping with the journey, including the practice of carrying religious artifacts of revered virgins, Christ, or patron saints for companionship. All the women reported that before departing their hometowns they had visited shrines to request protection from local patron saints. Several also requested final blessings from attending pastors. Three of the women had visited the sanctuary of Our Lady of Guadalupe in Mexico City. All but one of the women carried an array of religious artifacts in sealed plastic baggies to protect them on their journeys. One young woman from Venezuela produced a rosary and prayer book containing the prayers of St. Peter, who is known in her country as the guardian of travelers. She reported that when she found herself in a situation of danger or fear, she turned to her rosary for solace and safety. The women from Guadalajara carried rosaries along with holy cards of the town's Virgin of Zapopan who, as they said, was their spiritual companion during the journey. One young woman proudly displayed her medallion featuring the image of the Virgin of Guadalupe; inscribed on the back were the words "La Virgen siempre me cuida"—"The virgin always takes care of me."

The narrative of a familiar patron saint or icon as companion on the road was a recurrent one told by migrants. Recall that at the shrine of St. Toribio in the dusty town of Santa Ana de Guadalupe, Jalisco, we interviewed seasoned migrants, some of whom had a long history of migration to the United States. They frequently referred to their "coyote saint" as a "spiritual companion" on whom they relied during the journey. Several of the migrants referred to St. Toribio as a new saint, who in part now replaced or at least competed with the role of protector previously played by the Virgin of Guadalupe or the Virgen de San Juan de los Lagos, located in the nearby town of the same name. Carlos, a thirty-year-old man from Aguas Calientes, Jalisco, and a seasoned migrant, claimed that he "felt him" during the journey. The comfort of St. Toribio's companionship gave him the strength to "travel back and forth between California and Mexico without fear." Others firmly believed in the miraculous powers of St. Toribio who, they steadfastly assert, grants safe passage to migrants who travel with scant resources. These beliefs are reaffirmed through folklore and narratives of his unexplained appearance to stranded migrants and miraculous powers of guiding them to safety, which are recounted over and over by the shrine's priests, keeper of miracles, and throngs of devotees. As one young man related, "I hear of many people who have made it safely on their trip, and they all pray to San Toribio and the Lord. They believe they made it to the United States because of San Toribio. And so do I. It's a miracle." Like so many of the miracles recounted by migrants, these, too, are manifested during periods of crisis, episodes during the journey when migrants are spared death or apprehension. Their steadfast belief in the companionship powers of St. Toribio allows his believers to transcend place—the state-imposed boundaries separating Mexico from California—and enter into a spiritual space where they feel they can derive protection and companionship.

To fill the long stretches of time and loneliness during what must feel like an endless journey, both Catholic and Protestant migrants in the study drew strength and sustenance from reading familiar passages from their Bibles and prayers from the devotionals that were provided to them by their clergy or by religious workers at shrines and shelters they visited. From southern Mexico to the U.S. border, numerous Mexican churches, pilgrimage shrines, and migrant shelters sell to their departing Catholic flock for a few pesos the *Devocionario del Migrante* (Migrants Prayer Book), introduced in chapter 1. Each version of the devotional varies somewhat, reflecting the concerns and needs of individual dioceses, but most include at the very least a series of prayers to meet the needs and allay the concerns of journeying migrants, including individual prayers for parents, children, and spouses in home communities and for those who fall ill or perish on the road. The devotionals also contain prayers for migrants who miss services while traveling, and include prayers to encourage national and local level allegiance (for "my country and government") and an introductory letter from diocese archbishops in which migrants are encouraged to remember and to stay in touch with local patron saints or icons. The more recently published devotionals are more sophisticated in language and have been expanded to include special migrant rosaries, Migrants Acts of Contrition, and even a Migrant Way of the Cross.

All the devotionals include contact information for shelters and human rights and legal aid services along the border, and have empty lined pages for making notes and leaving messages to family and hometown priests, especially in case of death. These devotionals recognize and may even be said to embrace the mobility of migrant flows, especially their transnational character, and as such help migrants reproduce Catholic belief systems and local veneration. They help as well to keep the migrant spiritually and emotionally linked to Catholicism and home, both during the journey and in the places they eventually settle in the United States.

Some migrants we spoke to chose not to carry religious items with them, claiming no need for these artifacts since their savior was, as some put it, "in my heart when I traveled." For these migrants, some of whom are evangelical Protestants and believe that the spirit of God is within them, individual prayer alone was their coping strategy. Graciela left her hometown in the department of San Miguel, El Salvador, in 1992. She traveled the distance with a group of *paisanos* from her home community. Along the way, the group, which was largely Catholic, stopped at the Basilica of the Virgin of Guadalupe in Mexico City to pay homage to the patroness and request protection. Several of her companions purchased medallions of the virgin but Graciela chose not to. As she explained, "God is in my heart and my soul, and he was with me all the way. Every hour of every day I prayed to him for my safe arrival. I lost track of time on the journey, we all did, but at least I had God with me."

José, a young Mexican migrant, crossed the Nuevo Laredo-Laredo border in 2001. Before he left Nuevo Laredo, he, his companions, and their coyote attended mass and silently prayed for their safety. As he explained, prayer became his coping strategy to alleviate the unbelievably stressful situation in which he found himself once the group set out for Houston. "I was placed under the floorboard of the car, where passengers rest their feet. I lost track of time and all that kept me going was prayer. I prayed that I would not pass out, that we would not have a car accident. I counted the number of rosaries I said on the way to Houston."

Both José and Graciela experienced what Oscar Handlin referred to as a period in which a "prolonged lapse of unsettled time obscured the calendar."[10] Hours and days become indistinguishable and the journey can no longer be measured in terms of time. Numerous migrants in the study sample couldn't remember how long the journey took, but they could recall their regimens of prayer and ritual. At some point, then, only their faith, belief systems, and religious and spiritual practices sustain the migrants on their journey. In the case of Graciela and José, prayer defined time and structured the journey. For some, then, migration becomes a spiritual journey.

Group prayer was also a common resource on the road. In times of desperation, stranded migrants drew on their shared belief systems and the strength of the larger group to cope with the fear and gain some control over their situation. Praying together enhanced group solidarity through providing a common identity.[11] María, a young Protestant woman from Mexico City, traveled to the Arizona-Mexico border with a group of strangers and under the guidance of a coyote in 2000. Once they reached the border, they were transferred to a pair of coyotes, whom they followed across the desert. As she explained, "We were lost. We had been in the desert for too long and we all knew we were in trouble. We lost track of time. One among us asked that we pray together and so we did. Even one of the coyotes prayed with us, and then asked us to forgive him for the hardships he had inflicted upon us. We were at the point of passing out when I thought I saw a cross. The sign inspired us and we continued. We were saved."

A religious worker recounted another story in which a group of migrants were traveling together and found themselves in a near-death situation. One among the group asked the others to join him in prayer. He then told the group, "If you are not a believer, then leave the group." No one left the group; they arrived safely in the United States, but were later deported to Mexico. Here, a shared belief system established a sense of moral order and control within the group; believers provided both social support for one another and guidelines for religious observance on the road.[12] Again, common belief structures were essential to controlling the situation, and an important element in that structure is the belief in miracles. Stranded migrants repeatedly interpreted escapes from death and safe returns as miracles—as signs of hope that fortified them and agents that propelled them to try again. The powerful effect of miracles on hope, fortitude, and action was expressed over and over. "If I made it once, I can make it again, since God is watching over me," or, "We wouldn't have gotten as far as we did if we hadn't been watched over by God. Next time, he will let us get closer to Houston."

Summary

Faith, which nurtures hope, fortifies migrants with the strength to cope both psychologically and physically with their journey. Far from home communities and the familiar and trusted institutions on which they have always relied, they depend on one another and their common belief systems and familiar religious customs and practices, especially prayer, to help them overcome, understand, and make bearable the traumas and uncertainties they face. Whenever feasible, migrants seek out churches and shrines for spiritual sustenance from clergy and their revered icons. Visiting shrines along the migrant trail allow migrants to envision and re-create their relations with God

CHAPTER 5

La Promesa

After coyotes sealed Cecilia and her sister Margot in a poorly ventilated truck and then exposed them to a near-death experience with drug smugglers, they finally guided the two women across the Mexico-California border. There Cecilia was reunited with her husband, Juan, at the Days Inn in San Isidro, California. Juan had arrived without incident and a day ahead of the women; the extra protection purchased at considerable cost had not, after all, guaranteed a less dangerous journey for Cecilia and Margot. Upon their reunion at the hotel, the three migrants got down on their knees and gave thanks to God and the Virgin of Guadalupe for their good fortune. Cecilia then called her mother to let her know that her daughters and son-in law had arrived safely. When her mother heard the joyful news, she knelt before the home altar and also gave thanks to the Virgin of Guadalupe. Then she blew out the two white veladoras of the virgin's image that she had lit before her daughters' departure to illuminate the path that would guide them to safety in the United States. Her mother then relayed news of their arrival to the local priest in Puebla who had blessed the young women before their departure. Once family and clergy had been notified of safe passage, Cecilia, Margot, and Juan made their way to the home of Cecilia's aunt in Los Angeles, who accompanied them to her Catholic Church. Again Cecilia gave thanks to her savior for safe passage. "Each week while I was living in Los Angeles I went to mass and there I always thanked God and La Virgen for protecting me and making sure that nothing bad happened to me on the road."

When I first met Cecilia in 2003 and told her of my project, it was several months before she mustered up the strength to tell, for the first time, her harrowing experience in the desert. In her account, which she told in tears, she pledged a continued vigil to her guardians who had protected her during her journey. Until she could return home, she frequently prayed to her patroness and further honored her through weekly church services. Cecilia's vigil in the United States allowed her to experience the presence of her revered icon and remain connected to her homeland until she was able physically to make the pilgrimage to honor her patron saint. In February 2006, Cecilia received the long-awaited green card and she and her U.S.-born son, Armando, flew to Puebla, Mexico; it was the first time Cecilia had been back since her departure in 1998. One of the first things she did after a reunion with her mother and family was to fulfill her promesa to God and the Virgin of Guadalupe. She made her way to the local church, fell to her knees, and gave thanks to God and the virgin for providing her with a green card so that she could settle permanently and safely in the United States and return to Puebla to see her mother again.

The promesa is a private agreement between the believer and a sacred image. It is a popular cultural and religious practice among the people of South and Central America and Mexico, and among many immigrants and Latinos in the United States. In exchange for a favor granted, believers pledge a vow of reciprocity. These vows provide hope and solace to those facing danger, illness, poverty, and other events deemed out of the believer's control. The practices and rituals through which people fulfill their promises are informed by place and time and shaped by the social context of the petitioner's requested favors.

In this chapter, I explore migration promesas, the various vows of reciprocity observed by migrants in exchange for a successful migration experience, a process that is first marked by a safe arrival in the United States. As Cecilia's narrative illustrates, the migrant's promise of giving thanks in return for a safe passage is both a cultural and religious act that transcends national borders and manifests itself over an extended period of time. For Cecilia, her promise to the patroness of her homeland, La Virgen de Guadalupe, was fulfilled upon her return home, but her vigil actually began after she arrived in the United States, in conjunction with her mother's vigil in her homeland. It evolved into a lifelong religious practice, transforming along with circumstances, place, and time.

After arriving in the United States, many Latino migrants draw on familiar Christian traditions to express gratitude and to fulfill their departing pledges, such as falling to one's knees to pray and give thanks or saying a rosary. Fulfilling the promesa sometimes constitutes the final devotional act in a cultural ritual that family members or clergy initiated in the home community before the migrant's departure, as when Cecilia's mother lit and then extinguished the Virgin of Guadalupe candles that adorned her home altar. In this sense the promesa symbolizes the finality of the religious journey.

Often migrants cannot fully honor their promises for months or years; while forging a new life in the United States some migrants, like Cecilia, must wait to complete their pledges until they return home for a visit or acquire the legal authorization to travel freely between their U.S. homes and communities of origin. By then, they have achieved new successes for which they are thankful and these, too, are included in their observances. In this way migration promises are dynamic and ever changing, incorporating new migration milestones over time.

As in the earlier migration stages of preparation, departure, and journey, many of the spiritual expressions of devotion and gratitude for safe passage are private affairs that migrants and their families practice outside the institutional realm of religion and among family or clergy or in personal communion with God and popular icons. Unconnected to services, such as weekly masses provided by churches, these expressions of devotion and spirituality draw heavily on traditional and folk religious observances to regionally based icons and are framed in popular Christian discourse. They are culturally reproduced by family and community across generations and in spaces that transcend political borders. Just as Cecilia's mother taught her daughter about the meaning and power of promises, so shall Cecilia teach this ritual to her U.S-born son. The reproduction of these devotional practices by the second generation has important implications. As sociologist Rob Smith found in his ethnographic account of transnational practices among Ticuanenses in New York City, promises pledged and observed by youth can foster bonds between children and parents and encourage the second generation to sustain ties to the migrants' homeland and culture.[1]

The promesa practice is also observed among undocumented migrants. In conjunction with a humble prayer of thanks, three out of every four migrants in the study who successfully completed the journey north chose one or more special devotional practices to give thanks for safe passage. Upon arrival in their final place of destination in the United States, many visited a church to give thanks to God or to a revered icon or to seek private counsel with a cleric. This thanksgiving was then followed by prayer and home-centered religious practices. Some migrants reported visiting a church to give thanks at the first port of entry, and in a few cases, attending clergy there heard confessions and provided migrants with financial assistance. These, however, were the exceptions. In general, giving thanks for a successful arrival had to wait until migrants reached their final destination and the safety of family, friends, and clergy.

Such was the case for Perla, who departed her hometown of Trujillo, Honduras, in 1995 to join her brother and uncle in Houston. The trip would take her nine months. Robbed and left destitute in Mexico City, she found temporary work in a restaurant kitchen and, reared as a Catholic, naturally joined the thousands of daily pilgrims at the Basilica of the Virgin of Guadalupe. Perla beseeched the virgin to provide her with the necessary resources to continue her journey to the United States and vowed to honor her for safe passage. Eventually arriving safely in Houston, she called her mother to let her know and then asked her brother to take her to see the image of the virgin at the Church of Our Lady of Guadalupe in Houston's Eastside Latino barrio. There Perla repeated the familiar popular expression of devotion and sacrifice that she had practiced for so many months at the basilica in Mexico City: She made the laborious and painful journey down the sanctuary's center aisle on her knees and then veered left to the overflowing shrine dedicated to the Virgin of Guadalupe. She paid her respects and among the thousands of votive objects left by pilgrims, placed her small handwritten note of thanksgiving. Practicing this ritual of thanksgiving for a miracle enabled Perla to place value and meaning on her journey and to reconnect with what had been her world before migration and where she hoped one day to return.

Another young Mexican woman, Rocío from León, also made sense of her migration ordeal through her faith, which she says was renewed through the journey. Rocío experienced a harrowing monthlong passage to reach the United States, one fraught with multiple dangers. Lost and stranded in the desert for four days, she and her two traveling companions were eventually rescued by INS agents and were sent back to Mexico. After several failed attempts to reenter the United States, Rocío finally convinced a cousin whom she resembled to lend her a visa to cross and was eventually reunited with her grandparents in Houston. Raised a Catholic, Rocío rarely attended church in León (in the state of Guanajuato). In her youth, she had frequented the Sanctuary of El Señor de Villaseca (the Black Christ), the regional patron, and she and her cousins once visited the Basilica of the Virgin of Guadalupe to request guidance in their future plans. However, she told me, by the time she reached adulthood, she had lost her faith. "I was no longer very religious back home. If and when I went to mass my body was there but not my mind." In times of trauma during the northbound journey, she recalled her savior from youth, the Black Christ, and turned to the familiar as a source of comfort. "I pleaded with God and El Cristo Negro to help us, to save us from death. When I reached Houston, I went to a church and confessed to God. I thanked him for getting me here. From this point on, I began attending church." With time, Rocío also became more active in church activities, including directing a youth group and organizing services for those in need in the community. "I am now a member of the Guadalupanas (Society of Guadalupe) and work and pray for those who have less than me and those who are coming to the United States."[2] In a call she recently made to Mexico, she learned that a friend was on his way to the United States. "I pray for him daily. There are so many people dying that I pray that he will not be one of them . . . In all since I left home, I have become more spiritual, and now feel that the emptiness I once felt has been filled." For Rocío, the migration experience, especially surviving the journey, proved to be in some ways a spiritual journey that increased her faith and facilitated her recognition of an obligation to the larger community of those in need, including praying for the well-being of others who follow in her footsteps, an act that further sustains her faith. Membership in the Society of Guadalupe fosters her spirituality and enables her to reconnect with her Mexican Catholic identity.

Helen, a Catholic from San Vincente, El Salvador, also completed her migration experience and found its meaning through faith and popular cultural practices that transcended religious affiliation. In 1991 she joined siblings and an uncle who had settled in Houston some five years earlier. Once she had safely arrived, Helen and her relatives went to the Episcopal Church that was near their apartment and that offered services in Spanish. There she fulfilled the promesa that she had made before leaving El Salvador and, to the surprise of congregants not familiar with the Catholic tradition, she took the painful steps chosen by Perla, entering the church on her knees and slowly making her way to the altar to give thanks for the miracle of a safe arrival. Several days later, attending a Spanish service at the Episcopal Church, Helen received counsel from the attending priest who was very sympathetic to the experience of the migrants and offered special counseling to them. From that point on, this church became Helen's place of worship. What was very important to Helen at the end of her journey was to fulfill her promise and give thanks through a familiar cultural tradition that she valued highly, one that enabled her to comprehend emotionally and psychologically her safe entry into the United States. What was less important to Helen was the institutional context in which she observed her faith and spirituality.

Helen's religious adaptability is not unusual. It was a common practice among migrants in this study and it is a common practice among immigrants more generally. As sociologist Peggy Levitt observes, syncretism is often the norm, rather than the exception, among immigrant groups of various faiths.[3] Helen moved easily from a Catholic to an Episcopal church, a transition facilitated in part by her relatives who all attended the church and introduced her to their place of worship, and by a Spanish-speaking cleric who welcomed Helen into his flock. For Helen, Rocío, and Perla, the church provided a spiritual space in which they could each practice a culturally familiar ritual that renewed their links to their families and home communities. At the same time, the church provided a bridge into the new community in which they now lived.

María, a migrant from Guererro, Mexico, provides another illustration of the porous boundaries between faith traditions, cultural practices, and the dynamic nature of their intersections. Shortly after she arrived in the United States, she converted to Catholicism and then later reconverted to Protestantism. Despite her multiple conversions, she all the while observed the popular devotional practices that she brought with her from her home community and that had carried her safely through the journey north. María was raised a Catholic but had joined a Pentecostal temple, El Divino Redentor, in her late teens. When it came time for her to leave for the United States, however, it was to La Virgen de Guadalupe that she turned for protection. María purchased a medallion of the virgin that she wore around her neck throughout the journey. Once in New York and in the safety of family, her sister accompanied María to a Catholic Church to give thanks and to light a small ex-voto candle to La Virgen. While in New York, María occasionally accompanied her sister to services at the same Catholic Church and she continued to pray to an image of the Virgin of Guadalupe that sits on the home altar in her sister's apartment. In 1995, Maria moved to Houston and a year later joined a Pentecostal church, Iglesia de Dios, which she learned about through a friend and neighbor. Although she identified herself as Pentecostal when interviewed, like Helen and others who had formally left the Catholic Church after arriving in the United States, María continued to pray to the patroness of Mexico in the privacy of her own home and regularly thanked the virgin for the miracle of a safe arrival.[4]

Many of the Mexican migrants in this study gave their allegiance first to the Virgin of Guadalupe, regardless of their formal religious affiliation, suggesting that in many cases religion and culture go hand in hand, while at other times the latter trumps the former. María's narrative shows that for many migrants, their relationship with God and their patron saints and images is also a private affair, one that they prefer to practice alone or with trusted family and community in their own homes.

Not all the migrants interviewed were able to give thanks upon arrival in the comfort of family and friends. Many arrived alone or in the companionship of fellow travelers they had met on the road or in migrant shelters in Mexico and along the border. Lacking the personal networks from which to draw resources upon arrival, many turned once again to those organizations they had depended on during their journey—faith-based shelters. These religious shelters can be found in small towns and large cities situated along the most heavily traversed routes in U.S. border states. Once in Texas, many migrants turn for refuge to Casa Oscar Romero in Brownsville or the Casa del Migrante in Laredo. New arrivals in southern California find refuge in the Valley Missionary Program, an immigrant welcoming center in the Coachella Valley in southern California.[5] If these unattached newcomers gain entry to Houston, they usually will find their way to Casa Juan Diego, the most well-established migrant hospitality center in the city and one that religious workers and migrants along the migrant trail know well. The center, founded in 1980 and inspired by the Catholic Worker Movement, provides humanitarian, medical, and religious services to the migrants who stay there. Casa staff members provide an opportunity for arriving migrants to understand and, if necessary, make peace with their migration experiences[6] by telling their stories to the larger Juan Diego community.

Many of these testimonies, such as the following given by Carlos, a young Honduran who arrived in the shelter in 2002, describe the harrowing journey in detail and then close with humble words of thanks for being alive. "Since I had nowhere to go in Houston, the coyote dropped me off at a gas station. Asking people, I got the address of Casa Juan Diego, where they gave me a place to stay, food, and work. I am very grateful now that I have a permanent job and, above all, I give thanks to God because if it were not for him, I would not be alive."[7] A woman whose husband had been shot and killed for the $1,000 he was carrying, relayed the following after she arrived at the casa: "I thank the people who have helped me, especially Sister Fatima Mary in Casa Romero who gave me her unconditional help and had a mass celebrated for my husband. The other guests of Casa Romero all supported me and prayed with me. And thanks to Casa Juan Diego, this house of succor and assistance which gives all help and protection to immigrants."[8]

By encouraging these testimonies, what theologian Daniel Groody refers to as the "living documents of immigrants,"[9] shelters provide a safe space for migrants to share their experiences collectively and cope emotionally, psychologically, and spiritually with the losses and traumas of the journey. The shelters that welcome migrants might be said to rekindle or sustain the religious dimension of the journey in that they provide spiritual therapy for the migrant who has endured the hardships of the journey. These hospitality shelters also promote solidarity and group identity among a largely marginalized people—undocumented migrants—as they forge their way in a new society and culture that does not embrace their arrival.

Newly arrived migrants also relay news to the home community. Because so many back home invest spiritual and emotional energy in the migration of one of their own, it is not surprising that news of a migrant's safe arrival is relayed as soon as possible and often celebrated by family members and/or clergy. All but two of the migrants in the study who traveled without papers either called home or wrote to parents, spouses, or children to let them know promptly of their safe arrival. Many family members respond to the joyful news with a variety of regional and ethnic devotional expressions of gratitude, the majority of which are private, home-centered practices, similar to Cecilia's mother's act of extinguishing the candles of the Virgin of Guadalupe after hearing from her daughter. Sometimes, families and migrants fulfill their promises of thanksgiving simultaneously in the belief that the message of thanks will be more quickly received if it is relayed by multiple family members. When Jaime and his cousin migrated in 1991 from Mexico City, they crossed under the guidance of a coyote who took them to Houston. "I carried two white candles with me, to protect me. As I pledged to God before leaving, when I arrived in Houston I called my mother and asked her to light two candles to thank God and the virgin for helping me get here. I then took the candles that I brought from the church at home and lit them in a church here." By observing parallel rituals of thanksgiving in both home and host communities, Jaime and his mother remained spiritually linked to each other despite the jurisdictional boundaries that separated them.

When Amelia joined her husband in Durham, North Carolina, following a terrifying journey that took her and her sister through the Sonoran Desert, she immediately called her mother and children in her hometown of Huista, Guatemala, to let them know of her safe arrival. Upon hearing the news, her parents approached the home altar and blew out the two white candles of the town's patron saint, San Antonio Huista, that had illuminated the way to safety for her daughter. Mario also called his mother in a small town in the outskirts of Guadalajara to let her know of his safe arrival. His mother, too, extinguished the white candle that had illuminated the way for her son. As he was unable to return home because of his undocumented status, some months later Mario wired money for his cousin, Lucy, to make the pilgrimage to the chapel of St. Toribio, to give thanks to his patron saint who had guided him through the desert and to record his miracle in the sanctuary's room of miracles. We approached Lucy after mass one Sunday at the shrine of St. Toribio. She was waiting in line to share her migration miracle with Father Gabriel Pérez. Lucy told us that she had received a call from Mario shortly after his arrival in the United States. Mario told Lucy that St. Toribio came to his rescue when he was stranded in the desert. As she explained, "Mario and his friends were lost and disoriented in the desert. They prayed and prayed. When they had given up all hope, Mario saw a wet spot on the desert floor. He drank from it and the water continued to flow. He drank until he was full. It was a miracle."

Although most migrants relied on loved ones back home to relay news of a safe arrival to clergy, approximately two of every ten migrants—mostly evangelicals who had received personal counsel from clerics before departure— directly notified their pastors, some by calling them. When Henry lost his job in 1998, he felt that he had no choice but to leave his wife and two children in Monterrey, Mexico, to search for work in Texas. He was troubled by his decision because his wife did not want him to leave, fearing that he might not return. He recalled:

> My wife found some relief through our local priest who encouraged her to pray and support my decision. He continued to pray with her during my long journey north, when I was unable to contact her. When I crossed the border with little difficulty, I then knew God willed me to go. I had made the right decision for me and my family. As soon as I crossed the border, I called my wife and then my priest to let them know I was safe. I called them both again when I arrived in Houston.

Cultural tradition, ethnic identity, and church membership shape how migrants correspond with clergy in their home communities. In Catholic communities throughout Central America and Mexico, sometimes priests are notified of a safe arrival directly by the successful migrant, but usually the news is relayed by family to local clergy; the priests and pastors then share this news with their congregants during daily and weekly services. For example, during daily services at the Cathedral of Our Lady of Peace in San

Miguel, El Salvador, a major pilgrimage site for departing migrants who come to pray for a safe journey and for those they leave behind, priests regularly announce the safe arrival of a fellow parishioner. Other times attending parishioners voice the arrival of a family member during the "intention and thanksgiving period" of the service. As one attending priest explained, "Sometimes family members are reluctant to share in public the names of those who have arrived safely, so they tell me in private, after mass, and together we pray for their continued success. Sometimes the family makes an offering of thanks and we light a votive candle and pray together. These small counsels provide great comfort to family left behind."

In remote evangelical communities in the highlands of Guatemala, Maya departing migrants frequently receive guidance and counsel from local pastors. After arriving in the United States, it is to these trusted clergy and their ministries that they turn to announce their safe arrival and to give thanks.[10] In these ethnically homogenous and close-knit communities, news of a safe arrival is often shared among clergy, family, and community at ayunos—the fasting and prayer services led by independent and often traveling pastors that cater to the spiritual needs of the rural poor, many of whom are not connected to a formal church. Ayunos last anywhere from several hours to several days and adhere to Maya custom. They are convened in sacred places, such as on mountaintops and around altars in the homes of ministers. Consequently, ayunos are frowned on by clergy of established churches who compete for those who flock to the ayunos. More than once we heard ayunos referred to by other clergy as "witchcraft, voodoo, and false magic." To attending Maya, however, ayunos represent a private and spiritual experience that may or may not be observed along with church attendance.

At one ayuno that we attended in the home of a Maya woman who has presided over her home ministry in a small rural hamlet for two decades, several dozen participants squatted around a small altar and participated in group prayer and praise. After hearing about my research, the pastor reached under the draped home altar, retrieved several large envelopes, and emptied their contents: scores of photographs of young men and women. As the pastor explained, these were pictures that migrants had sent to her via family members to provide evidence of their safe arrival. As is customary, the attendees pray as a group, first to thank God for the miracle of a safe arrival and then for the continued success and well-being of the migrant. Pastors of small Pentecostal churches throughout the highlands regularly commented on their receipt of small donations for the church sent through family members by migrants in return for a safe arrival. In one church we visited in the department of Totonicapan, the walls were covered with letters of safe arrival and thanksgiving. The numerous pictures and monetary offerings are testimony to the important role that religion assumes in creating and re-creating transnational links between the home religious community and the migrant, even as the individual is forging a new life in the United States.

The history of immigrant America is full of accounts of immigrants who, because they intended to return home, continued to reach out to spiritual leaders in the home community, even while establishing roots in the United States.[11] The migrants in my study are no exception. Long after arriving in the United States, Guatemalan, Honduran, Salvadoran, and Mexican migrants continue to keep in touch with the clerics who sanctioned their migration, counseled their families, and helped them prepare spiritually and psychologically for the journey. These same clerics become spiritual lifelines to communities of origin. Pastors in Guatemala, El Salvador, and Mexico all reported receiving calls, letters, and financial donations from migrants whom they had counseled about migration long after these people had forged new lives in the United States.

Over time, some interpersonal ties between migrants in the United States and clergy in home communities have led to the development of organizational ties between churches in home and host communities that shared similar belief systems and religious practices. For example, the pastor of the Príncipe de Paz Church in San Cristóbal, Guatemala now regularly receives funding from a sister church in Houston where those he has counseled now attend. The relationship between the two churches was nurtured by a pastor who visited the Houston community and was further developed by couriers who travel between the communities, bringing with them donations and goods for the San Cristóbal church. Similarly, clergy from sending communities in El Salvador and Guatemala traveled to visit their flock in communities in the United States, a transnational practice that has been documented in many contemporary studies of Latin American migration.[12]

What is equally notable is how often migrants, especially women, contact and continue to keep in touch with clergy and religious workers they met on the road but who were not connected to their home communities, thus emphasizing the importance of religious guidance on the journey. Priests who care for popular shrines and religious workers at shelters report that they often receive calls and donations from transit migrants with whom they had had only brief contact. Clearly, successful migrants never forget the religious workers who provided them with humanitarian and spiritual assistance on their journey north. The comments provided by Sister Gemma, a Scalabrini missionary who runs a women's shelter for local, internal, and international migrants in Tijuana, were echoed by other religious workers along the migrant trail, especially by those who cared for the needs of the female journeyers:

> It always surprises me as I do not always remember all my girls. But they remember me long after they have left. My girls keep in touch with me. They call or write and tell me about their work, families, etc. They report their religious life to me in the United States. I hear from them often, be it from the United States or from other places in Mexico. For those that stay in Tijuana they drop by often. We are in fact trying to organize a monthly reunion for them but it's difficult locating a time when we can all meet because of their busy work schedules.[13]

As Sister Gemma's remarks illustrate, the shelters where migrants stop provide more than short-term humanitarian assistance; they also provide a social space in which migrants can receive spiritual nourishment and develop personal networks to sustain them on the trail. In some cases, the clergy and staff at these shelters will prove to be the last official religious persons with whom migrants have contact before embarking. Consequently, given the strong bonds that are formed among migrants and staff at the shelters, it is not surprising that some migrants would maintain close contact long after the journey is over.

Homecoming

Returning home to offer thanks for protection on the journey north proved difficult for most. Like Cecilia, many had to wait years until they received authorization to make this cross-border pilgrimage, and by then they had tallied additional migration milestones for which to thank their icons. However, regardless of the length of time it took migrants to fulfill these extraordinary promises, "coming home" to give an offering of thanks to an image of the virgin, Christ, or a saint who they believed had made it all possible, represented the final spiritual marker in their journey to the United States. By fulfilling the pledge to return home to the familiar—their customs, belief systems, and popular religious practices—migrants we spoke with had remained emotionally and spiritually connected to their home communities.

When returning migrants are finally able to carry out the promesa, they deposit ex-votos at the shrines of their revered icons to give thanks for the safe journey. Ex-votos can include a wide variety of objects, ranging from paintings to silver tokens called milagros to flowers. In observing this custom, they follow the steps taken by millions of supplicants throughout history and across cultures who have sought audiences with the divine to whom they have made pledges and who they believe control their fates.

The cultural tradition of depositing tokens and mementos at religious shrines in return for divine favors predates Christianity and can be traced to the pagan practices of the Greeks. In these ancient cultures, supplicants customarily visited shrines where they left small anatomical figures of clay, wood, or stone either to pray for relief from a physical ailment or to express thanks for health having been restored. By the fifteenth century, a more elaborate form of veneration had been adopted by the wealthy: the ex-voto painting. Derived from the Latin term "from a vow," the ex-voto painting emerged in Italy in the late fifteenth century among the wealthy but its popularity rapidly spread among all classes throughout Europe. The early ex-voto paintings favored scenes of the life of Christ, Mary, the saints, and biblical figures, and were typically hung alongside or behind a home shrine, or church altar. With time, the ex-voto paintings evolved to include images of the divine, the supplicant, and the miraculous event that brought the two together, all of which was explained in an accompanying textual narrative that was drafted by a wealthy patron who commissioned the ex-voto.[14]

The various votive traditions followed the Spanish to the New World where, in a new and diverse cultural context, they underwent considerable transformation over the centuries, ultimately giving way to popular forms of cultural and devotional expression that varied considerably by region and country.[15] In Mexico, for example, a vow of reciprocity at first manifested itself through the ex-voto painting tradition, which gained immense popularity in the eighteenth and nineteenth centuries, before undergoing important changes. At first the tradition was restricted to the wealthy who commissioned the paintings on canvas or wood, but with the introduction of tinplate in the nineteenth century, the tradition's popularity spread to the masses. By the early 1920s, the practice of painted ex-votos became largely concentrated in the western Mexican states of Guanajuato, Zacatecas, Jalisco, and San Luis Potosí, where the painted tin stories are referred to as *retablos*, from the Latin retro-tabula or "behind the altar."[16]

Today, these Mexican states house multiple shrines that overflow with retablos that have been left by supplicants to thank a religious icon. Among the scores of retablos are those that reflect a concern to many who live in western Mexico: international migration. The role of religious shrines and the images they house in the lives of Mexican migrants was a largely neglected topic among researchers until Jorge Durand and Doug Massey conducted a content analysis of votive paintings that had been commissioned by migrants and their families during the period 1900–1993. The results of their fascinating account, unfolded in narrative and pictorial detail, tell of some of migrants' most pressing concerns in each stage of the migration process: 1) heading north and making the trip; 2) finding the way; 3) legal problems; 4) medical problems; 5) getting by in theUnited States; and 6) homecoming. Collectively, concerns about the trip north and coming home to give thanks were represented on more than one-third of all these votive paintings on tin or retablos.[17]

Votive painting traditions continue to undergo transformation but they persist in reflecting the concerns of the people who observe them. Returning migrants carry on the tradition of visiting the devoutly honored Catholic shrines in southwest Mexico—La Virgen de San Juan de los Lagos, La Virgen de Zapopan, El Señor de la Misericordia, and St. Toribio—to give thanks for a safe arrival. When feasible, migrants return on the feast days of their patron saints. At the shrines, migrants and others still leave painted votive offerings of thanks for a safe arrival, though the practice of leaving commissioned paintings on tin has all but disappeared. The ex-votives they leave today integrate an assortment of materials and methods to create collages that mix traditional drawings with modern media.[18]

In the shrine of St. Toribio Romo, the "patron saint of migrants," located in what was once the desolate farming village of Santa Ana de Guadalupe in Jalisco, Mexico, scores of pilgrims with migrant concerns have passed through the daunting stone gates and along the "causeway of martyrs" to enter the chapel. Some visit the shrine to pray for the safety of family members who linger on the migrant trail. When we stopped at the shrine one busy Christmas season, when migrants were returning home to see family, many of the pilgrims we met told us that they had come to the shrine to give thanks to their patron saint for a safe arrival and to pray for those who would follow in their steps. A young man from Aguas Calientes, Mexico, had recently received permanent residency status in the United States. "Yes, I thanked St. Toribio for my green card but most of my prayers I say today are for others who were not so fortunate and for those who must still take the dangerous journey and need St. Toribio's company," he said.

Josefina, "the keeper of the miracles," escorted us to the shrine's retablo room, where many contemporary versions of the traditional ex-voto paintings hang from the walls. Several of the drawings included images of miraculous life-saving events along the migration trail. In one votive painted on wood, the picture story depicts two men, one in a sombrero, heading across cactus-dotted desert terrain and toward a barbed wire fence, beyond which are two American flags, a misspelled "Mcdonals" sign, and an armored tank. Looming large in the retablo is the priest like image of a St. Toribio. Unlike many of the older and more traditional retablos painted on tin in which the donor remained anonymous, the López brothers signed their names to their ex-voto:

> Santo Toribio, Rafael and David Lopez give you thanks for assisting them crossing the border to the United States. In gratitude, we offer you this humble retablo. Mexico. 9-Sep.-02

Other retablos were simple in design, often including only a paper drawing and written inscription of gratitude that has been framed in glass and wood. In one retablo, consisting of a colored-pencil drawing in a glass-encased frame, the donor has written alongside the image of St. Toribio a message of thanks for having survived the "Río Bravo." In another colored-pencil drawing on paper, the artist wrote his message of thanks alongside a photocopy of his visa. In yet another image, a young girl had drawn hands stretched upward in a gesture of prayer. Above the image, she inscribed a message thanking St. Toribio for a visa that would allow her to travel with papers and avoid the overland journey north.

In the nearby shrine of El Señor de la Misericordia (Lord of Mercy) in Tepatitlan, Jalisco, hangs a wooden retablo that was recently painted for el Señor, the reclining wooden Christ, in exchange for a miraculous escape from the deadly Sonoran Desert. In the simple wooden image, the Christ-like figure of El Señor de la Misericordia looms over a desert scene of cactus and sunlight. Across the remaining space of the retablo, two young migrants expressed in elegant gold lettering their humble gratitude to their protector and savior, whom they also credit with saving the lives of their anonymous fellow travelers:

> We give thanks, Lord of Mercy, for allowing us to escape with our lives after three days in the Altares Desert in Arizona. 26, 27, 28 of May, 2000. Jose Maria Gutierrez, Jose Juan Valazquez, and Friends

We saw the theme of thanksgiving for a successful migration journey depicted in many ex-votos adorning shrines in Jalisco. Tacked on a solitary space of wall in the Guadalajara shrine of La Virgen de Zapopan, a migrant had left a photocopy of his 2002 visa alongside a handwritten note thanking his revered virgin for safe and legal passage to the United States. Often the migration event depicted in the drawings includes markers of successes in the United States achieved long after the journey. Alongside the thousands of votive offerings that cover the walls of the Virgin's Chamber in the church of the Virgin of San Juan de los Lagos, migrant believers pin, nail, or tape handwritten offerings associated with such milestones as receiving a driver's license, graduating from high school, or successfully establishing a business. For all of these achievements, they credit their patroness. As these few examples show, in the Jalisco region of western Mexico from which many migrants hail, the ex-voto drawing of thanks remains alive in the culture as a way of fulfilling the promesa; only the materials have changed, from elaborate painted drawings on tin to more modest and less expensive depictions on wood and paper.

Retablos are but one of many gifts that believers leave in exchange for a favor granted by their sacred image. Most of the shrines that returning migrants visit in western Mexico also house flowers, ribbons, carvings, crutches, baby booties, clothing, silver milagros of body parts, and just about any other object that could symbolize a favor granted. At the shrine of St. Toribio, Josephina escorted us to a chamber beyond the retablo room where, as keeper of the miracles, she guards many of these votive offerings in cabinets and drawers. From one large drawer she pulled milagros (silver, tin, and metal medallions and tokens), dried flowers, ribbons, locks of hair, and articles of clothing. Safety-pinned to a cherished braid that appeared to have been cut off at the nape of a young girl's neck was a note in which the donor had written in a mixture of upper- and lowercase letters:

> Thank you, St. Toribio, for providing me with the long-awaited visa. I waited 90 days and on the 90th day it came. I can now travel to see my beloved grandparents. My hair is the only meaningful offering I have to give you in thanks.

Since votive practices are deeply associated with religious tradition and regional sacred images, it is not surprising that they vary by people and geography. Farther north along the U.S.-Mexico border where victim-intercessors are honored, supplicants regularly travel across the border from California to Tijuana to give thanks to their beloved folk hero, Juan Soldado. Although not sanctioned by the Catholic Church, two shrines to him have been erected by his believers in the city's public cemetery. To many, Juanito is also a border alma and a protector of crossing migrants. Adorning his shrines are multiple votive offerings—drawings, paintings, flowers, milagros—from residents of California. Some have left large plaques on which they engraved their thanksgiving. Frequently, the messages include migration-related themes, some of which, like the following one engraved on a large plaque, thank their alma for a safe crossing:

> Little Juanito, thank you for all the help that you have given us and for not abandoning us especially for the miracle of letting me cross when I most needed to. Mario and Carmen Macias

Leaving a gift at a shrine for a favor granted is also a common cultural practice in many communities in Central America. Although the retablo never gained widespread popularity there, a multitude of other ex-voto offerings adorn the area shrines, especially milagros: tiny wax, bone, tin, silver, or gold figures of body parts, animals, plants, and domestic items. The type of milagro employed and the tradition behind their offerings vary by region. In the shrine of La Virgin de Paz in San Miguel, El Salvador, tradition dictates that believers offer thanks by attaching tiny milagros of body parts to ribbons that are then safety-pinned to the gown of their patroness.

In many Central American countries, but especially in Guatemala and Honduras, believers have historically honored their sacred images by engraving words of gratitude on marble and wooden plaques that are then attached to the walls of shrines or faces of sanctuary altars. In the present day, many of these inscriptions are written on materials that are more accessible to the poor, such as cardboard and even simple lined white paper. In Iglesia de San Francisco el Grande in Antigua, Guatemala, the home of Guatemala's only saint, St. Pedro de San José Betancur, or Hermano Pedro as he is affectionately called, believers who have come to his shrine inscribe general messages of thanks on the many plaques that decorate the walls of the church: "En gratitud a San Pedro por favor recibido (In gratitude to Brother Pedro for a favor received)." Some of the faithful write more detailed descriptions of the favor received, such as these translated inscriptions left on marble and wooden plaques in exchange for safe passage:

> We offer our endless gratitude to Brother Pedro for having fulfilled my dream of going to Los Angles, California. Zulema Mazarigos. 25-6-2001

> Thank you San Pedro for allowing my family to join me safely in the United States. 26-2-2002

In some shrines in Mexico and Central America, believers also honor their spiritual contracts by recording their narratives of thanksgiving in large altar books, commonly referred to as Books of Miracles.[19] Believers who come to the Iglesia de San Francisco to pay homage to Hermano Pedro regularly record favors granted in the two-foot-long Book of Miracles that sits in front of the shrine's large altar. The four-hundred-page book is so heavily used by worshippers that it must be replaced every few months to accommodate the thousands of narratives that are recorded in it each year. Again, the theme of the dangerous crossing emerges among the entries of thanksgiving:

> I give thanks to Hermano Pedro for the miracle of safe travel across the waters of the Rio Bravo to Los Angeles. Sra Maro. May, 2003

Most migrants do not fulfill these special pledges for many years, until they obtain green cards or legal authorization to travel freely between their U.S. homes and communities of origin. Cecilia waited eight years before she could fully realize her contract with God. Fortunately, long before making the special pilgrimage to her hometown of Puebla, Mexico, Cecilia managed a temporary fulfillment of her obligation to honor the promesa through regular visits to her country's patroness, the Virgin of Guadalupe, in a Los Angeles sanctuary that houses the virgin's image and where Cecilia lit small votive candles in offering of thanks. In large cities and small towns throughout the United States, especially those with large Latino populations and situated close to the U.S.-Mexico border, multiple churches now house popular Mexican and Central American images of Christ and the virgin. These become important settings through which migrants nurture identity collectively, with religious companionship that transcends ethnic and national boundaries. Although Roman Catholics have long brought images of regional saints and icons from their home communities to the United States, a renewed interest has surfaced in recent years, in large part because of the large scale and sustained immigration from Mexico and Latin America.[20]

Mexican and Central Americans in the United States have transformed many of the churches housing regional images into shrines and popular sacred places where they can express their votive offerings and practice other religious rituals. And churches are accommodating popular devotional practices of these Catholic newcomers.[21] For many Central Americans and especially for Mexicans, the Virgin of Guadalupe is their everyday companion, and their cultural identification with her often trumps religious affiliation. Her protective arms reach easily across borders. As Timothy Matovina, an expert on Latino Catholicism, observes, "She represents the coming together of the indigenous and the Spaniard . . . More than Christians, Mexicans are Guadalupanos."[22] On December 12, the feast day of Our Lady of Guadalupe, migrants descend on shrines dedicated to the virgin throughout the United States to give thanks for their many migration milestones. On the same day, more than a thousand miles away, similar religious practices unfold at the mother shrine in Mexico City. In a small border town located along the Rio Grande, believers pay their respects and leave offerings of thanks to La Virgen de San Juan del Valle, a replica of the image of Our Lady of San Juan de los Lagos in Jalisco, Mexico. Images of El Señor de Esquipulas from Guatemala are revered by followers in the San Antonio Cathedral of San Fernando, California, the oldest cathedral in the United States, as well as the sanctuary of Our Lord of Esquipulas in Chimayo, New Mexico. Saints, once bound by local place, have become increasingly transnational and appropriated by believers throughout the world.[23]

So important are these icons to the faith and religious identities of Mexican and Central American communities in the United States that parish priests and the church hierarchy in Mexico, Guatemala, El Salvador, and Honduras accommodate their transnational followers by regularly bringing images of patron saints with them when visiting and tending to migrant communities and their places of worship in the United States. In 2003, for example, Cardinal Oscar Rodríguez of Honduras and his aide, Father Carlo Magno, the vicar of the Cathedral of Tegucigalapa, escorted the patroness of Honduras, the Virgin of Sayupa, to Honduran communities and sister parishes in Los Angeles and Houston during the week surrounding her feast day of February 3. "The Virgin went to visit her children in the United States," Cardinal Rodríguez said.[24] Several years earlier and a few days before the November 21 feast day of El Salvador's patroness, the Virgin of Peace, Bishop Angel Marajn of San Miguel and several of his aides carried an image of the tiny virgin to her faithful and sister parishes in Washington, D.C., home to one of the largest Salvadoran immigrant communities in the United States.[25]

Sometimes local community organizations facilitate cross-border religious activities with the church hierarchy and local parishes in Mexico and the United States. Among their activities is appropriating cherished images of patron saints from home communities and bringing them to the faithful in the United States. Often these images are linked to the plight of migrants.[26] For example, to identify publicly with the plight of the undocumented migrant, these sacred images sometimes take the same dangerous journey that their devotees traveled. In 2002, for example, 250 migrant runners took turns escorting two painted images of Our Lady of Guadalupe and Juan Diego overland from the mother shrine in Mexico City to her new home in Saint Patrick's Cathedral in New York City so that those who could not return to honor her could "be with her here."[27] Following the centuries old Mexican tradition of *antorcha* (the torch run), runners travel the length of Mexico, cross the U.S-Mexico border, and continued through eighteen U.S. states, a 3,133-mile journey, before arriving in New York on December 12, the feast day honoring Our Lady of Guadalupe.[28] The run is organized and sponsored by the Tepeyac Association of New York, a group of thirty community organizations advocating on behalf of Latino immigrants in the city, and in cooperation with church hierarchy and local parishes in Mexico and the United States, and provides a religious venue for Latino communities across the country to "display their identity," as the association's leader commented. Increasingly, Latino religious communities in the United States, like the Asociación Tepeyac in New York, view their mission as one that crosses borders: promoting civic engagement among immigrants in the United States while continuing to aid those in their home communities.

Migrants themselves participate in transnational rituals and form organizations and brotherhoods outside their homelands to bring their patron saints to them, to re-create the presence of their saints, so that the faithful in their new homes can honor them through established customs such as annual processions and everyday votive practices. In this sense, immigrants do not have to travel to the shrine to feel the presence of their revered icons. Second-generation Ticuanense in New York participate in religious rituals that commemorate their patron saint to identify with their Mexican home community.[29] Participants in Charismatic Catholic groups, for example, provide Dominicans with a sense of identity that works in multiple geographic locations.[30] The Peruvian Brotherhood of the Lord of Miracles regularly reproduces the procession to the Lord of Miracles to help Peruvian migrants maintain religious solidarity with their patron saint, as well as to create a distinctive public space for them.[31] The Hermandad of Hermano Pedro, a brotherhood discussed earlier, organizes religious festivals and celebrations in honor of Hermano Pedro that are attended by established and newcomer Guatemalan residents in communities throughout the United States. Moreover, in their collective and individual vigils, Hermano Pedro's global community of believers commemorate the plight of his undocumented followers as they pray over their petitions requesting assistance on their journeys.

Immigrants also reproduce their revered icons in their own images. Following the trail taken by many of her followers, each spring a twelve-inch wooden image of La Virgin de Zapopan is escorted from her hometown shrine in Guadalajara, Mexico, to Los Angeles, where throngs of believers welcome her.[32] They then escort her to Santa Isabel Parish in East Los Angeles. During her ten-day sojourn in the city, crowds of pilgrims descend upon the shrine. Her visit concludes with a procession in downtown Los Angeles during which her Plexiglas-encased image is carried by followers led by Aztec dancers. Sometimes the identities of these patron saints and the devotional practices to honor them are transformed to reflect the plight of the migrants and the undocumented status that has been imposed on them by the state and others.

In the spring of 2006, at the request of the Guatemalan community in Los Angeles, the Los Angeles-based Brotherhood of Esquipulas arranged for the consecration of an image of the Black Christ in St. Cecilia's Church in Los Angeles, a popular place of worship for many Guatemalans, Hondurans, and Salvadorans living in the area. Four Guatemalan members of the Brotherhood of Esquipulas carried on their backs over thousands of miles, from Guatemala to Los Angeles, a life-size image of their beloved Cristo Negro de Esquipulas. To commemorate the dangerous journey that many of his followers in Los Angeles had taken, the icon's escorts hired a Mexican coyote to take them across the U.S.-Mexico border, and in honor of those who crossed before them, renamed the image El Cristo Mojado, the Undocumented Christ. The journey took five days and, along the way, as is customary for many migrants journeying without papers, the group paid bribes to officials to assure safe passage.

The brotherhood had worked closely with the Asociacíon de Fraternidades Guatemaltecas (Association of Guatemalan Fraternities) and the church hierarchy in Guatemala and Los Angeles to bring the image of El Cristo Negro to his followers in Los Angeles. Subsequently, Catholic hierarchy in Guatemala arranged for the transportation of blessed images of the Virgin Mary, Mary Magdalene, and St. John to flank the Christ on the altar in his new home. On September 6, 2006, the Guatemalan metropolitan archbishop, Monseignor Rodolfo Quezada, and his aides traveled to Los Angeles where they joined Cardinal Roger Mahoney of Los Angeles and the local vicar of St. Cecilia's. Together they performed the ceremony of consecrating the images to an audience of almost three thousand devotees. Following the ceremony, a blend of indigenous Maya and Catholic religious practices celebrated the arrival of the Undocumented Christ and created a cultural space for his followers. For many, the ceremony represented the long-awaited reunion with their national patron from whom they had been separated since leaving their native land.

Summary

The promesa is a powerful force in the northbound migration of many to the United States. Before leaving their home communities to undertake the long and risky journey, most migrants, Catholic and Protestant alike, make vows of reciprocity. In exchange for a safe passage, migrants, their families, and their clergy pledge favors to sacred figures: to privately observe a religious ritual at a home altar; to publicly enter a sacred place on one's knees to demonstrate a sacrifice; to send an ex-voto of thanks to a religious shrine in the home community; and/or to observe simultaneous rituals with family in home and host communities. Some migrants promise the extraordinary—to embark on a costly and long pilgrimage to the home community to thank their protector personally and to leave an ex-voto drawing, a lock of hair, or other cherished object as fulfillment of the vow.

Migrants may temporarily fulfill these promises by visiting shrines that house replicas of familiar images that have been brought to the United States by other migrants, priests from home communities, and international brotherhoods. Sometimes immigrant devotees reproduce their revered icons in their own images, which indirectly promote civic engagement and common membership that cuts across ethnic and national groups. In recent years some of these images have been transformed by followers to reflect the plight of the undocumented people that honor them.

The promise is not completely fulfilled until the migrant returns home to pay homage to the sacred figure in the original shrine in which the pledge was made. By then vows of reciprocity have been transformed by new achievements and milestones for which the migrant may be thankful as well. These, too, are included in the promises that have now been transformed through the migration experience, becoming more expansive over time and all powerful in helping the migrant sustain ties to the homeland. In this way, promises nurture spirituality through the journey and beyond.

CHAPTER 6

Conclusion

Myrna left her home in El Salvador in 1990. Before departing for the dangerous overland journey to the United States, her mother gave her a cross to wear for protection and then together they went to the local church to pray. She, her cousin, and a friend traveled by bus to San Salvador and by air to Mexico City, where they planned to meet the coyote who would guide them through Mexico and across the Mexico-Texas border. While in Mexico City, the trio made their way to the Basilica of the Virgin of Guadalupe, where they joined other pilgrims and made their way to the image to pray for their safety. At the basilica's store, Myrna's cousin and friend bought holy cards of the virgin to accompany them on their journey. Myrna chose not to purchase a religious memento, instead relying on the cross given to her by her mother and on the presence of God, who she said is always in her heart and soul. The trip from El Salvador to Washington, D.C., their final destination, took several weeks. Along the trial, they experienced exhaustion, heat, and hunger, but survived, as she said, through God's will. Since Myrna's arrival in Washington, she has married, become a naturalized citizen, visited her mother in El Salvador, and arranged for her son to join her in the United States. She credits her safe journey and all her subsequent migration milestones to God.

Each year hundreds of thousands of unauthorized migrants come to the United States in search of work. Most are poor laborers from Mexico and the Central American countries of Honduras, Guatemala, and El Salvador, who usually have no recourse but to leave behind family and community and attempt the increasingly dangerous journey. Until now, scholars have explained their migration undertaking and experiences along the journey in economic and social terms, reflecting in large part the type of questions social scientists have developed to understand and justify migration experiences. I, too, found that under questioning, most migrants will cite some combination of push-pull economic factors to explain their migration, such as declining opportunities in the home community coupled with higher wages in the United States; when asked why they migrated to a particular U.S. town or city, they most often told me the choice was made because of friends and family who live there. But when I asked how they managed to survive the hardships of the crossing, their most frequent and fervent answer was, "God's help."

This book has focused on an unexplored dimension of the migration undertaking—the powerful influence of religion. Religion does not explain why the individual people decided to migrate, nor does it directly determine whether they successfully made it to the United States. Yet, as a powerful guiding, coping, protective, and mediating force, religion did shape how these migrants formed their decisions, how they decided on the timing of their departures, how they experienced the journey, and ultimately how they made sense of their place in the migration process. And, for some, their faith, expressed in the everyday religious and cultural practices along the migrant trail, and with the help of mediating religious institutions that provided for them, did, in fact, fortify them with the willpower to persevere and ultimately reach the United States.

To date, historic and contemporary literature on religion and migration has focused on how religious institutions shape the immigrants' incorporation experience, highlighting how places of worship comfort newcomers and ease their adaptation to the United States, while at the same time helping them to maintain their ethnic roots and stay connected to their homelands.[1] In their comprehensive survey of the scholarship on religion and migration, Alejandro Portes and Ruben Rumbaut show that the classic and contemporary literature offers abundant accounts of the buffering, integrative, and at times transformative roles of religion in immigrant incorporation. Absent from this scholarship are any studies devoted to how religion interacts with earlier stages of the migration process, in sending communities and along the journey.[2] In *Migration Miracle* I have illustrated the powerful reflexive role of religion in earlier and unexplored stages of the migration process, including decision making and the departure, the journey, and the arrival. I have also shown how religion—in its role as protector, companion, and mediator in the migration undertaking—is itself transformed, becoming stronger and more dynamic during the course of the journey.

Within this larger narrative, I have portrayed migrants as agents in the creation and transformation of religious and cultural practices, highlighting the centrality of practices that Central American and Mexican migrants perform outside the structure of organized churches, in sacred spaces, in public displays of commemoration, in the privacy of their homes, and in the long stretches of the northbound journey. For many Latinos, including migrants, religion is foremost about practicing folk, popular, and domestic activities that, while influenced by institutional context, are often expressed in ways that are shaped by place, time, and circumstance.[3] Reaching beyond traditional church membership lines, prospective and journeying migrants alike often undertake these cultural and everyday religious practices with those they most often depend on and have come to know and trust—spiritual companions, family, clergy, community, and fellow travelers. Thus this study not only moves beyond the story of religion in the settlement and adaptation experience of immigrants, but also represents a departure from denominational, congregational and institutional studies that have dominated much research on religion and migration.[4]

In this final chapter I revisit the stages of migration and discuss the ways in which the religious dimension of migration interacts with its economic, social and cultural dimensions. Within this discussion I highlight what I believe are the major mechanisms and processes through which religious institutions and local clergy, but especially the everyday religious and cultural practices of migrants, influence how and when migrants make the decision to migrate, prepare for the undertaking, negotiate the journey, and ultimately understand and interpret their migration experiences.

Religion as Guide and Support

Neoclassical theory and the new economics of migration are models that rely primarily on economic factors to explain why people move. According to these microlevel accounts, individuals alone or in conjunction with family members in the home community make a cost-benefit analysis between the places of origin and potential destinations, including an assessment of intervening factors, the psychological costs of leaving family and community, and the difficulty of making the trip; they migrate if the net benefit anticipated—usually higher wages—is greater at the destination.[5] Network theory complements economic models of decision making and broadens the social actors involved in decision making.[6] According to network theory, when migrants are all set to move, they will, if they can, activate their personal networks at areas of destination. That is, once the network connections linking sending and receiving communities reach a critical level, prospective departing migrants draw on the assistance provided by friends and family in the United States, which reduces the costs of migration and initiates departure. Cultural models of migration incorporate community tradition into the decision making process. According to the culture of migration explanation, in migrant sending communities with an established history and strong tradition of international migration, aspirations to migrate are elevated, and for many young adults the event becomes a rite of passage.[7]

Yet the decision to migrate in the contemporary world is even more complex than presented in economic or social network models of decision making. For the undocumented migrants in this study, intervening factors weighed painfully on their minds. The psychological cost of leaving family in the face of a real possibility of not seeing them again because of the risks of crossing two heavily-guarded borders was a fundamental consideration. Thus the decision as to whether to migrate was too great to leave solely to self or family. Even the practical help of seasoned family and friends in receiving communities could not resolve the balance of enormous psychological and human costs. In other words, the social capital—financial assistance and information about the journey—derived from the migrants' personal social networks seemed insufficient to substantially reduce the physical and psychological costs associated with today's more dangerous journey. As a result, these migrants increasingly turned to religion and its resources for spiritual support and guidance in the decision-making process, and clergy and places of worship in home communities adapted to the needs of their flock.

The presence of religion as a source of guidance and support reveals itself to different degrees and in various ways during the decision-making process that evolves as migrants' considerations shift with changing sets of opportunities, attitudes, and social relations.[8] Throughout these deliberations, migrants regularly turn to God and to clergy for counsel and sustenance. For some, this will consist of saying simple prayers for safety and fortitude, but for others who have a strong religious foundation in their home communities, the religious interaction is much greater and more intense—even to the point of perceiving divine intervention via a "sign" or "message from God" indicating that migration plans may move forward. The very religious may postpone trips until they receive these messages. Among migrants in this study, divine signs or messages took many forms, ranging from confirmation through reading the Scriptures, to approval by a local pastor, to endorsement from a family member, to securing a coyote and even borrowing a visa. Signs can be variable and are influenced by faith, place, and culture. Signs are important not only because people believe in them but because they are powerful agents of action, in this case influencing the timing of migration.[9]

Religion as a guiding and supporting force reveals itself in the second stage of the migration undertaking—leave taking. The decision to leave is more than an individual or household affair. Migrants rely heavily on migration counseling from those they know and trust: local clergy. Approval from local clergy, often in the form of final blessings, offers enormous psychological empowerment to prospective migrants. These official blessings constitute a spiritual travel permit that, in the mind of the receiver, may come close to if not exceed the value of an official visa or passport. Migration counseling sanctions what is otherwise an unauthorized act. So powerful is their faith in God's sanction that it is invoked in a popular Guatemalan ballad, "El Mojado" ("The Wetback"). The following verse was recounted to me by Aleksy: "If the universal visa is extended the day that we are born and expires at the time of our death, then why do they persecute you, el mojado, since the consulate of the heavens already gave you permission?"[10]

Migrants and their families are active agents in leave-taking rituals, practicing, reproducing, and even transforming popular religious rituals so that revered saints and icons will guide and accompany migrants on their journeys and so that travelers may remain connected to homeland and family. Like most of the religious practices observed by the migrants in this study, departure rituals are strongly shaped by place and culture. In rural Catholic communities in Mexico and Central America, for example, many mothers light candles and place them on a homemade altar alongside a revered icon before a family member's departure, and keep the flame burning until their child's safe arrival, providing hope, presence, and finality for the journeying migrant.

Migrants and their families also seek protection on the journey by traveling the sacred geography of their homelands, making pilgrimages to national and local shrines and sacred places seeking counsel before departure. These pilgrimages are also influenced by faith and culture. In evangelical sending communities in Guatemala and elsewhere, prospective migrants turn to ayunos, retreats, and prayer camps to prepare for the journey.[11] In Catholic communities throughout Central America and Mexico, departing migrants often make pilgrimages to familiar shrines where they deposit petitions requesting safety during their trip and well-being for their families, and make promises to national and local saints in exchange for safe travel.

The caretakers of these shrines and other churches throughout the region have also created rituals and transformed sacred images to mark the departures of their flock and to encourage them to stay close to home and to their faith. In this sense religious institutions in sending communities foster spirituality and sustain emigration. Recognizing that migration is a way of life in their communities and motivated to keep their flocks linked to the home community, local dioceses, parishes, and the priests who care for these shrines increasingly accommodate emigration. In many parishes, clergy counsel migrants and provide departing blessings to them. In many parishes throughout Mexico and in some sending communities in El Salvador and Honduras, clergy celebrate the Day of the Migrant to commemorate in part the hardships that journeying migrants endure; the Day of the Absent Sons is celebrated to provide solace to parents and to encourage a homecoming. Increasingly, dioceses, churches, and clergy have adapted to the realities of undocumented migration and the dangers of the migrant trail. Some churches and shrines also promote migration devotion through framing migration miracles, and profit from its material aspects by selling to migrants physical mementos—medals, devotionals, scapulars—to comfort them on their long trek north. Local religious leaders, especially in well-established sending communities, also promote migration by incorporating the plight of migrants into their weekly services and transforming and then framing local saints as protectors and companions of migrants.[12] In Santa Ana Guadalupe, the local diocese transformed St. Toribio, a martyr of the Cristero Wars, into a coyote saint, thus providing a powerful spiritual and moral narrative for undocumented migrants.

Devotion to saints to commemorate the plight of the migrant, however, is not always bound by place, time, and in the control of the church. Hermano Pedro, for example, has been symbolically appropriated from the local shrine in Antigua, Guatemala, by his believers and transformed into a transnational saint, worshipped by members of a global brotherhood who pray for the safe passage of undocumented followers. Other times, churches and religious leaders in sending and receiving communities work across borders and with these transnational brotherhoods to mark the danger of the journey and commemorate the migrants. In some cases, the journey is reproduced by the migrant at the spiritual level and fortified by the church.[13] In other cases, the dangers of the journey are symbolized by holy images and icons actually carried on undocumented journeys, such as was done in the 2003 trek by foot and bus of El Cristo Mojado (the Undocumented Christ) from his home in

Esquipulas, Guatemala, across two international borders, to the largely Latino congregation of St. Cecilia Church in Los Angeles, California. Created in the image of the undocumented, these holy figures tell us much about the ways in which migrants turn to religion for the strength to leave all they hold dear and embark on the uncertain journey that will carry them to a new land.

Religion as Mediator

The significance of social networks in reducing the costs of migration extends beyond decision making to the journey. Scholars have largely conceptualized the journey from Central America and Mexico to the United States as a social process and have used social network theory to explain how unauthorized migrants gain entry into the United States. Social networks consisting of family and friends, built on notions of trust and reciprocity, provide journeying migrants with the companionship of seasoned travelers, contacts, and information about how to cross, sometimes including access to coyotes.[14] Sometimes these networks are so powerful that they overcome attempts by the state to control migration.[15]

Yet, as many scholars have noted, migrant networks are not foolproof. Like all human relationships, they can change over time and, under particular circumstances, can weaken and erode. Sometimes seasoned migrants exploit their newcomer counterparts. Other times, because of gender inequalities and sex-based work patterns, networks may provide differential resources to group members. Moreover, under conditions of poverty and marginality, these networks may be inaccessible to many, or they may be unable to provide resources to those who need them. In short, in particular situations, migrants' personal networks simply cannot deliver the social capital that the literature assumes.[16]

The means and strains of the undocumented journey further test the weakness of migrants' networks. The increased enforcement in recent years along the US.-Mexico and Mexico-Guatemala borders has raised the human costs of undocumented migration, resulting in enhanced risks of physical and social problems, including death. Because the crossing experience has become more dangerous and more expensive, seasoned family and friends are far more reluctant than in the past to accompany first-time crossers or are unable to provide the necessary social and financial support to mitigate danger. Migrants who possess the financial resources (which network members often supply) rely increasingly on the crossing services of both trusted and unfamiliar coyotes who have grown in number and kind and have raised their fees according to demand.[17] Yet, as this study demonstrates, many first-time crossing migrants, especially young, unattached, and unseasoned migrants from Central America, do not have access to either personal networks or financial resources to hire coyotes to assist them on their journeys. Lacking the social protection and support that family, friends, and even coyotes provide, many transit migrants suffer at the hands of gangs, corrupt officials, and predatory coyotes, all of whom are part of a for-profit transit migration industry that exploits the conditions of transit migration in the context of fortified borders. The migration industry that operates along the migrant trail from Central America to the United States represents a local and contemporary expression of a global enterprise composed of for-profit entrepreneurs and businesses, often with the participation of national governments that provide services to facilitate and sustain international labor migration.[18]

It is at this juncture in the migration process that religion as mediator takes on importance. The changing conditions and social infrastructure of the undocumented journey—disrupted and weak personal networks, militarized borders and increased dangers, the rise of a migration industry that preys on transit migrants—has resulted in the growth of religious and humanitarian organizations that provide for transit migrants. Many migrants, lacking the resources or personal networks to assist them in their travels, now turn to churches, shelters, and religious workers to perform network functions. In recent years, these organizations have become part of the social infrastructure that sustains transit migration in the region. As the number of transit and returning migrants has increased in the region, so has the number and type of institutional resources available. Once limited to occasional churches offering migrants help, now multiple organizations, churches, and migrant programs along the migratory route provide for the needs of journeying and deported migrants. These social actors and the social capital they provide are important in understanding how the undocumented navigate the journey and crossing experiences, a process that has largely been explained through social network theory.

Faith-based shelters provide numerous services to migrants to facilitate their journey north. First and foremost, these faith-based and humanitarian migrant programs provide direct material assistance in the way of food, shelter, clothing, and medical attention. But these shelters and the faith workers who staff them do more than offer material assistance. They also provide migrants with the spiritual, psychological, and social capital to continue on their journey. The clergy who care for these shelters offer services, blessings, and counsel to migrants to sanction their migration, help them endure the separation from family and community, and fortify them for the hardships of the remaining journey. Prayer and consultation with clergy along the journey gives meaning to suffering and strength to persevere and continue. From trusted faith workers and lay staff who run the shelters, migrants learn about the dangers of crossing international borders and, in some cases, are directed to alternative and safer routes than they would otherwise use. At these shelters, migrants also receive devotionals that include a directory of shelters and legal services that migrants may draw on if necessary during their journey, when human support alone is not enough to sustain the travelers through the hardship of the journey. Indeed, sometimes these small religious items are the only things found in the pockets of dead migrants pulled from the Rio Grande or picked up in the Arizona deserts.

New migrant-based networks are also created and nourished along the journey. Migrant shelters such as the Scalabrini Casas del Migrante offer a networking resource to transit migrants where they can connect with one another and exchange ideas and information about the journey. From deportees who are returned to the shelters by government officials who rely on the shelters, unseasoned migrants learn the ropes of crossing the border. Those who travel alone sometimes link up with other migrants at these shelters. Such nonkin migrant networks, forged in the shelters, buffer against the disruption and isolation, offering solidarity, social support, and protection on the road. They also provide first-time emigrants with access to a host of emotional, psychological, and material resources, from companionship to financial help from their more seasoned fellow travelers. In sum, religious institutions and organizations assume a constant mediating role in the migration process. They provide guidance and counsel to departing migrants in sending communities, material assistance, social capital, and spiritual sustenance on the journey, and, as others have found, comfort and assistance on arrival.

Religion as Sanctuary and Advocate

Religious organizations in the region that provide for the needs of undocumented travelers have also become advocates for the rights of migrants and watchdogs of state policy. At multiple levels of church hierarchy, from bishops conferences to interfaith organizations, to local churches and shelters in Central America, Mexico, and along the U.S.-Mexico border, faith workers are increasingly involved in issues of human rights and international and transit migration that often challenge the rights of states to regulate and control migration. Transnational in scope, the public face of these organizations and their mobilization efforts have grown substantially in recent years as they have developed their own migrant programs and human rights offices along the migrant trail, from Guatemala to the southwest United States. Motivated by a theology of migration, and advocacy for the rights of migrants to cross borders to find work, these religious workers and the transnational hierarchies in which they operate have emerged as important vehicles for contesting nation-state activities and monitoring the regulatory practices of state institutions and policies. They challenge the state by documenting human rights abuses and the crossing risks associated with current border enforcement policies.[19] These organizations have become so effective that in some countries, such as Mexico and Guatemala, governments invite them to the table when formulating migration policy. Along the U.S-Mexico border, cross-border interfaith coalitions challenge U.S. immigration policy by providing humanitarian assistance to crossing migrants and encouraging social and political protest among followers.[20]

Collectively, these religious groups and organizations assume an important responsibility in the organization of undocumented migration in the region and their activities suggest the emergence of a new cross-border sanctuary movement that resists state policy. This new movement is unlike the Sanctuary Movement in the 1980s in the southwest United States and southern Mexico, which was largely limited to national efforts and geared toward providing refuge for Central Americans fleeing political strife.[21] Today's sanctuary efforts transcend national borders, focusing on the human rights of transit migrants and receiving the sanction of multiple levels of church hierarchy, from the Vatican to transnational religious congregations, bilateral bishops conferences and diocesan efforts, and local religious workers. In the absence of a retreat in state enforcement policy, these sanctuary efforts are unlikely to recede as they constitute a countervailing refuge from the transit migration industry and military operations with which they share the migratory route.

Religion as Companion

Yet migrants are not always able to find sanctuary on the road. To understand how they cope with the despair and danger along the trail we must shift attention from the mediating role of institutional actors and examine how, as

Peter Berger suggests, individuals live through religion to find meaning and create order in times of crisis.[22] This change in perspective reflects the agency component of the migration experience and also constitutes what scholars call "everyday religion," or "lived religion."[23] Religion as practiced emphasizes how people in particular social contexts live with or through the religious idioms available to them.

To help them with the loneliness, despair, and danger, undocumented migrants do indeed live religion on the road—both as a means to survive and as a way to find meaning in the journey. The ways in which migrants live their religion on the journey reveal much about their undocumented identity and the struggles that shape their individual and collective experiences. During their long journey across nations and over mountains and deserts they turn to the familiar and reproduce, borrow, and even create a rich diversity of cultural and religious practices to help them cope and ultimately survive their migration. Indeed, as large numbers of migrants told me, their faith was their sustenance during the journey and their relationship with their revered icons was strongest then, when they were stripped of all resources, including the identities they had left behind in their home communities.

When feasible, migrants turn to churches and clergy for help and blessings that fortify them for the path ahead, when specific religious affiliations become increasingly less relevant as Protestants and Catholics, believers and nonbelievers alike, turn to the same clergy and pray under the same roof. More often than not, however, journeying migrants practice religion outside the institutional walls of churches and their representatives. While some visit shrines and popular saints recognized specifically for protecting migrants, others spontaneously erect popular shrines to revered icons from their home communities to reproduce those cultural practices with which they are most familiar and comfortable. Many rely on their spiritual companions for protection, the images pasted on holy cards carried in their pockets or engraved on medallions worn around their necks. Recall Arturo in chapter 4, the young Honduran who purchased an international phone card adorned with the image of his revered Virgen de Guadalupe. Though the phone account had long been spent by the time he showed it to me in 2003, the laminated card remains safely in his wallet where Arturo has kept it since the day he had purchased it some two years before.

Migrants also draw on their memories and recreate companions, engraving their images on stone features. Some, facing the possibility of impending death, turn to group prayer and later interpret their rescue or successful journey as a miracle from God. These miracles provide meaning and hope to migrants who believe their trips have been sanctioned by God. They also propel and sustain action by providing migrants the psychological will to move forward. Migrants also leave religious artifacts—rosaries, devotionals, crosses—along the journey as personal testimonies of faith and markers of their imposed undocumented identities.

Religion as the Link to Past and Future

After arriving in the United States, the migrants in this study continued to make sense of their migration experience through religion, drawing once again on familiar cultural practices. A number of migrants, like Samuel, described their migration outcomes in religious terms and interpreted their safe arrival as divine intervention: "If God and La Virgen didn't want me here, I wouldn't have survived the journey and I wouldn't be here talking to you now." Some, then, believe that religion actually made migration happen, and so in return for protection and safe passage to the United States they now must pay their debts to God, the virgin, or a saint. These devotional rituals manifest themselves over time and through multiple individual, family, and group activities, most of which occur without institutional support. Some observe a ritual at a home altar; others enter a sacred place on their knees in a sign of reverence and sacrifice; still others send ex-votos of thanks to a religious figure in the home community.[24] Many migrants pledge the extraordinary: to return home one day to give thanks to their revered icon. While unable to do so because of their undocumented identity, some will call on family members, such as Aleksy, who asked her mother to perform this ritual for her. "I couldn't make the trip, but she could in my place," Aleksy said. "Now I send her money each year to make the pilgrimage where she regularly thanks El Cristo Negro for my safety, Emilio's safety [her brother who has since joined Aleksy in North Carolina], and the good fortune of our lives."

Yet immigrants do not need to go to shrines in their home communities to feel the presence of their saints. They can visit churches in the United States where images of their revered icons have been reproduced by believers. In these re-created shrines they come to give temporary thanks for safe passage. So important are these icons to the faith and the religious practices and identities of Mexican and Central American communities in the United States that parish priests and the church hierarchy in sending and receiving communities regularly arrange for images of patron saints to be brought to immigrant communities and their places of worship in the United States. Sometimes immigrant devotees reproduce their revered icons in their own images. As this book has shown, the plight of the undocumented has been personified in the construction of popular saints such as St. Toribio and Juan Soldado, whose followers believe them to be protectors of migrants, and the dangers of the border crossing are symbolized by holy images and icons actually carried on undocumented journeys, such as was done in the 2003 trek of El Cristo Mojado.

Facing an uncertain period of family separation and life in the shadows of an illegal residency, the act of fulfilling the promise enables undocumented migrants to maintain an ongoing sense of belonging to their home communities, to their faith, and to their culture. In this sense, promises reach across time and space, linking past with future and children with their parents. Some migrants, like Cecilia, are unable to make it home for a year or more. With the passage of time vows of reciprocity are transformed by new achievements for which the migrant may be thankful as well. These are also included and in this way the promises are transformed into processes that nurture spirituality through the journey and beyond.

Faith Reaffirmed

At each stage of the migration process, many migrants practice familiar cultural and religious acts to cope with the traumas of the undocumented journey. With each religious practice and each small success along the way their faith is reaffirmed. Religious institutions in sending communities and on the migrant trail promote and foster this spirituality. In unexpected ways, then, the migration journey strengthens and intensifies religious commitment and becomes a spiritual journey. It is this strengthened faith that then fortifies migrants with the willpower to persevere and ultimately reach the United States. Fulfilling the promesa represents the final religious marker in the journey, but faith persists long past this ritual act. In a new and sometimes hostile land, migrants continue to seek refuge and find solace in the familiar. None of those in the study completely abandoned their faith after arriving in the United States, though some converted while others "mixed and matched" religious practices and denominations.[25] While some reported attending formal religious services with less frequency over time, most continued to practice their religion away from institutionalized settings. Faith and the construction and reproduction of familiar cultural and religious practices help many migrant believers not only endure their journeys but also face challenges and overcome misfortunes as they struggle forward in the United States; the sense of still being a part of their home communities and the spiritual fabric of their lives there, provides a powerful anchoring and integrative force during the psychological and emotional disruptions of adaptation. The narrative told in this book helps us to understand why, for many, migration is very much a religious experience.[26]

Certainly Cecilia believes her relationship with God accounts for escape from the deadly Arizona desert and the success she and her husband now enjoy: they eventually moved from California to their current home in New York where they joined family and friends who had already settled in the emerging Mexican community in Newburg. There, Cecilia and Juan have thrived. They became active members of a local Catholic Church that provides religious and social services for the Mexican residents in the area, and Cecilia helped form the church-sponsored Mexican folk dancing group that has performed around the state. She believes it has helped her maintain her Mexican and Catholic identity. Cecilia established her own domestic cleaning business and Juan became a cook and then a truck driver. Together, they bring home $6,000 a month, all through legal means. They have one young son and another on the way. She admits that she is no longer as active in her church as she once was, but still attends services and prays every day to God and La Virgen de Guadalupe. Despite all her good fortune since settling in the United States, she has never forsaken her "guardian angels" who she believes made it all possible. It was only natural, then, that Cecilia should include her good fortune in observances of thanks at the local church when she made the pilgrimage home to Puebla in 2006 after receiving her green card. Cecilia, like others, credits her success in the United States to her faith, which she says has grown deeper and stronger through the migration experience. "If you have faith," Cecilia insists, "you can do anything."

NOTES

REFERENCES

ACKNOWLEDGMENTS

INDEX

Notes

Introduction

1. Personal interview with Pastor Sapon in his home, San Cristóbal, Totonicapán, Guatemala, June 2000.
2. Hagan (2002); Hagan and Ebaugh (2003).
3. Eschbach, Hagan, Rodriguez, Hernández-León and Bailey (1999); Eschbach, Hagan, and Rodriguez (2003); U.S. General Accountability Office (2006); Sapkota et al (2005); Massey, Durand, and Malone (2003).
4. Handlin (2002).
5. Smith (1978, pp. 1155–1185; quotation from p. 1175).
6. Handlin (2002); Herberg (1955).
7. Handlin (2002).
8. Ebaugh and Chafetz (2000); Levitt (2007); Wuthnow (2005); Warner and Wittner (1998); Bankston and Zhou (1996); Ammermon (2005). For a review of the research on the role of religion in the lives of post-1965 immigrants in the United States, see Cadge and Ecklund (2007). Also see Hirschman (2004). For research on the role of religion and spirituality in the adaptation of refugees and other forced migrant populations, see a special issue of *Journal of Refugee Studies* (2002), edited by Gozdziak and Shandy.
9. Wuthnow (2005); Kurien (1998); Warner and Warner (1998). Also see Cadge and Eckland (2007) for a synthesis of the literature on immigration, religion, and ethnicity in the United States today.
10. See Levitt (2004; 2005; 2007) for overviews of literature that look at religion from a transnational perspective.
11. For an overview of religion in Latin America, and particularly the popular and orthodox practices of poor Latin Americans, see Martin (1990); Burdick and Hewitt (2000); Smilde (2007); Levine (1986; 1992); Stoll (1990); Garrard-Burnett (1998); Berryman (1987; 1996); Chestnut (1997); Cleary (1985).
12. Van Dijk (1997).
13. Hagan (2006; 2007); Fitzgerald (2008); Espinosa (1999; 2000); Martinez (2001).
14. Coutin (1993); García (2006).

15. See, e.g., Handlin (1951); Herberg (1955); Dolan (1975); Greeley (1972); Menjívar (2003); Ebaugh and Chafetz (2000); Ebaugh and Pipes (2001).
16. Durand and Massey (1995).
17. Hagan (2002); Hagan and Ebaugh (2003).
18. This nonofficial and deinstitutionalized dimension of religion, which emerges not from above but from the everyday actions and creative responses of women and men, is sometimes referred to as popular, lived or everyday religion. See Orsi (2002); Hall (1997); Ammerman (2007).
19. The migrant interviews were conducted in Spanish and then translated into English by the interviewers. The interviews with religious leaders and faith workers, which were conducted by me, were done in Spanish in some cases and in English in other cases. For purposes of confidentiality, most of the names of the migrants interviewed have been changed, with the exception of Cecilia, Amelia, Myrna and Aleksy, who asked that their first names be used. All four women were proud of their migration experiences and wanted their children to able to read about them one day. I have used the actual names of clergy and faith workers.
20. Garrard-Burnett (1998); Hagan (1994).
21. Passel (2006).
22. See Passel and Suro (2005) and Passel (2006) for a profile of the unauthorized population in the United States. See Hernández-León and Zúñiga (2005) and Singer (2004) for an overview of new immigrant destinations in the United States.
23. Andreas (2000); Grayson (2002; 2003).
24. Ackerman, Loughna, and Castles (2004); García (2006).
25. Nazario (2006).
26. Cevallos (2007); Ollmos and Muello (2005).
27. Dow (2005) discusses the difficulty in quantifying the growth in Protestantism in Mexico and Central America, arguing that at least part of the problem stems from the different figures provided by anthropological (Stoll 1990) and evangelical (Holland 1997) sources. Nonetheless, as he points out the general trend is an impressive increase in Protestantism, regardless of the source.
28. Stoll and Garrard-Burnett (1993); Wilson (1997); Green (1999); Hallum (2002).
29. Griffith (1987; 1992).
30. The Casa del Migrante in Ciudad Juarez is now under the direction of the Dominicans, and in 2006 Father Pellizzari relocated to Nueuo Loredo, where he directs the city's Casa del Migrante.
31. Huntington (2004); Brimelow (1995).

1. Decision Making and Leave-Taking

1. There is large body of literature that focuses on the ways in which individuals can effectively use religious resources (e.g., prayer, participation in religious institutions) to cope with life problems and circumstances, including health problems, depression and anxiety, and bereavement and loss events. For a com-

prehensive review of this literature and the broader scholarship on the relationship between religion and health, see Chatters (2000).

2. For a comprehensive review of migration theories, see Massey et al. (1993). For a review of macro and micro neoclassical theories, see Todaro (1976); Todaro and Marusko (1987); Ranis and Fei (1961); and Sjaastad (1962). See Stark and Bloom (1985) and Taylor (1986) for "the new economics of migration," and Piore (1979) for dual labor market theory. More recent scholarship on transnational activities also addresses the role of global institutions and organizations, including religious ones, in sustaining international movement. See, e.g., Casanova (1994); Levitt (2001; 2007); Guarnizo and Smith (1998); Ebaugh and Chafetz (2002).

3. See, e.g., Gamio (1930); Macdonald and Macdonald (1974); Lomnitz (1977); Tilly (1978); Roberts (1974).

4. Massey, Alarcón, Durand, and González (1987).

5. Increasingly, scholars recognize that migrants' personal networks reach beyond trusted family and paisanos to include for-profit actors in the migration process, including employers and coyotes. See, e.g., Krissman (2005); Hernández-León (2008); and Spener (2005; 2006; 2007).

6. Kandel and Massey (2002) were the first to document, through quantitative analysis, the existence of a culture of migration in Mexican migrant sending communities, but a tradition of migration has long been described in field studies of migration. See, for example, Mines (1981); Reichart (1981). Others have observed that this tradition may be gendered, in that women and men aspire to migrate for different reasons. (Kandel & Massey 2002; Hondageu-Sotelo 1994; Hagan 1994).

7. An earlier version of parts of this chapter are published in a chapter titled "Faith for the Journey: Religion as Resource" in *A Promised Land, A Perilous Journey: Theological Perspectives on Migration*, eds. Daniel Groody and Gioacchino Campese (Notre Dame, IN: University of Notre Dame Press, 2008). Some of the statistics have been updated and recalculated for this book.

8. This insight into the subjective dimension of human action is often referred to as the "the Thomas Theorem," namely, if people define situations as real, then they are real in their consequences (Thomas and Thomas 1928).

9. International Bible Society (1984).

10. The large majority of the Protestants in the sample were evangelical, who theoretically do not recognize the Virgin Mary or saints in their religious practices, limiting their worship to God.

11. See Lafaye (1976) and Durand and Massey (1995) for a discussion of the long-standing Mexican tradition of veneration icons of God and the virgin. Holy images worshipped by the masses in Mexico did not include the saints and their relics as was the case in Europe and in Central America.

12. For a discussion on the devotion in western Mexico see Giffords (1974). Durand and Massey (1995), in their analysis of migration retablos in western Mexico, identify some of the most important shrines in the area. See also Meyer (1976).

13. Pope John XXIII, *"Pacem in Terris* (Peace on Earth) (April 11, 1963) (Washington, DC: USCCB, 1963), no. 25; USCCB, "Strangers No Longer: Together on the Journey (January 22, 2003).

14. For a survey of the dangers of the Guatemala-Mexico border, see Grayson (2002). For a comparative overview of the dangers experienced by Central American and Mexicans migrants, see Rodriguez (2002; 2007). Menjívar (2000), in her study of Salvadoran migration, also documents the dangers incurred to Salvadorans en route to the United States, including their experiences along the Guatemala-Mexico border. See also Guacin (2003), and Hagan (2006; 2007).

15. For an understanding of the role of social networks in sustaining undocumented migration from Mexico, see Massey, Alarcón, Durand, and González (1987); Massey and Espinosa (1997). See also Singer and Massey (1998) for a discussion of the role of seasoned travelers, including family and friends, in crossing assistance. Menjívar (2000) also demonstrated the important role that family and paisanos in the United States assume in the migration of Salvadorans to the United States. For a similar pattern among the Guatemalan community in Houston, see Hagan (1994, 1998).

16. See also Donato and Patterson (2004).

17. For a discussion of family separation during the Bracero Program, see Chávez (2007). For an analysis of family separation and immigration today, see Hondagneu-Sotelo and Avila (1997); Brycesson and Vuerela (2002); Hagan, Eschbach, and Rodríguez (2008); Salzar Parreñas (2005); Priblisky (2004).

18. See Orsi (1991) for a discussion of the origin and meaning of lighting candles and other devotional practices among Catholic Americans.

19. Numerous shrines and sacred places throughout the region are visited by pilgrims, many of which are not described here. I have included only those major shrines and sacred places repeatedly identified by the study sample or visited by me during the study period.

20. Fitzgerald (2008).

21. Popular devotions have long been a reliable means of revenue for churches. Orsi (1991).

22. In his historical analysis of the Mexican Catholic Church's policies toward emigration, Fitzgerald (2008) reviews a 1920 play, titled *Vamos pal norte!* (Let's Go North), and finds that Toribio was actually very critical of emigration and that returnees were in essence traitors to their homeland. Ironically, as Fitzgerald notes, the last survivors in the Romo family line now reside in California.

23. The 10:30 a.m. mass is the most popular because it was the time at which Father Toribio delivered his *cantamisa* (first mass) nearly eighty years earlier.

24. The three-foot reclining image of the Black Christ, carved from dark balsam wood, dates back to 1595, when the Portuguese sculptor Quiro Catano presented it to the mayor of the city of Esquipulas, who placed it in a church in a mountain valley adjacent to the town of Esquipulus. During the years, the image darkened to its present-day black color, perhaps from the smoke of hundreds of burning candles left by pilgrims. In 1737, the Guatemalan Bishop Pardo de Figuero ordered the basilica built and Christian pilgrims began to flock to the shrine.

25. Celestino and Meyers (1981).
26. Our Lady of Suyapa is believed to have appeared to a young peasant boy. In 1747, on the way home from work in the fields, a young boy and his friend decided to rest along the Piliguin Ravine, a short distance from the village of Suyapa. After awaking from their nap, one of the boys, Alejandro Colindres, found next to him the tiny image of Our Lady carved in cedar wood. The image has been visited by two popes, Pius XII in 1925 when Our Lady of Suyapa was declared patroness of Honduras, and in 1983, when John Paul II visited Honduras.
27. Tradition has it that when the virgin was discovered in 1883, the country was undergoing a civil war. After the discovery of the image, the divided nation made peace and on November 21, now her feast day, the image was named after the peace for which she was credited and placed in the church of San Miguel.
28. Egan (1991).
29. Espin (2000).
30. See also Fitzgerald (2008).

2. The Dangerous Journey

1. Castles and Miller (2003).
2. Although I am concerned in this book with the human costs of U.S. and Mexican enforcement policies, there is a burgeoning literature on the tragedies resulting from enforcement polices in other areas of the world. For example, Jorgen Carling's analysis of Spain's high-tech border (2007), which shares many similarities with the U.S.-Mexico border, shows that as the government increases its enforcement efforts, smuggling routes have become longer, which lead to more migrant deaths.
3. Although there is no single work that systematically and completely explores the multiple types of danger that migrants are exposed to during their journey, there are a number of studies that identify and describe aspects of the increasing dangers associated with undocumented travel from Latin America. Chávez (1992) writes about the undocumented experience in general, including the perilous journey. See Annerino (1999) and Urrea (2004) on the dangers in crossing the desert borderlands. Eschbach and his colleagues began documenting deaths of migrants crossing the Mexico-U.S. border in the mid-1990s (1999; 2001; 2003). Massey, Durand, and Malone have converted these figures into annual death rates (2003). Grayson (2003), Nazarío (2006), and Menjívar (2000) focus on the dangers experienced by undocumented Central American migrants on the journey. Guacin (2003), Angeles Cruz (2003), Casillas (2001), and Chávez (2006) have written on the particular dangers associated with crossing the Mexico-Guatemala border. Urrutia-Rojas and Rodríguez (1997) focus on the particular perils confronting young unaccompanied migrants. Rodríguez and Hagan (2004), Rodríguez (2002), and Liu (2002) provide preliminary comparisons of the comparative risks of Central Americans and Mexicans.
4. Lee (2003).
5. García (1980); Annerino, (1999).

6. Annerino (1999).
7. Eschbach, Hagan, Rodriguez, Hernández-León and Bailey (1999); Eschbach, Hagan, and Rodriguez (2003); Nevins (2002); Reyes, Johnson and Van Sweatingen (2002).
8. Massey, Durand, and Malone (2002).
9. Cornelius (2006).
10. Andreas (2000).
11. Lipton (2006).
12. For a comprehensive overview of these operations and the militarization of the U.S.-Mexico border, see Dunn (1996); Andreas (2000); and Nevins (2002).
13. Eschbach, Hagan, Rodriguez, Hernández-León and Bailey (1999); Massey, Durand, and Malone (2002).
14. With the establishment of the Department of Homeland Security (DHS) in 2003, the Immigration and Naturalization Service (INS) moved from the Department of Justice to the DHS. Its immigration service responsibilities (e.g., naturalization and asylum) became the charge of the U.S. Citizenship and Immigration Services (USCIS), and its enforcement operations (e.g., deportations, investigations) were combined with U.S. customs investigations to create the U.S. Immigration and Customs Enforcement.
15. Eschbach, Hagan, Rodriguez, Hernández-León and Bailey (1999); U.S. Government Accountability Office (2006).
16. Pupouac (2007).
17. Hanson and Spilimbergo (1999); Reyes, Johnson and Van Sweatingen (2002); U.S. Government Accountability Office (1997; 1999; 2001).
18. Andreas (2003).
19. Massey, Durand, and Malone (2003); Massey (2005).
20. U.S. General Accounting Office (1999; 2001; 2006).
21. Spener (2001; forthcoming).
22. The deadliest smuggling attempt along the southwest border occurred in May 2003 when seventeen migrants were found dead in the back of an abandoned tractor-trailer rig in Victoria, Texas, about one hundred miles southwest of the truck's final destination of Houston. Two other migrants died several days later. All nineteen victims died from dehydration, overheating, and suffocation. See Ramos (2005).
23. Archibold (2006).
24. Lipton (2006).
25. We know that just because the United States deports people, it doesn't mean that those people won't return. Mass deportations of Mexicans have always been a regular part of our immigration history. During the Depression and later through Operation Wetback in 1954, the United States deported a million Mexican migrants. This policy was resurrected with the passage of the 1996 Immigration Act. Before 1996 fewer than 50,000 immigrants were deported annually; after the new law added more categories for which immigrants can be deported, deportations increased dramatically, reaching more than 200,000 by 2007. Nonetheless, our research, based on a random sample of three hundred migrants deported to

El Salvador, indicates that these deportations do not permanently remove all deportees but instead simply expand their migration careers. For example, many Salvadoran deportees have established work histories and family ties in this country. Indeed, 52 percent of the deportees in our sample reported that either a spouse or child remained in the United States. Many of these children were born in the United States. These family ties, rarely acknowledged in immigration debates, largely explain why 38 percent of all those interviewed who had been deported intended to return to the United States, while an additional 20 percent had not decided whether to return. See Phillips, Hagan, and Rodriguez (2006) and Hagan, Eschbach, and Rodriguez (2008).

26. This route is also increasingly used by non-Central Americans, including Ecuadorians, Peruvians, Chinese, Indians, and Russians. According to some reports, these groups often fly to Central American countries and then follow the migration route of Central Americans to the United States. See Ackerman, Loughna, and Castles (2004).

27. García (2006).

28. Two groups of Guatemalans are officially permitted to cross the Guatemala-Mexico border: first, Mexican-born children of Guatemalan refugees who were living in exile in Mexico in the 1980s during the armed conflict that swept Guatemala; Second, Guatemalans from the border region that is eligible to apply for local visas to work in Mexico on a temporary basis. See Ackerman, Loughna, and Castles (2004).

29. García (2006).

30. See Ogren (2007) for an overview of the role of the U.S. government in Mexico's enforcement and inspection campaigns along its southern border.

31. Ogren (2007).

32. Flynn (2002).

33. Casillas (2001).

34. Indeed, Mexico's President Fox reportedly assured President Bush that "no terrorists will come through Mexico to go the United States (Brusa, as cited in Ogren 2007).

35. Ackerman, Loughna, and Castles (2004); Cruz (2003).

36. Many of the gang members, considered a product of the civil war in El Salvador, fled to Los Angeles during the crisis and were later deported from the United States. They have since established a visible presence along the El Salvador-U.S. migrant trail where they prey on migrants as they hide in concealed train compartments or jump off the trains as they approach check points.

37. Grayson (2002). Retrived July 2003 from http://www.cis.org/articles/2002/back 702.html.

38. Ortiz Pinchett, as cited in Grayson (2003).

39. Personal interview with Father Flor María Rigoni, Notre Dame University, September 22, 2004.

40. Interviewees were asked to answer all applicable responses to the question, "What kinds of problems did you encounter on the trip?" Besides an "other" option, the problems enumerated were sexual/physical assault; theft/robbery;

problems with law enforcement officials; injury; sickness; extreme temperatures; hunger/ thirst. The first three responses comprise our measure of social dangers, the last four physical dangers.

41. Jeffrey (2002).

42. Thompson and Ochoa (2004); Jeffrey (2002).

43. See, e.g., Guacin (2003); Nazario (2006); Ogren (2007). When the UN Special Rapporteur for Migrants' Rights, Gabriella Rodriguez Pizarro, visited southern Mexico in 2002, she reported that the majority of the detained migrants with whom she spoke reported that they had been detained and extorted by officials (Ogren 2007).

44. Jordan (2004).

45. Organización Internacional para las Migraciones (2002).

46. Guacin (2003).

47. According to personnel at the National Commission of Human Rights (NCHR), a Mexican organization charged with investigating complaints against authorities, some of the abuses that migrants report are at the hands of authorities working with the Mexican National Institute of Migration (Guacin 2003).

48. According to Salvadoran law, any person eighteen years of age may leave the country (Menjívar 2000). Of course, the government stands to benefit from its open emigration stand. Emigration is a source of currency for a country through the remittances it receives from migrants abroad. By some estimates, by the mid-1990s, remittances to El Salvador surpassed national exports as a source of foreign exchange, comprising between 6 and 17 percent of household income (de la Garza, Baraona, Orozco, Pachon, and Pantoja 1997).

49. In her account of Salvadorans journeying to the United States, Menjívar (2000) also reported that some of respondents left the country on flights bound for Mexican cities. This strategy, however, is becoming less of an option for many undocumented Salvadorans and Central Americans more generally, who are now regularly apprehended at major points of entry, including airports, by Mexican officials and sent back across the border, either to Guatemala or their countries of origin. The Mexican enforcement efforts, which are partially financed by the U.S. government, are geared toward curtailing transit migration through the country.

50. Ackerman, Loughna, and Castles (2004).

51. The Chiapas-Mayab railway was acquired by the U.S.-owned Genesee & Wyoming Railroad in 1999. Reportedly, the company has failed to meet the required security measures, and some of the guards hired by the company are known to exploit and abuse migrant passengers (United Nations, as cited in Ogren 2007).

52. Marroquin, as cited in Ogren, 2007:223.

53. According to the Mexican National Institute of Migration (MNIM), during the two-year period, from 2003 to 2005, almost two hundred migrants were injured while riding the trains. See Guacin (2003) for tallies of migrant fatalities and injuries documented by MNIM for the period 2000–2003.

54. Angeles Cruz (2003).

55. In one tragic incident, five migrants riding the train suffocated when the temperature in the locked car in which they were trapped soared above 120 degrees Fahrenheit (Ruiz 2000).

56. Guacin. (2003).

57. Nazario (2006).

58. See, e.g., Donato and Patterson (2004); Casillas Bermúdez (1998); Lopéz Castro (1998); Singer and Massey (1998); Kyle (2000); Kyle and Koslowski (2001).

59. Casillas Bermúdez (1998); Kyle and Koslowski (2001); López Castro (1998); Singer and Massey (1998).

60. For a recent overview of Mexican migration to the United States, including crossing patterns and strategies, see Durand and Massey (2004).

61. Massey (2005).

62. Increased enforcement efforts along the southern borders of Mexico and the United States have further increased migrants' reliance on coyotes. The guides have grown in number, type, and cost, all of which influence the dangers migrants are exposed to when entrusted to their care. In his analysis of *coyotaje* (smuggling practices) along the Texas-Mexico border, Spener (2005; forthcoming) identifies a far more multifaceted coyote or what he refers to as coyotaje—the many different strategies adopted by undocumented migrants that include the hiring of an intermediary to cross the U.S.-Mexico border to work and live in the United States. Spener identifies ten types of coyotaje practiced along the Texas-Mexico border. Some involve little risk for crossing migrants, such as relying on an expensive document rental or working with coyotes who have collaborators within the U.S. border enforcement bureaucracy who will let them pass unobstructed; other strategies pose enormous danger, such as the low-cost fee of hiring a "short distance coyote," whose job it is to take the migrant across the border only, leaving the migrant to rely on his or her wits to survive the long trek on foot around interior immigration checkpoints. As Spener notes (2005, 2007), migrants have long relied on multiple coyotajes to reach the United States. In the contemporary context of a militarized border, the human costs have increased.

63. Other scholars have also documented the rising costs and range of fees paid from Latin America, depending on the type of service and distance involved. See, e.g., Genicot and Senesky (2004); Spener (2001; 2005); and López Castro (1998); Lee (2006); Massey, Durand, and Malone (2003); Massey (2005).

64. The strategies adopted by parents in the sample varied considerably. One Salvadoran mother, for example, secured visas for her and her daughter, which enabled them to travel legally by air to Mexico City. Once there, they stayed with friends until they purchased green cards that belonged to permanent residents of the United States. The arrangements, which cost her about $10,000 (which she was still paying off at the time of the interview), assured her and her daughter a safe trip and reunification with her husband. Several women reported paying multiple trusted coyotes to bring their children to the United States. Most,

however, refused to expose their children to the dangerous journey, and accepted temporary separation as part and parcel of the harsh reality of international labor migration. Tragically, the temporary separation that most parents accepted when they left their families and home communities has evolved, for some, into an increasingly permanent one. Unable to cross freely because of the militarization of the northern and southern borders of Mexico, more parents are either unwilling to expose their children to the perilous journey or to return home for a visit for fear of not being able to cross back into the United States.

3. Churches Crossing Borders

1. Hagan (1987); Aguayo and Fagen (1988).
2. For example, Jim Corbett, one of the founders of the U.S. Sanctuary Movement, traveled to Chiapas from Arizona and gave religious workers the names and addresses of churches along the U.S.-Mexico border that would provide safe haven to refugees (García 2006). For an overview of the 1980s U.S.-based Sanctuary Movement, see Coutin (1993).
3. See Hagan (1987); Smith (2001); Mahler (2000); Hamilton and Chinchilla (1991); and García (2006) for discussions of the origins of historical and contemporary migration flows from Central America. Largely unrecognized as refugees in the United States, Mexico, or the Central American nations, most Central Americans displaced by the economic and social effects of political conflict in the region have become unauthorized migrants. For example, the number of displaced persons from Central America granted refugee status in the United States, Canada, Mexico, Costa Rica, Panama, Belize, and Guatemala has declined significantly in recent years. See Ackerman, Loughna, and Castles (2004); García (2006).
4. Casanova (1994).
5. In their report on the human rights of migrants in Central America, Ackerman, Loughna, and Castles (2004) identify these organizations along with a number of research institutions that work on behalf of migrants and human rights. In her study of migration and human rights along the border, Ogren (2007) identifies the many national, regional, state, and local level Mexican agencies involved in regulating transit migration.
6. Civil society organizations encompass a broad range of NGOs that increasingly work not only on local social issues, but also with international organization such as the United Nations and the World Bank. Other examples of CSOs not mentioned here include foundations, professional associations, and trade unions. As intermediaries between large national and international organizations and social groups at the local level, they have been increasingly successful in recent decades in transforming global polices through advocacy and mobilization efforts. According to Keck and Sikkink (1998), common concerns, values, and exchanges of information are what constitute a transnational advocacy network.
7. Rodriguez and Hagan (2004).
8. In 2003, Mexico deported 150,000 migrants, almost all of whom (98 percent) were from Central America (Ackerman, Loughna, and Castles 2004). The Human

Rights Commission of Mexico has found that one of every ten detentions is arbitrary. In response, the Working Group on Arbitrary Detention visited Mexico to investigate both the detention of ordinary prisoners as well as the situation of detained migrants (UN Economic and Social Council. Commission on Human Rights 2002).

9. U.S. Customs and Border Protection (2003).

10. Ackerman, Loughna, and Castles (2004).

11. For additional information on NGOs with migrant programs in the region, see Ackerman, Loughna, and Castles (2004); Mahler (2000); García (2006).

12. Hoover (1998).

13. Kerwin (2006).

14. Casanova (1994).

15. In 1952, in *Exsul Familia* (the Magna Carta on migration), Pope Pius XII became the first pontiff to state an explicit but conditional right to migrate when he argued that when conditions worthy of human life are not present, then people and their families have the right to migrate. In *Pacem in Terris,* Pope John XXIII reaffirmed this right when he stated, "Every human being has the right to freedom of movement and of residence within the confines of his own country; and, when there are just reasons for it, the right to emigrate to other countries and take up residence there" (1963, p. 25). Subsequent Vatican documents on the migration question include *De Pastorali Migratorum Cura* (1969, www.vatican.org), *Church and People on the Move* (1978, www.vatican.org), *Refugees: A Challenge to Solidarity* (1992, www.vatican.org), and *Era Caritas Christi* (2004, www.vatican.org).

16. There are also numerous international conventions concerning migrants and refugees. The United States, Mexico, and all countries of Central America are party to the 1951 Refugee Convention and the 1967 Protocol that provide international standards for the treatment of refugees and that specify their rights and obligations, including those of states toward them. The 1990 UN convention on the Protection of the Rights of All Migrant Workers is the international standard concerning irregular migrants. Implemented in July 2003, it extends human rights law to all migrant workers and their families. Belize, El Salvador, Guatemala, and Mexico are among the twenty-one signatories to the UN convention, but the United States is not (United Nations 2003).

17. The Catholic Church has long taken care of its own, including Mexican Catholics entering the United States. Indeed, when Pope John Paul II delivered *Ecclesia in America* in Mexico City in 1999, he called on the Catholic Church to position itself as both advocate and protector of the right to migrate, regardless of the legal status of the migrant. Implicit in this statement was the reality that undocumented migrants from Mexico are an important source of labor in the developed world, including the United States, a comment he explicitly referred to in the 1995 message for World Migration Day. See Hagan (2006; 2007).

18. U.S Conference of Catholic Bishops (2003).

19. To provide a theological basis for their position, they draw on many biblical scriptures from the Old and New Testaments; among these is the reminder that Jesus, Mary, and Joseph themselves were refugees from Egypt (Mathew 2:15).

20. Blume (2003).

21. In the United States, the Bishops Conference established the national office of Migration and Refugee Services (MRS) to coordinate national and diocesan immigration-related activities. See Kerwin (2006).

22. Since the 1960s, the Catholic Church's outreach program to immigrants in the United States has also expanded substantially, paralleling a simultaneous expansion in state-sponsored social service activities. MRS was established to administer these various services. See Mooney (2006).

23. Other policy recommendations include: 1) an expansion of NAFTA agreements to include policies that regularize the movement of people between Mexico and the United States; 2) reforms in U.S. immigration policy to enable Mexican families more opportunities to reunite with families in the United States; 3) a legalization program for undocumented migrants living in the United States; and 4) the development of a fair and humane employment-based immigration program for Mexican workers (U.S. Conference of Catholic Bishops 2003).

24. Kerwin (2006).

25. U.S. Conference of Catholic Bishops (2003).

26. Casanova (1994).

27. Comisión Episcopal para la Pastoral de la Movilidad Humana Conferencia del Episcopado Mexicano (2003).

28. The northern dioceses include Hermosillo, La Paz, Mexicali, Tijuana, Ciudad Juárez, Nuevo Casas Grandes, Matamoros, Nuevo Laredo, Satillo, and Piedras Negras. The central dioceses include Autlán, Ciudad Guzmán, Guadalajara, San Juan de los Lagos, Tepic, Zacatecas, Morelia, León, San Luís Potosí, México D. F., Cuernavaca, Texcoco, Tula, and Tulancingo. The southern dioceses include Coatzacoalcos, Papantla, San Andreas Tuxtla, Veracruz, Acapulco, Tabasco, San Cristóbal de las Casas, and Tapachula.

29. Ackerman, Loughna, and Castles (2004).

30. Personal communication with Michael A Blume, SVD, Mexico City, Sept. 9, 2003. Father Blume was ordained Archbishop in August, 2005. He is now the apostolic noncio to the West African countries of Togo and Benin.

31. The responses of the remaining 17 percent were not reported.

32. The total percentage exceeds 100 since some respondents gave multiple combinations.

33. Tuscan Diocese Newsletter, 2007. Accessed at www.diocesetucson.org/May07 memo.html.

34. The historical and sociological basis for the pastoral work of Scalabrinians in Central America and Mexico is best understood by examining the social teachings of Bishop John Baptiste Scalabrini, the founder of the congregation, referred to by his followers as the Apostle to the Migrants. According to Birollo (2003), as superior general of the Missionaries of St. Charles, Bishop Scalabrini identified emigration as a natural and human right, one that should be free to those in need who are seeking well-being and opportunity. Alarmed by the rise in emigration from Italy and the conditions of the migrants, his primary pastoral concern was migration intervention at all stages of the process, from decision making to arrival. Bishop Scalabrini believed in immigration reform; he was vehemently critical of

immigration laws since he believed that although such laws could never eliminate emigration, they had the adverse effect of placing migrants at the mercy of what he referred to as unscrupulous persons enforcing it, which he referred to as "merchants of human flesh." (Birollo 2003, p. 13).To this end he founded the Congregation of the Missionary Priests and Brothers; later, he founded a lay society and religious congregation of sisters. The first mission of these religious groups was to maintain Catholic faith and practice among Italian emigrants in the new areas of settlement and to ensure their moral, civil, and economic welfare. The congregation established churches, hospitals, and other institutions to assist in the settlement of Italian migrants in various established destinations around the globe, from New York to Brazil. The second mission was to oversee the migration process. Recognizing that emigration was an inevitable social question that would incorporate persons of various cultures over time, he called on his missionaries to counsel the departing migrants and if necessary to direct them toward safe passage. He also requested that his congregation monitor those officials who regulate the process to assure that they do not violate the law or exploit migrants. The Vatican's current program for migrants, the Pontifical Council for the Pastoral Care of Migrants and People on the Move, which was established in 1970, is partially based on the Scalabrini model (personal interview with Michael A. Blume, SVD, Mexico City, Sept. 9, 2003). For a complete history of the Scalabrini fathers and the Italian emigrant church, see D'Agostino (1997).

35. D'Agostino (1997). The Scalabrini congregation missionaries also direct Centers for Migration Studies, publish newspapers and magazines (Migrantes) for migrants and conduct television and radio programs for them.

36. Campese (2007).

37. Fitzgerald (2008).

38. Espinosa (1999), as cited in Fitzgerald (2008); Hagan 2007.

39. The Casa de Atención al Migrante in Guatemala City includes two sections: the Casa del Migrante, which is a shelter. and the Migration Information Center, which is charged with educating area youth about migration.

40. Ackerman, Loughna, and Castles (2004).

41. Gutiérrez (2004).

42. Campese (2007).

43. In her analysis of religion, culture, and agency in the Central American solidarity movement, Nepstad (2004) moved beyond studying the mechanisms of political action to linking the meaning systems of individual movement participants to their protests. Meaning systems include values, beliefs, and socialization experiences. She referred to this subjective dimension of movements as meanings of protest.

44. See, for example, Hondagneu-Sotelo, Gaudinez, Lara, and Ortiz 2004; Hondagneu-Sotelo, Gaudinez, and Lara 2007. In these analyses, Hondagneu-Sotelo and her colleagues document the growing number of posadas organized by interfaith coalitions along the U.S.-Mexico border and in the interior United States in recent years.

45. Coutin (1993).

46. Hagan (2006).

47. See, for example, Nepstad (2004); Guth, Green, Smidt, Kellstedt, and Poloma (1997); Hagan (2006); Wuthnow (2005); Wuthnow and Evans (2002).

48. The political efforts of the Christian Right have largely been restricted to issues associated with the regulation of reproductive activities, sexual practices, and marriage. These include political, church, and faith-based efforts to restrict abortion, homosexuality, and gay marriage.

49. Eschbach, Hagan, Rodriguez, Hernández-León and Bailey (1999).

50. American Friends Service Committee (2005). The AFSC continues to promote social justice along the U.S.-Mexico border. In the spring of 2005 it trained volunteer observers to document any abuse of migrants along the Arizona-Mexico border by members of the Minuteman Project, a civilian-led border-watch effort that was founded in 2004.

51. Not all religious groups along the border have responded to the current immigration crisis with political protest. A number of religious groups working along the border have developed comprehensive border ministries in which challenging and reforming immigration policy is only a small component of a much larger vision. One such organization is Frontera de Cristo, a binational ministry that works to address border problems. While Frontera de Cristo does participate in advocacy for immigration reform (e.g., it is a member of Humane Borders whose binational board of directors recently sent a letter to the U.S. president and Congress urging immigration reform), its leaders believe that they are also challenged to address root causes of U.S.-bound labor migration from Latin America. Recently, for example, they established a coffee cooperative—Just Coffee—in an area in southern Mexico that advocates fair prices for individual farmers who grow coffee. The cooperative hopes the effort will allow people to stay on their land rather than trek north.

52. Personal communication with Father Carney, Douglas, Arizona, June 12, 2002.

53. Marchi (2006).

54. Stop Gatekeeper! (2004).

55. Santino (2006) draws on the work of J. L. Austin, who makes a distinction between the commemorative and performative functions of shrines and symbols. While the commemorative aspect is obvious and static, the performative encompasses the public dimension of the ritual, the component that addresses a social issue.

56. Humane Borders was the brain child of members of Borderlinks, a binational faith-based NGO organized to raise the consciousness of U.S. citizens about migration issues through educational programs. In this capacity they regularly guide groups of U.S. citizens across the border to witness firsthand the implications of enforcement operations for the conditions of journeying migrants.

57. Personal communication with Rev. Hoover; September 2004.

58. Hoover (2002).

59. International Bible Society (1984).

60. Rev. Hoover would eventually pull out of the organization, claiming that he "wanted to work within the boundaries of the law."

61. Personal communication with Rev. Fife, June 13, 2002.
62. No More Deaths (2005).
63. International Bible Society (1984).
64. No More Deaths (2005).
65. No More Deaths (2006).
66. It is important to note that a countermovement has also emerged in response to what many feel is an invasion of the border. Dressed in military fatigues and sometimes armed, these groups of private citizens patrol the border, rounding up migrants and turning them over to the U.S. Border Patrol. The official Minuteman web site (*www.minutemanhq.com/hq/html*) details their present and future activities along the U.S.-Mexico border.
67. Interview with Fife, June 2002.
68. Nazario (2006).

4. Miracles in the Desert

1. Handlin (2002, p. 112).
2. Berger and Luckmann (1966).
3. Hall (1997, p. vii). The focus on everyday practices of women and men has a history in the French tradition of the sociology of religion. For a review of this tradition, see Hervieu-Leger (1997), Davie (2004), and Dobbelaere (1987). Luckmann (1967) introduced a reorientation of institutionally diffuse religion among American scholars. In recent years, this perspective has gained increased currency. See, e.g., the collection of studies of everyday religion or lived religion by Hall (1997) and Ammerman (2005).
4. Orsi (1997, p. 7).
5. Egan (1991); Vidal (1972).
6. Griffith (1992); Durand and Massey (1995); Vanderwood (2004).
7. Durand and Massey (1995, p. 21).
8. For a fascinating account of Juan Soldado and the pilgrims who visit his shrine, see Vanderwood (2004).
9. See Annerino (1999).
10. Handlin (2002, p. 112).
11. Pepitone (1994).
12. Here I draw on Durkheim (1912), who argued that communities of faithful are far more demanding than other groups since they provide both support (integrative function) and guidelines as to how to live (regulative function). See Fields (1995) for translated text.

5. La Promesa

1. In his analysis of Ticuanese in New York, Smith (2006) provides a rich discussion of religious practices among the second generation, in which he identifies significance of promesas for intergenerational bonds and transnational life.

2. Sociedades Guadalupanas (Guadalupe Societies) are locally based religious associations founded and organized by largely Mexican-American Catholics in Texas to meet both the secular and religious educational needs of the people. In some Texas communities they have been instrumental in meeting the needs of the poor and teaching members and parishioners how to read and write in English. In time, the sociedades evolved into a support system for Mexican-American women. Becoming a Guadalupana involves a series of rituals; participants cite a series of prayers, declare a public commitment to the virgin, and are the presented with the Guadalupe medal. In some societies, members are given an official rose-colored cape. Members usually maintain home altars of La Nuestra Señora de Guadalupe. For many Guadalupanas, participation in the association ends only at death. Some, like Rocio, credit their increased spirituality to their membership and years of devotion (Acosta, Teresa, "Sociedades Guadalupanas," The Handbook of Texas (2008). See also Sullivan (2000).

3. Peggy Levitt (2007, p. 109).

4. In her study of religious practices among Mexican Catholics in a Houston barrio, Sullivan (2000) found that members of a local Catholic Church regularly attended Pentecostal, Methodist, and Baptist churches, all the while maintaining their domestic Catholic practices in the privacy of their homes.

5. Groody (2002).

6. Mark and Louise Zwick founded the Casa Juan Diego in Houston, Texas in 1980 to serve immigrants and refugees. More than 50,000 immigrants have stayed at least one night in the Houses of Hospitality. The Zwicks are coeditors of *Houston Catholic Worker,* a bimonthly newspaper. www.cjd.org/cjd.html.

7. Carlos (2001).

8. Lucia (1997).

9. Groody (2007, p. 193).

10. Both Wellmeier (1998) and Menjívar (1999) also found that Protestant migrants, who come from ethnically homogenous communities, continued to identify strongly with ministries in the home community long after arrival in the United States, often redirecting funds and energy toward these ministries.

11. Levitt (2007).

12. The Catholic Church has long sent its clergy from sending communities to care for migrants in receiving areas. For a historical overview of Mexican priests traveling to the United States to attend to the Mexican origin populations, see, for example, Dolan and Hinojosa (1994) and Fitzgerald (2008). For a more contemporary account of this cross-border practice, see, among others, Levitt (2003; 2005); Cook (2002); Fortuny-Loret de Mola (2002); Hagan (2002); and Fitzgerald (2008).

13. Personal interview with Sister Gemma in Tijuana, Mexico, May 30, 2003.

14. Egan (1991); Vidal (1972); Durand and Massey (1995, p. 21); Cousin (1982); Sanchez (1990).

15. Giffords (1974); Durand and Massey (1995); Egan (1991).

16. Durand and Massey (1995).

17. Ibid.

18. Ibid, p. 26.
19. These altar books are also found in some Mexican shrines, including the Chapel of la Noria, situated on the highway linking Mexico City with Querétaro, and the Chapel of San Sebastián de Aparacio in Puebla (Durand and Massey 1995).
20. Immigrants have long transferred religious rituals, holy images and ideas from communities of origin to the host country, confirming their continued membership in the home community (Orsi 1985). Ethnic congregations in the United States in the eighteenth and nineteenth centuries were important settings for the reproduction of a groups' religious heritage. German Catholic immigrants and Italian Catholics in New York are but a few of the ethnic congregations that helped newcomers retain their religious identities (Dolan 1975). In more recent times, Cubans in Miami erected familiar shrines that welcome newcomers to the community and provide a sense of belonging in an otherwise unfamiliar and new society (Tweed 1997). With the growth of immigration from Latin America in recent decades, countless shrines of the Virgin of Guadalupe and other revered saints in the region have been erected in Latino neighborhoods throughout the United States.
21. Levitt (2007); personal interviews with several Scalabrini priests, Notre Dame, Indiana, September 21, 2004.
22. Navarro (2002).
23. Levitt (2007).
24. Personal interview with Cardinal Rodriguez, Tegucigalpa, December 7, 2004.
25. Personal interview with Father Chapa, San Miguel, El Salvador, December 10, 2004.
26. Bada, Fox, and Selee (2005).
27. Broadway (2002).
28. The Tepeyac brought the Anorcha Guadalupana tradition to New York in 1999 when it initiated annual runs from St. Patrick's Cathedral to local parishes. In 2001, Cardinal Edward Egan of New York challenged the association to organize a Mexico City-New York run (Broadway 2002).
29. Smith (2006).
30. Levitt (2007).
31. See Paerregaard (2001), for example, for a detailed discussion of the development and implications of Peruvian migrants' organization of religious brotherhoods to honor the country's patron, the Lord of the Miracles.
32. Pratt (2006).

6. Conclusion

1. See, e.g., Handlin (2002); Herberg (1955); Smith (1978); Orsi (1997; 2002); Warner and Wittner (1998); Ebaugh and Chafetz (2000); Levitt (2000; 2007); Guest (2003).
2. Interestingly, in their review of the literature on the relationship between religion and immigration, Portes and Rumbaut (2006, p. 301) acknowledge the role of places of worship in sending communities in guiding emigration, but do

not cite any studies or provide any data as evidence of the role of religion in the departure stage of migration.

3. See the writings of Elizondo (1975; 1980; 1986; 1993) for a discussion of the cultural context of Latino/religious folk and popular practices, especially the role of these practices as a source of identity.

4. There are, of course, exceptions. For a more dynamic understanding of how religion is lived, transformed, and redefined by immigrants themselves, see Orsi (1997; 2002); and Levitt's extensive scholarship on religion and transnationalism (2001; 2007); Also, see Smith (2006); Paerregaard (2001); Levitt (2007); Tweed (1997). See Ammerman (2005), Hall (1997), and Hervieu-Leger (1997) for a more general understanding of the concept of lived religion.

5. See, for example, neoclassical economics (Todaro 1976; Todaro and Marusko 1987; Ranis and Fei 1961); Sjastad 1962, the new economics of migration (Stark and Bloom 1985), and segmented labor market (Piore 1979).

6. Massey, Alarcón, Durand, and González (1987).

7. Kandel and Massey 2002; Mines 1981; Reichart 1981.

8. There is scholarship on migrant decision making during other stages of the migration process. See, e.g., Portes and Truelove (1987) and Hagan (1994) for a discussion of decision making and regularizing one's migration status. See Grasmuck and Pessar (1991) for an early discussion on gender, decision making, and return migration.

9. Orsi (2007) refers to these events as abundant events.

10. Arjona (2005).

11. Also see Van Dijk (1997).

12. Popular devotions have long been a reliable means of revenue for churches (Orsi 1991).

13. For example, just sixty miles north of the California-Mexico border town of Calexico, California, in the brutally hot Coachella Valley, a Catholic Church responded to the dangerous crossing and spiritual struggles of migrants by developing welcoming ceremonies (Groody 2002).

14. See, e.g., Taylor (1986); Browning and Rodriguez (1985); Massey, Alarcón, Durand, and González (1987); Hagan (1994); Singer and Massey (1998); Menjívar (2000).

15. Massey, Durand, and Malone (2003); Hagan (1994).

16. See, Hernández-León (2005); e.g., Hagan (1998); Menjívar (2000); Gilbertson (1995); Portes and Jensen (1989); Portes and Sensenbrenner (1993); Krissman (2005); Mahler (1995); Hondagneu-Sotelo (1994); and Gonzalez de la Rocha (1994).

17. Kyle and Koslowski (2001); Massey, Durand and Malone (2002); Spener (2005).

18. This transit migration industry is one segment of a larger migration industry composed of entrepreneurs and businesses that financially gain from providing services that facilitate and sustain international migration. Castles and Miller (2003) coined the term "migration industry" to describe the for-profit aggregate of recruitment organizations, lawyers, smugglers, and agents that facilitate international migration. Hernández-León (2008) applies this concept to the case of

Mexican-U.S. migration and explores the conditions under which these for-profit actors complement or replace migrants' social networks.

19. Zolberg (2006); Hollifield (2004).

20. A growing body of work focuses on the political and civic face of American religion, underscoring the role of religion in facilitating political and civic participation. See, for example, the edited volume by (Hondagneu-Sotelo 2007; Ammerman 2005; Wuthnow 2005) and challenging state institutions (Casanova 1994; Hagan 2007).

21. The cross-border sanctuary movement that I describe in the book is different and broader in scope than the recently formed (2007) U.S. based New Sanctuary Movement. The U.S. based movement includes a coalition of interfaith religious leaders and congregations who advocate on behalf of immigrants residing in the United States.

22. Berger and Luckmann (1966).

23. Ammerman (2007); Hall (1997).

24. Durand and Massey (1995).

25. Levitt (2007); Wuthnow (2005).

26. Smith (2006).

References

Ackerman, Lisanne, Sean Loughna, and Stephen Castles. "Assessing the Human Rights of Migrants in Central America and Mexico." Report commissioned by Project Counseling Service (PCS). Lima, Peru, August 2004.

Aguayo, Sergio, and Patricia Weiss Fagen. "Central Americans in Mexico and the United States: Unilateral, Bilateral, and Regional Perspectives." *Refugee Survey Quarterly* 7(4) (1988): 36–31.

American Friends Service Committee. "Immigrants' Rights: AFSC." Accessed December 2007 from www.afsc.org/immigrants-rights/default.htm.

Ammerman, Nancy. *Pillars of Faith: American Congregations and Their Partners.* Berkeley: University of California Press, 2005.

———, ed. *Everyday Religion: Observing Modern Religious Lives.* New York: Oxford University Press, 2007.

Andreas, Peter. *Border Games: Policing the U.S.-Mexico Divide.* Ithaca, NY: Cornell University Press, 2000.

———. "A Tale of Two Borders: The U.S-Mexico and the U.S.-Canada Lines after 9/11." Working paper 77, The Center for Comparative Immigration Studies, University of California, San Diego, 2003: Accessed March 2008 at: http://www.ccis-ucsd.org/publications/wrkg77.pdf.

———. "The Transformation of Migrant Smuggling across the U.S.-Mexico Border." In *Global Human Smuggling: Comparative Perspectives,* ed. D. Kyle and R. Koslowski, pp. 108–125. Baltimore: Johns Hopkins University Press, 2001.

Annerino, John. *Dead in Their Tracks: Crossing America's Desert Borderlands.* New York: Four Walls Eight Windows, 1999.

Archibold, Randal C. 2006, September 20. "Border Fence Must Skirt Objections from Arizona Tribe." *New York Times,* September 20, 2006, p. A24.

Arjona, Ricardo. "Mojado." On *Adentro.* 2005 Sony International.

Bada, Xóchitl, Jonathan Fox, and Andrew Selee, eds. "Invisible No More: Mexican Migrant Civic Participation in the United States." Report published by the Woodrow Wilson Center Press and University of California Press, 2006.

Bankston, C. L., and M. Zhou. (1996). "The Ethnic Church, Ethnic Identification, and the Social Adjustment of Vietnamese Adolescents." *Review of Religious Research* 38 (1996): 18–37.

Barrett, Barbara. "Immigration Duel Persists: Panel Juggles Competing Interests While Drafting Legislation." *The News & Observer* (Raleigh, NC), March 12, 2006, p. A17.

———. "Rival Bills Prescribe Ways to Treat Illegal Immigration." *The News & Observer* (Raleigh, NC), March 27, 2006, A1.

Basch, Linda G., Nina Glick Schiller, and Cristina Blanc-Szanton. *Nations Unbound: Transnational Projects, Postcolonial Predicaments, Deterritorialized Nation-states.* Langhorne, PA: Gordon and Breach, 1994.

Berger, Peter, and Thomas Luckmann. *The Social Construction of Reality: A Treatise in the Sociology of Knowledge.* Garden City, NY: Anchor Books, 1966.

Bernstein, Nina. "In the Streets, Suddenly, Immigrants' Sound and Fury." *New York Times,* March 27, 2006, p. A14.

Berryman, Phillip. *Liberation Theology: Essential Facts About the Revolutionary Movement in Latin America and Beyond,* Philadelphia: Temple University Press, 1987.

———. *Religion in the Megacity: Catholic and Protestant Portraits from Latin America.* New York: Orbis Books, 1996.

Birollo, I. "The Legacy of Blessed John Baptist." In *Migration, Religious Experience, and Globalization,* ed. Gioacchino Campese and Pietro Ciallella, pp. 11–16. Staten Island, NY: Center for Migration Studies, 2003.

Blume, Michael. 2003. "Migration and the Social Doctrine of the Church." *Migration, Religious Experience, and Globalization,* ed. Gioacchino Campese and Pietro Ciallella, pp. 62–75. Staten Island, NY: Center for Migration Studies, 2003.

Boyd, Monica. "Family and Personal Networks in International Migration: Recent Developments and New Agendas." *International Migration Review* 23(3) (1989): 638–70.

Brimelow, Peter. *Alien Nation: Common Sense About America's Immigration Disaster,* Random House, 1995.

Broadway, Bill. "Carrying a Torch for Hope: Bearers of Flame from Our Lady of Guadalupe Relay Message to Immigrants in U.S." *The Washington Post,* November 30, 2002, B9.

Browning, Harley, and Nestor Rodriguez. "The Migration of Mexican Indocumentados as a Settlement Process: Implications for Work." In *Hispanics in U.S. Economy*, ed. George Borjas and Marta Tienda, pp. 277–292. New York: Academic Press, 1985.

Brycesson, D. F., and U. Vuerela. "Transnational families in the Twenty-first Century." In *The Transnational Family: New European Frontiers and Global Networks*, ed. D. F. Brycesson and U. Vuerela, pp. 3–30. Oxford: Berg Publishers, 2002.

Burdick, John, and W. E. Hewitt, eds. *The Church at Grassroots in Latin America: Perspectives on Thirty Years of Activism*. Westport, CT: Praeger Publishers, 2000.

Cadge, Wendy, and Elaine Howard Ecklund. "Immigration and Religion" *Annual Review Sociology* 33:359–379.

———. "Religious Service Attendance among Immigrants: Evidence from the New Immigrant Survey—Pilot." *American Behavioral Scientist*, 49 (11) (2006): pp. 1574–1595.

Calavita, Kitty. *Inside the State: The Bracero Program, Immigration, and the I.N.S.* New York: Routledge, 1992.

Campese, Gioacchino. "Beyond Ethnic and National Imagination: Toward a Catholic Theology of U.S. Immigration." In *Religion and Social Justice for Immigrants*, ed. Pierrette Hondagneu-Sotelo, pp. 175–190. Piscataway, NJ: Rutgers University Press, 2007.

Carlos. "How I came from Honduras to Casa Juan Diego" Houston Catholic Worker, vol. XXI, no. 9. December 2001. Also available online at www.cjd.org/stories/honduras.html.

Casanova, J. 2001. Religion, the New Millennium, and Globalization: 2000 Presidential Address. *Sociology of Religion* 62(4): 415–441.

Casanova, Jose. *Public Religions in the Modern World*. Chicago: University of Chicago Press, 1994.

———. "Globalizing Catholicism and the Return to a 'Universal' Church." In *Transnational Religion and Fading States*, ed. S. H. Rudolph and J. Piscatori, pp. 121–143. Boulder, CO: Westview Press, 1997.

Casillas Bermúdez, Karla. "La Frontera México-EU, la más dínamica del mundo: A los 12 años inician la aventura migratoria muchos mexicanos, revela estudio." *El Financiero*, May 9, 1998, p. 38.

Casillas, R. 2001. "Semblanza de la frontera sur de mexico." In *Migracion-Mexico entre sus Dos Fronteras 2000–2001*, pp. 22–28. Mexico City: Foro Migraciones, 2001.

Castles, Stephen, and Mark J. Miller. *The Age of Migration: International Population Movements in the Modern World,* 3rd ed. New York: Guildford Press, 2003 (originally published, 1993).

Celestino, Olinda, and Albert Meyers. *Las Cofradias en el Peru: Region central.* Frankfurt am main: Verlag Klaus Dieter Vervuert, 1981.

Cevallos, Diego. "Religion-Latin America: Catholic Church Losing Followers in Droves." Accessed October 21, 2004, from http://ispnews.net/new_nota.asp?idnews=25966.

————. "Central American Migrants Face Death in Bid to Reach U.S." InterPress Service, January 24, 2007. vol. 45 (4):203–243.

Chafetz, Janet, and Jacqueline Hagan. "Dangerous Journey: Does Gender Matter?" Unpublished paper. Houston, Texas: Center for Immigration Research, University of Houston, 2005.

Chatters, Linda M. "Religion and Health: Public Research and Practice." *Annual Review of Public Health* 21 (2000): 335–367.

Chávez, Leo. *Shadowed Lives: Undocumented Immigrants in American Society.* Orlando: Harcourt Brace Jovanovich, 1992.

Chávez, Lillian. "Solidarity and the Process of Migration: A Case Study of Central Americans and Mexicans." M.A. thesis, University of Houston, 2006.

Chávez, Sergio. "The Making of a Border Labor Migration System: Government Policies, Labor Markets, and Social Networks in Tijuana." Ph.D. dissertation, Cornell University, 2007.

Chestnut, R. Andrew. 1997. *Born Again in Brazil: The Pentecostal Boom and the Pathogens of Poverty.* Piscataway, NJ: Rutgers University Press, 1997.

————. *Competitive Spirits: Latin America's New Religious Economy.* New York: Oxford University Press, 2003.

Christensen, Drew. 1996. "Movement, Asylum, Borders: Christian Perspectives." *International Migration Review* 30 (1996): 7–17.

Cleary, Edward L. *Crisis and Change: The Church in Latin America Today.* New York: Orbis Books, 1985.

Comisíon Episcopal para la Pastoral de la Movilidad Humana Conferencia del Episcopado Mexicano. *Autodiagnóstico . . . en Búsqueda del Rostro del Fenómeno Migratorio en México.* Mexico, September 2003.

Conover, Ted. *Coyotes: A Journey through the Secret World of America's Illegal Aliens.* New York: Random House, 1987.

Cook, David A. 2002. "Forty Years of Religion across Borders: Twilight of a Transnational Field?" In *Religion across Borders,* ed. Helen Rose Ebaugh and Janet Chafetz, pp. 51–74. Walnut Creek, CA: AltaMira Press, 2002.

Cornelius, Wayne. "The Impact of Border Enforcement on Unauthorized Mexican Migration to the United States." Accessed September 2006 at http://borderbattles.ssrc.org.

Cousin, Bernard. *Le Miracle et le Quotidien: Les Ex-votos Provencaux, Image d'une Societe.* Paris: Societes, Metalites, et Cultures, 1982.

Coutin, Susan Bibler. *The Culture of Protest: Religious Activism and the U.S. Sanctuary Movement.* Boulder, CO: Westview Press, 1993.

Cruz, Angeles, H. "La migracion internacional a traves de la frontera sur: la dimension de las estadisticas para la region del soconusco." In *Ecofronteras: Las Migraciones en al Frontera Sur de Mexico.* Mexico: El Colegio de la Frontera Sur, 2003.

D'Agostino, Peter R. "The Scalabrini Fathers, the Italian Emigrant Church, and Ethnic Nationalism in America." *Religion and American Culture* 7(1) (Winter 1997): 121–159

Davie, Grace. 2004. "Creating an Agenda in the Sociology of Religion: Common Sources/Different Pathways." *Sociology of Religion* 65(4) (Winter 2004): 323–340.

de la Garza, R., M. Baraona, M. Orozco, H. P. Pachon, and A. D. Pantoja. "Binational Impact of Latino Remittances." Policy brief from the Tomas Rivera Policy Institute, Washington, DC, 1997.

Dobbelaere, Karel. "Social Trends in European Sociology of Religion: The Secularization Debate." *Sociological Analysis* 48(2) (1987): 107–137

Dolan, Jay P. *The Immigrant Church: New York's Irish and German Catholics, 1815–1865.* Baltimore: Johns Hopkins University Press, 1975.

Dolan, Jay P., and Gilberto Hinojosa. 1994. *Mexican Americans and the Catholic Church, 1900–1965.*Notre Dame, IN: University of Notre Dame Press.

Donato, Katharine, and Evelyn Patterson. "Women and Men on the Move: Undocumented Border Crossing." In *Crossing the Border: Research from the Mexican Migration Project,* ed. by Jorge Durand and Douglas S. Massey, pp. 111–130. New York: Russell Sage Foundation, 2004.

Dow, James W. "The Growth of Protestant Religion in Mexico and Central America." Revised draft of paper presented at the Society for the Scientific Study of Religion annual meeting, October 23–26, 2003, Norfolk, Virginia. Accessed from http://personalwebs.oakland.edu/~dow/personal/papers/meso/sssr_.Accessed July 10, 2005.

Dunn, Timothy J. *The Militarization of the U.S.-Mexico border, 1978–1992.* Austin: University of Texas Press, 1996.

Durand, Jorge, and Douglas S. Massey. *Miracles on the Border: Retablos of Mexican Migrants to the United States.* Tucson: University of Arizona Press, 1995.

———, eds. *Crossing the Border: Research from the Mexican Migration Project.* New York: Russell Sage Foundation, 2004.

Durkheim, Emile. *The Elementary Forms of Religious Life.* Trans. Karen E. Fields. New York: Simon & Schuster, 1995 (originally published, 1912).

Ebaugh, Helen Rose, and Janet Saltzman Chafetz. "Agents of Cultural Reproduction: The Ironic Role of Women in Immigrant Congregations." *Social Forces* 78 (1999): pp. 585–612.

———. *Religion and the New Immigrants: Continuities and Adaptations in Immigrant Congregations.* New York: AltaMira Press, 2000.

———. *Religion across Borders: Transnational Immigrant Networks.* New York: AltaMira Press, 2002.

Ebaugh, Helen Rose, and Paula Pipes. "Immigrant Congregations as Social Service Providers: Are They a Safety Net for Welfare Reforms?" In *Religion and Social Policy for the 21st Century,* ed. P. D. Nesbitt, pp. 95–110. Walnut Creek, CA: AltaMira Press, 2001.

Egan, Martha. *Mílagros: Votive Offerings from the Americas.* Santa Fe: Museum of New Mexico Press, 1991.

Elizondo, Virgilio. *Christianity and Culture: An Introduction to Pastoral Theology and Ministry for the Bicultural Community.* Huntington, IN: Our Sunday Visitor, 1975.

———. *La Morenita: Evangelizer of the Americas.* San Antonio, TX: Mexican American Cultural Center Press, 1980.

———. "Popular Religion as Support of Identity." In *Beyond Borders: Writings of Virgilio Elizondo and Friends,* ed. Timothy Matovina, pp. 126–132. Maryknoll, NY: Orbis Books, 2000.

———. "Hispanic Theology and Popular Piety: From Interreligious Encounter to a New Ecumenism." In *Beyond Borders: Writings of Virgilio Elizondo and Friends,* ed. Timothy Matovina, pp. 278–291. Maryknoll, NY: Orbis Books, 2000.

Eschbach, Karl, Jacqueline Hagan, Nestor Rodriguez, Ruben Hernández-León, and Stanley Bailey. "Death at the Border." *International Migration Review* 33 (1999): 430–454.

Eschbach, Karl, Jacqueline Hagan, and Nestor Rodriguez. "Causes and Trends in Migrant Deaths along the Mexico-U.S. Border, 1985–1998." Working paper. Houston, Texas: University of Texas, Center for Immigration Research, 2001.

———. 2003. "Deaths during Undocumented Migration: Trends and Policy Implications in the New Era of Homeland Security." *In Defense of the Alien* 26 (2003): 37–52.

Espenshade, T. J., J. L. Baraka, and G. A. Huber. "Implications of the 1996 Immigration Reforms." *Population and Development Reviews* 23(4) (1997): 769–801.

Espin, Orlando. "Pasíon y Respeto: Elizondo's Contribution to the Study of Popular Catholicism." In *Beyond Borders: Writings of Virgilio Elizondo and Friends*, ed. Timothy Matovina, pp. 101–108. Maryknoll, NY: Orbis Books, 2000.

Espinosa, Victor M. "El Dia del Emigrante y el Retorno del Porqatorio: Iglesia, Migración a los Estados Unidos y Cambio Sociocultural en un Pueblo de los Altos de Jalisco." *Estudio Sociológos* 50 (1999): 119–135.

Fife, J. "A Theology of Sanctuary" Paper presented at the International Conference on Migration and Theology. Notre Dame, IN. (2004, Sept.).

Fitzgerald, David. *A Nation of Emigrants: How Mexico Manages Its Migration.* Berkeley: University of California Press, 2008.

Flora, Cornelia Butler. 1984. "Religiosity among Working Class Catholic Colombians." In *The Catholic Church and Religions in Latin America*, ed. Thomas C. Bruneau, Chester E. Gabriel, and Marty Mooney, pp. 66–87. Montreal: McGill University, 1984.

Flynn, Michael. "U.S. Anti-Migration Efforts Move South." Accessed July 2002 at http://americas.irc-online.org/pdf/articles/0207migra.pdf.

Fortuny-Loret de Mola, Patricia. "The *Santa Cena* of the *Luz Del Mundo* Church: A Case Contemporary Transnationalism." In *Religion across Borders*, ed. Helen Rose Ebaugh and Janet Chafetz, pp. 15–50. Walnut Creek, CA: AltaMira Press, 2002.

Gamio, Manuel. *Mexican Migration to the United States.* Chicago: Chicago University Press, 1930.

García, Juan Ramón. *Operation Wetback: The Mass Deportation of Mexican Undocumented Workers in 1954.* Westport, CT: Greenwood Publishing Group, 1980.

García, Mária Christina. *Seeking Refuge: Central American Migration to Mexico, the United States, and Canada.* Los Angeles,: University of California Press, 2006.

Garrard-Burnett, Virginia. *Living in the New Jerusalem: Protestantism in Guatemala.* Austin: University of Texas Press, 1998.

Genicot, Garance, and Sarah Senesky. "Determinants of Migration and 'Coyote' Use among Undocumented Mexicans in the United States." Mimeo, Georgetown University, 2004.

Giffords, Gloria K. *Mexican Folk Retablos: Masterpieces on Tin.* Tucson: University of Arizona Press, 1974.

Gilbertson, Greta. "Women's Labor and Enclave Employment: The Case of Colombian and Dominican Women in New York City." *International Migration Review* 29(3) (1995): 657–670.

Glick-Schiller, Nina Linda Basch, and Christina Szanton Blanc. "Transnationalism: A New Analytical Framework for Understanding Migration" In Glick-Schiller, Basch & Szarton Blanc, eds. *Towards a Transnational Perspective on Migration: Race, Class, Ethnicity and Nationalism Reconsidered*, pp. 1–24. New York: Annals of the New York Academy of Sciences, 1992.

Gonzalez de la Rocha, Mercedes. *The Resources of Poverty: Women and Survival in a Mexican City.* Cambridge: Blackwell Publishers, 1994.

Gozdziak, Elzbieta and Dianna Shandy. Special issue on "Religion and Spirituality in Forced Migration." *Journal of Refugee Studies* 2002(15).

Grasmuck, Sherri, and Patricia R. Pessar. *Between Two Islands: Dominican International Migration.* Berkeley: University of California Press, 1991.

Grayson, George W. "Mexico's Forgotten Southern Border: Does Mexico Practice at Home What it Teaches Abroad?" Accessed July 2002 from www.cis.org/articles/2002/back702.html.

———. "Mexico's Southern Flank: A Crime-ridden 'Third U.S. Border.'" *Hemisphere Focus* 6(32) (2003): pp. 1–4.

Greeley, A. M. *The Denominational Society: A Sociological Approach to Religion in America.* Glenview, IL: Scott, Foresman, 1972.

Green, John C., James L. Guth, Lyman A. Kellstedt, Margaret M. Poloma, and Corwin E. Smidt. *The Bully Pulpit: The Politics of Protestant Clergy.* Lawrence: University Press of Kansas, 1997.

Green, Linda. *Fear as a Way of Life: Mayan Widows in Rural Guatemala.* New York: Columbia University Press, 1999.

Griffith, James S. "El Tiradito and San Juan Doldado: Two Victim-Intercessors of the Western Borderlands." *International Folklore Review* 5 (1987): 75–81.

———. *Beliefs and Holy Places: A Spiritual Geography of the Pimería Alta.* Tucson: University of Arizona Press, 1992.

Groody, Daniel G. *Border of Death, Valley of Life: An Immigrant Journey of Heart and Spirit.* New York: Rowman & Littlefield, 2002.

———. "Globalization Spirituality and Justice: Navigating the Path to Peace." Maryknoll, NY: Orbis, 2007.

———. "A Theology of Migration." Paper presented September 21, 2004, at the International Conference on Migration and Theology, University of Notre Dame, Notre Dame, IN.

Groody, Daniel G., and Gioacchino Campese. *A Promised Land, A Perilous Journey: Towards a Theology of Migration.* Notre Dame, IN: University of Notre Dame Press, 2008.

Guacin, Edgar. "Dangerous Crossing: Undocumented Migration across the Mexican-Guatemalan Border." M.A. thesis, University of Houston, 2003.

Guarnizo, Luis, and Michael Peter Smith. "The Locations of Transnationalism." In *Transnationalsim from Below,* eds. Michael Peter Smith and Luis Guarnizo, pp. 3–34. New Brunswick, NJ: Transaction, 1998.

Guest, Kenneth J. *God in Chinatown: Religion and Survival in New York's Evolving Immigrant Community.* New York: New York University Press, 2003.

Guth, J. L., J. C. Green, C. E. Smidt, L. A. Kellstedt, and M. M. Poloma. *The Bully Pulpit: The Politics of Protestant Clergy.* Lawrence: University Press of Kansas, 1997.

Gutierrez, Gustavo. *A Theology of Liberation: History, Politics and Salvation.* Trans. by Caridad Inda and John Eaaleson. Maryknoll, NY: Orbis, 1973.

———. "Poverty, Migration, & OFP." Paper presented in September 2004 at the International Conference on Migration and Theology, University of Notre Dame, Notre Dame, IN.

Hagan, Jacqueline Maria. "The Politics of Numbers: Central American Migration during a Period of Crisis, 1978–1985." M.A. thesis, University of Texas at Austin, 1987.

———. *Deciding to Be Legal: A Maya Community in Houston.* Philadelphia: Temple University Press, 1994.

———. "Social Networks, Gender, and Immigrant Incorporation: Resources and Constraints." *American Sociological Review* 63 (1998): 55–67.

———. "Religion and the Process of Migration: A Case Study of the Maya Transnational Community." In *Religion Across Borders: Transnational Religious Networks,* ed. Helen Rose Ebaugh and Janet Chafetz, pp. 75–92. Walnut Creek, CA: AltaMira Press, 2002.

———. "Making Theological Sense of the Migration Journey from Latin America: Catholic, Protestant, and Interfaith Perspectives." *American Behavioral Scientist* 49(11) (2006): 1554–1573.

———. "The Church vs. the State: Borders, Migrants, and Human Rights." In *Religion and Social Justice for Immigrants,* ed. Pierrette Hondagneu-Sotelo, pp. 93–103. Piscataway, NJ: Rutgers University Press, 2007.

———. "Faith for the Journey: Religion as Resource for Migrants." In *A Promised Land, A Perilous Journey: Theological Perspectives on Migration,* ed. Daniel Groody and Gioacchino Campese, pp. 3–19. Notre Dame, IN: University of Notre Dame Press, 2008.

Hagan, Jacqueline Maria, and Helen Rose Ebaugh. "Calling upon the Sacred: The Use of Religion in the Migration Process." *International Migration Review* 37(4) (2003): 1145–1162.

Hagan, Jacqueline Maria, Karl Eschbach, and Nestor Rodriguez. "U.S. Deportation Policy, Family Separation, and Circular Migration." *International Migration Review* 42(1) (2008): 64–88.

Hall, David, ed. *Lived Religion in America.* Princeton, NJ: Princeton University Press, 1997.

Hamilton, Nora, and Norma Stolz Chinchilla. "Central American Migration: A Framework for Analysis." *Latin American Research Review* 26(1) (1991): 75–110.

Handbook of Texas Online, s.v. "Sociedades Guadalupanas." Accessed January 15, 2008 from http://www.tshaonline.org/handbook/online/articles/ss/ics10.html.

Handlin, Oscar. *The Uprooted: The Epic Story of the Great Migrations That Made the American People.* Philadelphia: University of Pennsylvania Press, 2002 (originally published, 1951).

Hanson, G., and A. Spilimbergo. "Illegal Immigration, Border Enforcement, and Relative Wages: Evidence from Apprehensions at the U.S.-Mexico Border." *American Economic Review* 89(5) (1999): 1337–1357.

Hellum, Anne Motley. "Looking for Hope in Central America: The Pentacostal Movement." In *Religion and Politics in Comparative Perspective: the One, the Few, and the Many,* eds. Ted G. Selen, Clyde and Clyde Wilcox. Cambridge University Press, 2002, pp. 225–242.

Herberg, W. *Protestant, Catholic, Jew: An Essay in American Religious Sociology.* Garden City: Doubleday and Company, 1955.

Hernández-León, Rubén. "The Migration Industry in the Mexico-U.S. Migratory System." On-Line Working Paper for California Center for Population Research. Accessed October 2005 from www.ccpr.ucla.edu/ccprwpseries/ccpr_049_05.pdf.

———. *Metropolitan Migrants: The Migration of Urban Mexicans to the United States.* Berkeley: University of California Press, 2008.

Hervieu-Leger, Daniel. "'What Scripture Tells Me': Spontaneity and Regulation within the Catholic Charismatic Renewal." In *Lived Religion in America: Towards a History of Practice,* ed. David Hall, pp. 22–40. Princeton, NJ: Princeton University Press, 1997.

Hirschman, Charles, Philip Kasinitz, and Josh DeWind, eds. *The Handbook of International Migration: The American Experience.* New York: Russell Sage Foundation, 1999.

Holland, Clifford. "Estimated Size of the Protestant Population in Spanish and Portuguese-Speaking Countries of the Americas." *World Data Sheet,* Population Reference Bureau. Washington, DC, February 22, 1997.

Hollifield, James. "The Emerging Migration State." *International Migration Review* 38(3) (2004): 885–912.

Hondagneu-Sotelo, Pierette (ed). *Religion and Social Justice for Immigrants.* NJ: Rutgers University Press, 2007.

Hondagneu-Sotelo, Pierette. "Regulating the Unregulated: Domestic Worker's Social Networks." *Social Problems* 41 (1994): 60–64.

———. *Gendered Transitions: Mexican Experiences of Immigration.* Berkeley: University of California, 1994.

Hondagneu-Sotelo, Pierette, and Ernestine Avila. "I'm Here but I'm There: The Meaning of Latina Transnational Motherhood." *Gender & Society* 11(5) (1997): 548–571.

Hondagneu-Sotelo, Pierette, Genelle Gaudinez, and Hector Lara. "Religious Reenactment on the Line: A Genealogy of Political Religious Hybridity." In *Religion and Social Justice for Immigrants,* ed. Pierrette Hondagneu-Sotelo, pp. 122–140. New Brunswick, NJ: Rutgers University Press, 2007.

Hondagneu-Sotelo, Pierette, Genelle Gaudinez, Hector Lara, and Billie C. Ortiz. "There's a Spirit That Transcends the Border: Faith, Ritual, and Postnational Protest at the U.S.-Mexico Border." *Sociological Perspectives* 47(2) (2004): 133–159.

Hoover, Robin. "Social Theology and Religiously Affiliated Non-Profits in Migration Policy." PhD diss., Texas Tech University, Lubbock, 1998.

———. "Crossing the Line in Faith Interpretation." Sermon delivered June 9, 2002, at First Christian Church in Tucson, Arizona.

Humane Borders. Accessed June 2006, 2007, at www.humaneborders.org.

Huntington, Samuel. *Who are We: The Challenges to Americas National Identity.* Simon & Schuster, 2004.

Innes, Stephanie. "Entrant-Helping Case Is Targeted." *Arizona Daily Star,* October 20, 2005, Accessed November 10, 2005 from http:www.azstarnet.com/dailystar/metro/98701.

———. "Former Arizona Chief Justice Will Represent One of Two Defendants in Entrant-Aid Case." *Arizona Daily Star,* February 7, 2006. 1A.

International Bible Society. *Holy Bible, New International Version.* Grand Rapids, MI: Zondervan, 1984.

Jeffrey, Paul. "Migrants: The Word of God that Walks." *National Catholic Reporter,* April 5, 2002.

Jordan, Mary. "Sex Often the Price for Passage to the U.S.: Central American Women Face Coercion Along Path to Freed." Accessed December 6, 2004 from www.msnbc.msn.com/id/66851.

Jørgen, Carlina. "The Merits and Limitations of Spain's High-Tech Border." Calrol. Migration Information Source. Washington, D.C., Migration Policy Institute. June, 2007. Retrieved August 2007, from www.migrationinformation.org/ Fecture/display.cfm?id-605.

Kandel, William and Douglas Massey. "The Culture of Migration: A Theoretical and Empirical Analysis." *Social Forces* 80(3)(2002): 981–1004.

Kearney, Michael. "The Local and the Global: The Anthropology of Globalization and Transnationalism." *Annual Review of Anthropology* 24 (1995): 547–565.

Keck, Margaret E., and Katherine Sikkink. *Activists across Borders: Advocacy Networks in International Politics.* Ithaca, NY: Cornell University Press, 1998.

Kerwin, Donald. "Immigration Reform and the Catholic Church." In *Migration Information Source,* Washington, DC: Migration Policy Institute, May 2006. Retrieved from www.migrationinformation.org/Feature/display.cfm?ID-395.

Kossoudji, Sherrie A. "Playing Cat and Mouse at the U.S.-Mexican Border." *Demography* 29(2) (1992): 159–180.

Krissman, Fred. "*Sin Coyote Ni Patrón:* Why the 'Migrant Network' Fails to Explain International Migration." *International Migration Review* 39(1) (2005): 4–44.

Kurien Prema. 1998. "Becoming American by Becoming Hindu: Indian Americans Take Their Place at the Multicultural Table." In *Gatherings in Diaspora: Religious Communities and the New Immigration.* eds. R. S. Warner and J. G. Wittner, pp. 37–70. Philadelphia: Temple University Press, 1998.

Kyle, David. *Transnational Peasants: Migrations, Networks, and Ethnicity in Andean Ecuador.* Baltimore: Johns Hopkins University Press, 2000.

Kyle, David, and Rey Koslowski, eds. *Global Human Smuggling: Comparative Perspectives.* Baltimore: Johns Hopkins University Press, 2001.

Lafaye, Jacques. *Quetzalcoatle and Guadalupe: The Formation of Mexican National Consciousness, 1531–1813.* Chicago: University of Chicago Press, 1976.

Lee, Erika. "Enforcing the Borders: Chinese Exclusion along the U.S. Borders with Canada and Mexico, 1882 to 1924," *Journal of American History* 89(1) (2002): 54–86.

———. *At America's Gate: Chinese Immigration during the Exclusion Era, 1882–1943.* Chapel Hill: University of North Carolina Press, 2003.

Lee, Jennifer S. "Human Smuggling for a Hefty Fee" *New York Times Week in Review,* May 28, 2006, p. 2.

León, Luis D. "Metaphor and Place: The U.S.-Mexico Border as Center and Periphery in the Interpretation of Religion." *Journal of the American Academy of Religion* 67(3) (1999): 541–568.

Levine, Daniel H., ed. *Religion and Political Conflict in Latin America.* Chapel Hill: University of North Carolina Press, 1986.

———. 1. "Religion, the Poor, and Politics in Latin America Today." In *Religion and Political Conflict in Latin America,* ed. Daniel Levine. Chapel Hill: University of North Carolina Press, 1986.

———. *Popular Voices in Latin American Catholicism.* Princeton, NJ: Princeton University Press, 1992.

Levitt, Peggy. "Local-Level Global Religion: U.S.-Dominican Migration." *Journal for the Scientific Study of Religion* 37 (1998): 74–89.

———. "Redefining the Boundaries of Belonging: The Instititional Character of Transnational Life." *Sociology of Religion* 65:1–18.

———. *The Transnational Villagers.* Berkeley: University of California Press, 2001.

———. "You Know, Abraham Was Really the First Immigrant." *International Migration Review* 37(3) (2003): 847–873.

———. "Immigration." In *The Handbook of Religion and Social Institutions,* ed. Helen Rose Ebaugh, pp. 391–440. New York: Springer Science and Business Media, 2005.

———. *God Needs No Passport: Immigrants and the Changing American Religious Landscape.* New York: The New Press, 2007.

Liu, Gan. "Dangers on the Journey: Physical and Social Problems Experienced by Undocumented Migrants." M.A. thesis, University of Houston, 2002.

Lipton, Eric. "Bush Turns to Giant Military Contractors," *New York Times,* May 18, 2006, 1A.

Lomnitz, Larissa Adler. *Networks and Marginality: Life in a Mexican Shantytown.* Trans. Cinna Lomnitz. New York: Academic Press, 1977.

López Castro, Gustavo. 1998. "Coyotes and Alien Smuggling." *The Binational Study on Migration Between Mexico and the United States* 3 (1998): 965–974.

Lozano, Juan. "Three Convicted in Immigrants' Deaths." *Houston Chronicle,* February 9, 2006, p. A1.

Lucia. "A Tragic Journey." Houston Catholic Worker, 27(1) January–February 1997. Also available online at www.cjd.org/stories/journey.html.

Luckmann, Thomas. *The Invisible Religion: The Problem of Religion in Modern Society.* New York: Macmillan, 1967.

MacDonald, John S., and Leatrice D. MacDonald. "Chain Migration, Ethnic Neighborhood Formation, and Social Networks." Milbank Memorial Fund Quaterly 24(1964):82–97.

Mahler, Sarah. *American Dreaming.* Princeton, NJ: Princeton University Press, 1995.

———. 2000. "Migration and Transnational Issues: Recent Trends and Prospects for 2020." Accessed 2004 from http://ca2020.fiu.edu/Themes/Sarah_Mahler.html.

Marchi, Regina. "El Dia de los Muertos in the USA: Cultural Ritual as Political Communication." In *Spontaneous Shrines and the Public Memorialization of the Dead*, ed. Jack Santino, pp. 261–284. New York: Palgrave Macmillan, 2006.

Martin, David. *Tongues of Fire: The Explosion of Protestantism*. Oxford: Basil Blackwell, 1990.

Martinez, Ruben. *Crossing Over: A Mexican Family on the Migrant Trail*. New York: Metropolitan Books, 2001.

Massey, Douglas S. "Why Does Immigration Occur? A Theoretical Synthesis." In *The Handbook of International Migration*, ed. Charles Hirschman, Philip Kasinitz, and Josh DeWind, pp. 34–52. New York: Russell Sage Foundation, 1999.

———. 2005. "Backfire at the Border: Why Enforcement without Legalization Cannot Stop Illegal Immigration." Center for Trade Policy Studies: Cato Institute.

Massey, Douglas S., Rafael Alarcón, Jorge Durand, and Humberto González. *Return to Atzlan: The Social Process of International Migration from Western Mexico*. Berkeley: University of California Press, 1987.

Massey, Douglas S., Joaquín Arango, Graeme Hugo, Ali Kouaouci, Adela Pellegrino, and J. Edward Taylor. "Theories of International Migration: A Review and Appraisal." *Population and Development Review* 19(3) (1993): 431–466.

Massey, Douglas S., Jorge Durand, and Nolan J. Malone. *Beyond Smoke and Mirrors: Mexican Immigration in an Era of Economic Integration*. New York: Russell Sage Foundation, 2003.

Massey, Douglas S., and Kristin E. Espinosa. "What's Driving Mexico-U.S. Migration?: A Theoretical, Empirical, and Policy Analysis." *American Journal of Sociology* 102 (1997): 939–999.

Menjívar Cecilia. "Religious Institutions and Transnationalism: A Case Study of Catholic and Evangelical and Salvadoran Immigrants." *International Journal of Politics, Culture, and Society* 12 (4) (1999): 589–612.

———. *Fragmented Ties. Salvadoran Immigrant Networks in America*. Berkeley: University of California Press, 2000.

———. "Religion and Immigration in Comparative Perspective: Catholic and Evangelical Salvadorans in San Francisco, Washington, D.C., and Phoenix." *Sociology of Religion* 64(1) (2003): 21–45.

Meyer, Jean A. *The Cristero Rebellion: The Mexican People between Church and State, 1926–1929*. New York: Cambridge University Press, 1976.

Mines, Richard. *Developing a Community Tradition of Migration: A Field Study in Rural Zacatecas, Mexico, and California Settlement Areas.* U.S.-Mexican Studies no. 3. La Jolla, California. Program in U.S.-Mexican Studies, University of California, San Diego, 1981.

Mooney, Margarita. 2006. "The Catholic Bishops Conferences of the United States and France: Engaging Immigration as a Public Issue." *American Behavioral Scientist* 49(11) (2006): 1447–1454.

Navarro, Mireya. "In Many Churches, Icons Compete for Space: Multiple Shrines to Patron Saints Testify to a Rivalry of the Devout." *New York Times,* May 29, 2002, A17.

Nazario, Sonia. *Enrique's Journey.* New York: Random House, 2006.

Nepstad Erickson, Sharon. *Convictions of the Soul: Religion, Culture, and Agency in the Central America Solidarity Movement.* New York: Oxford University Press, 2004,

Nevins, Joseph. *Operation Gatekeeper: The Rise of the "Illegal Alien" and the Making of the U.S.-Mexico Boundary.* New York: Routledge, 2002.

No More Deaths. Accessed June 2007 from www.nomoredeaths.org.

No More Deaths. Press release. Accessed September 2006 from www.nomoredeaths.org.

Ogren, Cassandra. "Migration and Human Rights on the Mexico-Guatemala Border." *International Migration* 45(4) (2007): 203–243.

Olivarez, Isaac. "Spanish Speakers Face Challenges, Opportunities in United States Sulture," Today's Pentecostal Evangelical Assemblies of God USA, May 16, 2004.

Olmos, Harold, and Peter Muello. "Next Pope Faces Loss of Latin American Faithful to Evangelical Churches." *The Detroit News.* Accessed April 16, 2005, from www.detnews.com/2005/religion/0504/17/relig-152283.htm.

Orsi, Robert A. *The Madonna of 115th Street: Faith and Community in Italian Harlem, 1880–1950.* New Haven: Yale University Press, 2nd ed., 2002.

———. "The Center Out There, In Here, and Everywhere Else: The Nature of Pilgrimage to the Shrine of Saint Jude, 1929–1965." *Journal of Social History* (1991): 213–232.

———. "Everyday Miracles: The Study of Lived Religion." In *Lived Religion in America,* ed. David Hall, pp. 3–21. Princeton, NJ: Princeton University Press, 1997.

———. "When 2 + 2 = 5: Can We Begin to Think about Unexplained Religious Experiences in Ways That Acknowledge Their Existence?" The Ameican Scholar Phi Beta Kappa. Spring, 2007. Also available online at www.theamericanscholar.org/archives/sp07/225-orsi.html.

Organización Internacional para las Migraciones (OIM). "Explotación Sexual Comercial de Niñas, Niños y Adolescentes en Guatemala." *Cuadernos de Trabajo Sobre Migración.* Accessed November 2002 at www.oim.org.gt/Cuaderno %20de%20Trabajo%20No.%2008.pdf.

Paerregaard, Karsten. "In the Footsteps of the Lord of Miracles: The Expatriation of Religious Icons in the Peruvian Diaspora." Working Paper, Transnational Communities Programme, 2001.

Parreñas, Rhacel Salazar. *Children of Global Migration: Transnational Families and Gendered Woes.* Stanford University Press, 2005.

Passel, Jeffrey. "Size and Characteristics of the Unauthorized Migrant Population." Report prepared Maruch 2006 by the Pew Hispanic Center, Washington, D.C.

Passel, Jeffrey, and Roberto Suro. September. *Rise, Peak, and Decline: Trends in U.S. Immigration 1992–2004.* Washington, DC: Pew Hispanic Center, 2005.

Pepitone, A. "Beliefs and Cultural Psychology." In *Cross Cultural Topics in Psychology,* ed. L. L. Adler and U. P. Gielen, pp. 185–200. Westport, CT: Praeger Publishers, 2nd ed., 2001.

Phillips, Scott, Jacqueline Hagan, and Nestor Rodríguez. "Brutal Borders: Examining the Treatment of Deportees during Arrest and Detention." *Social Forces* 85(1) (2006): 93–110.

Piore, Michael J. *Birds of Passage: Migrant Labor in Industrial Societies.* New York: Cambridge University Press, 1979.

Poepsel, Mark. "Border Patrol Arrests No More Deaths Volunteers." KOLD News–13, July 9, 2005.

Pope John XXIII. *Pacem in Terris* (Peace on Earth). Accessed June 2005 from www.vatican.va/holy_father/john_xxiii/encyclicals/documents/hf_j-xxiii_ enc_11041963_pacem_en.html.

Pope John Paul II. *Message for World Migration Day* (1995–1996, Undocumented Migrants No. 2). Available from the Vatican Web site: www.vatica.va.

Pope John Paul II. *Ecclesia in America* (The Church in America). Washington, DC: U.S. Conference of Catholic Bishops, 1999.

Portes, Alejandro, and Josh DeWind. "A Cross-Atlantic Dialogue: The Progress of Research and Theory in the Study of International Migration." *International Migration Review* 38(3) (2004): 828–851.

Portes, Alejandro, and Leif Jensen. "The Enclave and the Entrants: Patterns of Ethnic Enterprise in Miami Before and After Mariel." *American Sociological Review* 54(6) (1989): 768–771.

Portes, Alejandro, and Ruben Rumbaut. *Immigrant America,* 3rd ed. Berkeley: University of California Press, 2006.

Portes, Alejandro, and Julia Sensenbrenner. "Embeddedness and Immigration: Notes on the Social Determinants of Economic Action." *American Journal of Sociology* 98(6) (1993): 1320–1350.

Portes, Alejandro, and Cynthia Truelove. "Making Sense of Diversity: Recent Research on Hispanic Minorities in the United States." *Annual Review of Sociology* 13 (1987): 359–385.

Pratt, Mary. "Por que la Virgen de Zapopan fue a Los Angeles? Algunas reflexiones sobre la movilidad y la globalidad." *Contracorriente* 3(2) (2006): 1–13.

Priblisky, J. "Aprendemos a Convivir: Conjugal Relations, Co-Parenting, and Family Life among Transnational Migrants in New York City and the Ecuadorian Andes." *Global Networks* 4(3) (2004): 313–334.

Pupovac, Jessica. "Number of Migrants Deaths along the Border to Reach Record Numbers in 2007, says Mexican Official." *AHN News* November 6, 2007. Accessed: January 2008 at www.allheadlinenews.com/articles/7009072172.

Ramos, Jorge. *Morir en el intento: La peor tradegia de immigrantes en la historia de los Estados Unidos.* New York: Harper Collins, 2005.

Ranis, Gustav, and John C. H. Fei. "A Theory of Economic Development." *American Economic Review* 51 (1961): 533–365.

Reyes, B., H. P. Johnson, and R. Van Swearingen. "Has Increased Border Enforcement Reduced Unauthorized Migration?" Research Brief, Public Policy Institute of California, 2002.

Reichert, Joshua S. "The Migrant Syndrome: Seasonal U.S. Wage Labor and Rural Development in Central Mexico." *Human Organizations* 40 (1981): 56–66.

Rives, Karin. "Illegal Immigration: Who Profits, Who Pays?" *The News & Observer* (Raleigh, NC), February 26, 2006, p. A1.

Rodriguez, Nestor. "Crossing the Mexican Gauntlet: Trials and Challenges of Central American Migration to the United States." Paper presented at the Latin American Conference on "The Other Latinos" at Harvard University, April 2002.

———. "Mexican and Central Americans in the Present Wave of U.S. Immigration." Pp. 81–100 in Jose Luis Falconi and Jose Antonio Mazzoti (eds.) *The Other Latinos: Central and South Americans in the United States.* Cambridge, MA: Harvard University David Rockefeller Center for Latin American Studies, distributed by Harvard University Press, 2008.

Rodriguez, Nestor, and Jacqueline Hagan. "Fractured Families and Communities: Effects of Immigration Reform in Texas, Mexico and El Salvador." *Journal of Latino Studies.* Volume 2(3) (Fall 2004): 453–473.

Ruiz, A. "Migrants' dangerous trek north ends in death and deportation." *The Associated Press,* April 14, 2000.

Sánchez Lara, Rosa María. *Los Retablos Populares: Exvotos Pintados.* México, D.F.: Universidad Nacional Autónoma de México, Instituto de Investigaciones Estéticas, 1990.

Santino, Jack, "Performative Commemoratives" in *Spontaneous Shrines and the Public Memorialization of Death.* New York: Pelgrave, 2006, pp. 5–16.

Sapkota, Sanjeeb, Harold W. Kohl III, Julie Gilchrist, Jay McAuliffe, Bruce Parks, Bob England, Tim Flood, C. Sewell, Dennis Perrotta, Miguel Escobedo, Corinne E. Stern, David Zane, and Kurt B. Nolte. "Unauthorized Border Crossings and Migrant Deaths: Arizona, New Mexico, and El Paso, Texas, 2002–2003." *American Journal of Public Health* 96(7) (2006): 1282–1287.

Sigmund, Paul. *Religious Freedom and Evangelization in Latin America: The Challenge of Religious Pluralism.* New York: Orbis Books, 1999.

Sikkink, Kathryn. "Human Rights, Principled Issue-Networks, and Sovereignty in Latin America." *International Organization* 47(3) (1993): 411–441.

Singer, Audrey. "The Rise of New Immigrant Gateways." Accessed February 2004 from www.brookings.edu/urban/publications/20040301_gateways.htm.

Singer, Audrey, and Douglas S. Massey. "The Social Process of Undocumented Border Crossing." *International Migration Review* 32(3) (1998): 561–592.

Sjaastad, Larry A. "The Costs and Returns of Human Migration." *Journal of Political Economy* 70 (1962): S80–93.

Smidt, Corwin E. *Pulpit and Politics: Clergy in American Politics at the Advent of the Millennium.* Waco, TX: Baylor University Press, 2004.

Smilde, David. "Let God Govern: Supernatural Agency in the Venezuelan Pentecostal Approach to Social Change." *Sociology of Religion* 59(3) (1998): 287–303.

———. *Reason to Believe: Cultural Agency in Latin American Evangelicalism.* Berkeley: University of California Press, 2007.

Smith, Robert. *Mexican New York: Transnational Lives of New Immigrants.* Berkeley: University of California Press, 2006.

Smith, Timothy L. "Religion and Ethnicity in America." *American Historical Review* 83 (1978): 1155–1185.

Spener, David. "Smuggling Migrants through South Texas: Challenges Posed by Operation Rio Grande." In *Global Human Smuggling in Comparative Perspective,* ed. David Kyle and Rey Koslowski, pp. 129–165. Baltimore: Johns Hopkins University Press.

———. "Mexican Migration to the United States: A Long Twentieth Century of Coyotaje." Working Paper No. 124. Center for Comparative Immigration Studies, University of California at San Diego, 2005.

————. "Coyotaje as an Everyday Strategy of Resistance to Apartheid at the Mexico-U.S. Border." Paper presented October 28, 2006, at Segundo Coloquio Internacional Sobre Migración y Desarrollo in Cocoyec, Morelos, Mexico.

————. "Clandestine Crossings: Coyotaje on the South Texas-Northeast Mexico Border at the Beginning of the Twentieth Century." Paper presented April 27, 2007, at Latin American Demography: Past, Present, and Future: Contributions of the U.T. Population Research Center Alumni (1968–2006), held at the University of Texas at Austin.

————. "Cruces Clandestinos: Migrantes, coyotes y capital social en la frontera el noreste de México-sur de Texas." In *La Migración a los Estados Unidos y la Frontera Noreste de México*, ed. Socorro Arzaluz. Tijuana, Baja California: El Colegio de la Frontera Norte.

Stark, Oded. "Migration Decision-Making." *Journal of Developmental Economics* 14 (1984): 251–259.

Stark, Oded, and David E. Bloom. "The New Economics of Labor Migration." *American Economic Review* 75 (1985): 173–178.

Stoll, David. *Is Latin America Turning Protestant? The Politics of Evangelical Growth.* Berkley: University of California Press, 1990.

Stoll, David, and Virginia Garrard-Burnett, eds. *Rethinking Protestantism in Latin America.* Philadelphia: Temple University Press, 1993.

Sullivan, Kathleen. "St. Mary's Catholic Church: Celebrating Domestic Religion." In *Religion and the New Immigrants*, ed. Helen Rose Ebaugh and Janet Chafetz, pp. 125–140. Walnut Creek, CA: AltaMira Press, 2000.

Taylor, J. Edward. "Differential Migration, Networks, Information, and Risk." In *Migration Theory, Human Capital, and Development*, ed. Oded Stark, pp. 147–171. Greenwich, CT: JAI Press, 1986.

Thomas, W. I., and Dorothy S. Thomas. *The Child in America: Behavioral Problems and Programs*, New York: Knoph, 1928.

Thompson, Ginger, and Sandra Ochoa. "By a Back Door to the United States: A Migrant's Sea Voyage." *New York Times*, June 13, 2004, p. A1.

Tilly, Charles. "Migration in Modern European History." In *Human Migration*, ed. McNeil and Adams, pp. 48–72. Bloomington: Indiana University Press, 1978.

Todaro, Michael P. 1976. *Internal Migration in Developing Countries: A Review of Theory, Evidence, Methodology and Research Priorities.* Geneva, Switzerland: International Labor Office, 1976.

Todaro, Michael P., and L. Maruszko. "Illegal Migration and U.S. Immigration Reform: A Conceptual Framework." *Population and Development Review* 13 (1987): 101–114.

Tomasi, Silvano M. *Piety and Power: The Role of the Italian American Parishes in the New York Metropolitan Area, 1880–1930.* Staten Island, NY: Center for Migration Studies, 1975.

Tucson Diocese Newsletter, vol. 5, no. 8. May 7, 2007. Accessed January 2008 at www.diocesetucson.org/May07.html.

Tweed, Thomas A. *Our Lady of Exile: Diasporic Religion at a Cuban Shrine in Miami.* New York: Oxford Univeristy Press, 1997.

UN Press Release. "Convention on Protection of Rights of Migrant Workers to Enter Into Force Next July." Accessed June 2003 from www.un.org/news/Press/docs/2003/LT4371.doc.htm.

UN Economic and Social Council. Commission on Human Rights. "Report of the Working Group on Arbitrary Detention on Its Visit to Mexico." Accessed December 17, 2002, from www.unhcr.ch/huridocda/huridoca.

U.S. Conference of Catholic Bishops. *Strangers No Longer: Together on the Journey of Hope.* Washington, DC: IUSCCB, 2003.

U.S. Customs and Border Protection. "Search and Rescue Operations." Accessed June 6, 2003, from www.cbp.gov/xp/cgov/border_security/border_patrol/borstar/search_rescue.xml.

U.S. General Accountability Office. "Illegal Immigration: Southwest Border Strategy Results Inconclusive; More Evaluation Needed. GAO/GDD-98-164." Washington, DC: U.S. Government Printing Office, July 31, 1997.

———. "Illegal Immigration: Status for Southwest Border Strategy Implementation, GAO/GGD-99-44." Washington, DC: U.S. Government Printing Office, May 19, 1999.

———. "INS' Southwest Border Strategy: Resource and Impact Issues Remain After Seven Years." Washington, DC: U.S. Government Printing Office, 2001.

———. "Illegal Immigration: Border Crossing Deaths Have Doubled Since 1995; Border Patrol's Efforts to Prevent Deaths Have Not Been Fully Evaluated." Washington, DC: U.S. Government Printing Office, August 2006.

Urrea, Luis Alberto. *The Devil's Highway.* New York: Little, Brown, 2004.

Urrutia-Rojas, Ximena, and Néstor P. Rodriguez. "Unaccompanied Migrant Children from Central America: Sociodemographic Characteristics and Experiences with Potentially Traumatic Events." In *Health and Social Services among International Labor Migrants: A Comparative Perspective,* ed. Antonio Ugalde and Gilberto Cárdenas, pp. 151–166. Austin: University of Texas Press, 1997.

Vanderwood, Paul. *Juan Soldado: Rapist, Murderer, Martyr, Saint.* Durham, North Carolina: Duke University Press, 2004.

Van Dijk, Rijk A. "From Camp to Encompassment: Discourses on Transsubjectivity in the Ghanaian Pentecostal Diaspora." *Journal of Religion in Africa* 27 (1997): 135–159.

Vidal, Teodoro. *Los Milagros en Metal y en Cera de Puerto Rico*. San Juan: Ediciones Alba, 1974.

Warner, R. Stephen, and Judith G. Wittner, eds. *Gatherings in Diaspora: Religious Communities and the New Immigration*. Philadelphia: Temple University Press, 1998.

Watson, Julie. "Migrants Trek Gets Grimmer: Routes are Shifting as Border Tightens." *The News and Observer* (Raleigh, NC), May 3, 2006, A11.

Wellmeier, Nancy. "Santa Eulalia's People in Exile: Maya Religion, Culture, and Identity in Los Angeles." In *Gatherings in Diaspora: Religious Communities and the New Immigration*, ed. R. S. Warner & J. Wittner, pp. 97–122. Philadelphia: Temple University Press, 1998.

Wilson, Everette. "Guatemalan Pentecostals: Something of Their Own." In *The Pentecostals of Latin America*, ed. Edward L. Cleary and Hannah Stewart-Gambino, pp. 139–162. Boulder CO: Westview Press, 1997.

Wuthnow, Robert. *America and the Challenges of Religious Diversity*. Princeton, NJ: Princeton University Press, 2005.

Wuthnow, Robert, and John H. Evans, eds. *The Quiet Hand of God: Faith-Based Activism and the Public Role of Mainline Protestantism*. Berkeley and Los Angeles: University of California Press, 2002.

Yang, Fenggang, and Helen Rose Ebaugh. "Transformations in New Immigrants Religions and Their Global Implications." *American Sociological Review* 66(2) (2001): 269–288.

Zhou, Min, Carl L. Bankston, and Rebecca Y. Kim. "Rebuilding Spiritual Lives in the New Land: Religious Practices among Southeast Asian Refugees in the United States" in *Religion in Asian America*, ed. P. G. Min and J. H. Kim, pp. 37–70. New York: AltaMira Press, 2002.

Zolberg, Aristide R. "Matter of the State: Theorizing Immigration Policy." In *The Handbook of International Migration*, ed. Charles Hirschman, Philip Kasinitz, and Josh DeWind, pp. 71–93. New York: Russell Sage Foundation, 1999.

———. *A Nation by Design: Immigration Policy in the Fashioning of America*. Cambridge, MA: Harvard University Press, 2006.

Zolberg, Aristide. R., Astri Suhrke, and Sergio Aguayo. *Escape from Violence: Conflict and the Refugee Crisis in the Developing World*. New York: Oxford University Press, 1989.

Zúñiga, Victor, and Rubén Hernández-León. *New Destinations: Mexican Immigration in the United States*. New York: Russell Sage Foundation, 2005.

Acknowledgments

This project, like many field projects, began as a case study with a particular focus. Over time it expanded in scope and moved in unexpected directions. I am grateful to the many organizations, communities, and individuals who supported and assisted me along this long, sometimes rocky, but always challenging and rewarding research road. Initial fieldwork in Guatemala in summer 2000 was supported by the Pew Charitable Trusts, which funded the Houston-based Religion, Ethnicity, and New Immigrant Research (RENIR) project, one of several research projects supported by Pew to study religion and immigration. Under the prodding of my friend and colleague, Helen Rose Ebaugh, the principal investigator of the project, I traveled to Totonicapan, Guatemala (a highland area where I had done fieldwork some years earlier), to identify and explore different levels of religious links between a migrant-sending community and its sister community in Houston. Although I did identify some organizational- and individual-level links between Houston and Totonicapan, the idea for this book emerged from several visits to mountaintop and home-based *ayunos* (fasts) where I observed departing migrants pray for safe passage to the United States. When I returned to Houston, I designed and launched a larger project to study how migrants draw on religion as a resource and coping strategy to endure the travel north. This second phase of the project, which involved three hundred interviews with migrants, was funded by RENIR and several small grants provided by the University of Houston. From these interviews I learned of churches and sanctuaries visited by departing and transit migrants to seek counsel and support. My initial visits to sanctuaries in Costa Rica, Guatemala, and Mexico were funded by RENIR and several in-house grants from the University of Houston. My final field trip, to El Salvador and Honduras in 2004, was funded by a grant provided by Taryn Higashi of the Ford Foundation.

Two academic institutions helped me through the writing stages of the book. I would like to thank my previous academic home, the Department of Sociology at the University of Houston, for providing me with the space and time to develop research ideas and begin writing. I also extend warm appreciation to my present home, the Department of Sociology at the University of North Carolina at Chapel Hill, for the intellectual environment to complete the book.

I am grateful to the Scalabrini community, through which I met a number of priests, faith workers, and lay staff, many of whom provide for transit migrants from Central American and Mexico and assist in the integration of many migrants when they are deported to their home communities. I am especially grateful for the time and insights provided by Fathers Flor Maria Rigoni, Francisco Pellizzari, and Pedro Corbellini. Other religious leaders and faith workers also supported my field research. I am greatly indebted to Reverend Robin Hoover and Susan Goodman of Humane Borders, who introduced me to their humanitarian work and guided Helen Rose Ebaugh and me along the most dangerous crossing corridors situated on the Mexico-Arizona border and, in the process, revealing to me the many ways in which migrants, far from the walls of churches, practice everyday religion to cope with the arduous journey north. Humane Borders also supported two of my research assistants who interned with the organization. My deep gratitude also extends to Pastor José Sapon, who first illustrated to me, through visits to several Pentecostal prayer camps in Guatemala, the important and interrelated role of religion and culture in the decision and departure stages of the migration journey. Pastor Sapon spent many days and evenings with the research team, introducing us to other pastors who are engaged in migration counseling. I would like to thank Cardinal Oscar Rodriguez and his aide, Father Carlo Magno, for their hospitality and assistance in Honduras. Cardinal Rodriguez welcomed me and my husband into his home for several days, and Father Magno, the vicar of the national cathedral, guided us through the religious landscape of the Tegucigalpa area.

I am grateful for the following students and persons who devoted countless hours of their time interviewing immigrants, coding data, and assisting with the final presentation of the book: Anita Bondar, Lillian Chavez, Parker Chestnut, Cecilia Cook, Virginia Gallardo, Edgar Guacin, Leo Hernandez, Martha Krick, Ana Lui, Brianna Mullis, Debbie Munoz, Norma Perez, Michelle Pearsons, Vanesa Ribas, Reyna Thomas-Brown, and Javier, Cary, Samuel, and Maria. Many thanks also to my mother, Maria Teresa Hagan, and to Erin Lynch, Susan McCollum, and Luis Salinas for the many hours they spent in the field with me, interviewing migrants and visiting sacred shrines.

Writing this book would have been extremely difficult without the assistance and support of my editor, my colleagues, and my friends. A special thanks goes to my dear friend and colleague, Helen Rose Ebaugh, without whom I would never have launched this project. Helen Rose also read an early draft of my work and provided many suggestions for improvement. I owe much to my longtime and very dear friend and colleague, the late Janet Chafetz, who pushed me along the way and would certainly be gratified and relieved that I finally finished. My appreciation also goes to colleagues and friends who read parts of this work and offered advice, including Harley Browning, Karl Eschbach, Chris Smith, and especially to Nestor Rodriguez, who has always been on hand to discuss and clarify my field observations and ideas. I am especially grateful to Robert Smith, who read a draft of my manuscript and provided invaluable suggestions that pushed me forward and ultimately took the book one step further. My appreciation is also extended to my editor, Sharmila Sen, who believed in the book and pushed it to completion. I would also like to thank the anonymous reviewers for their very useful comments and suggestions.

A very warm and special thanks goes to Leslie Banner, who provided friendship and support throughout the writing stages of the project. During early morning walks in our woodsy Chapel Hill neighborhood, she patiently listened to the previous day's progress. Her intellectual curiosity clarified a number of ideas on which this book is based, and her exceptional editing skills and critical eye certainly polished the overall style of this book and the presentations of its narratives.

I am indebted to the many migrants from Central America and Mexico who shared their time and their difficult migration experiences, which were often painful to tell. Among the 350 immigrants whose stories are woven into this narrative, I would like to extend a very special thanks to Cecilia, Amelia, Aleksy, and Myrna, who spent many hours listening to my ideas and giving me feedback. These women and mothers have asked me to include their real names here in the hopes that they can one day share their migration histories with their children.

Most important, I want to thank my husband, Joe Glatthaar, who believed in this project and provided unparalleled companionship throughout its long life. Joe accompanied me on numerous research trips, sometimes sacrificing vacations along the way. He read countless drafts of chapters, all the while working on his own manuscript. Our household was not without its bumps, but through his patience, laughter and love, Joe always reminded me of what was most important in life.

Index